THE
ARTISTRY
OF
MIXING DRINKS

THE ARTISTRY OF MIXING DRINKS

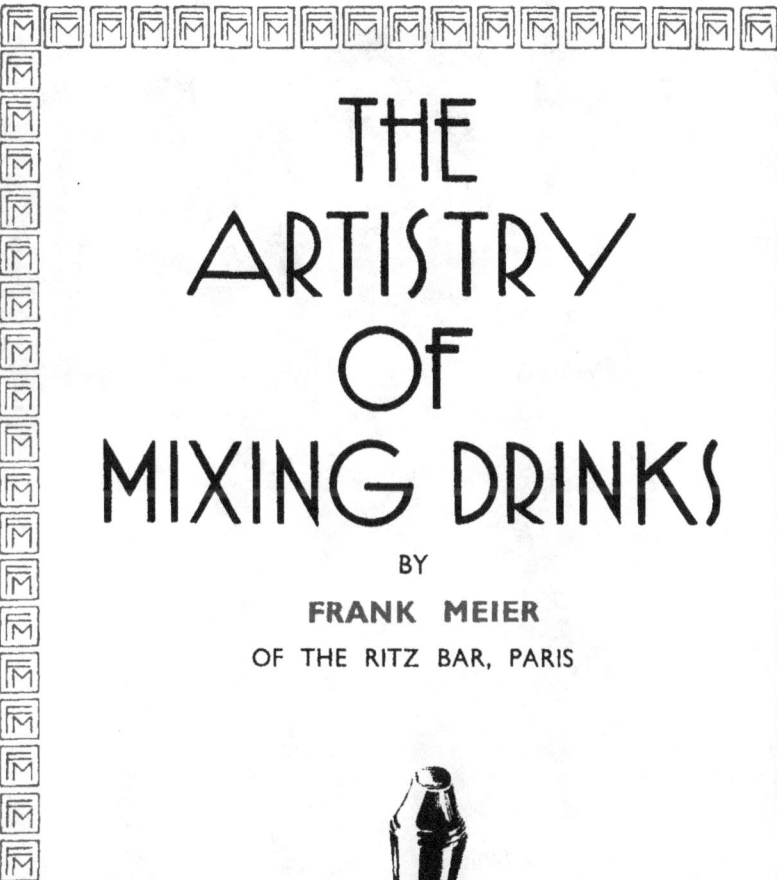

BY

FRANK MEIER

OF THE RITZ BAR, PARIS

MCMXXXVI

Copyright © 1936 Frank Meier

Published by Seven Star Publishing

ISBN (Hardcover): 978-1-62654-227-3
ISBN (Paperback): 978-1-62654-151-1
ISBN (Spiralbound): 978-1-62654-226-6

Printed and bound in the United States of America

FOREWORD

Though Frank Meier's primary object is to expound the art of mixing drinks which he has studied and practised so long, I feel that some mention should be made in the book regarding the institution of the American bar and the rare qualities which the man behind it should possess.

What Europeans call an American bar is in fact international in its true sense. Visitors from all countries expect, and can have, their own special drinks and whilst cocktails are perhaps the main " raison d'être " this institution has various other points. It is in a way a meeting-place where acquaintanceship and introductions are easy and where, in consequence, the barriers of many inhibitions and shyness disappear without great formality. This definition is not intended to accuse American bars of democracy, or to deny the merits of " pubs ", " bistros " or " weinstuben ". Many readers undoubtedly have their pet pub or beer garden to back against any bar.

Few people realize that the mood of the man when having his drink is of the greatest importance; if the drink, the atmosphere of the place, and the barman's smile and amiability are conducive to putting its patron in the right frame of mind, the success of such a place is certain.

The successful barman must be a chemist, a physiologist and a psychologist of the first order, in other words the true mixologist is a man of science. Furthermore, he requires an understanding of humanity, and ability to sympathize with his patrons' real or fancied troubles, and laugh when they repeat a story which he had told them the day before. He must be able and willing to advise on almost any subject from the proper diet for pet dogs or goldfish to selection of a restaurant or theatre which would please their aunts or their business associates. He must see that they are served promptly and with good drinks, and remember their individual preferences. He must develop some of the qualities of the chameleon, yet retain a personality of his own. Tact is essential, as misunderstandings have a way of arising after the ...nth drink. A good barman really requires everything a diplomat should have and something more, genuine knowledge of food and drink.

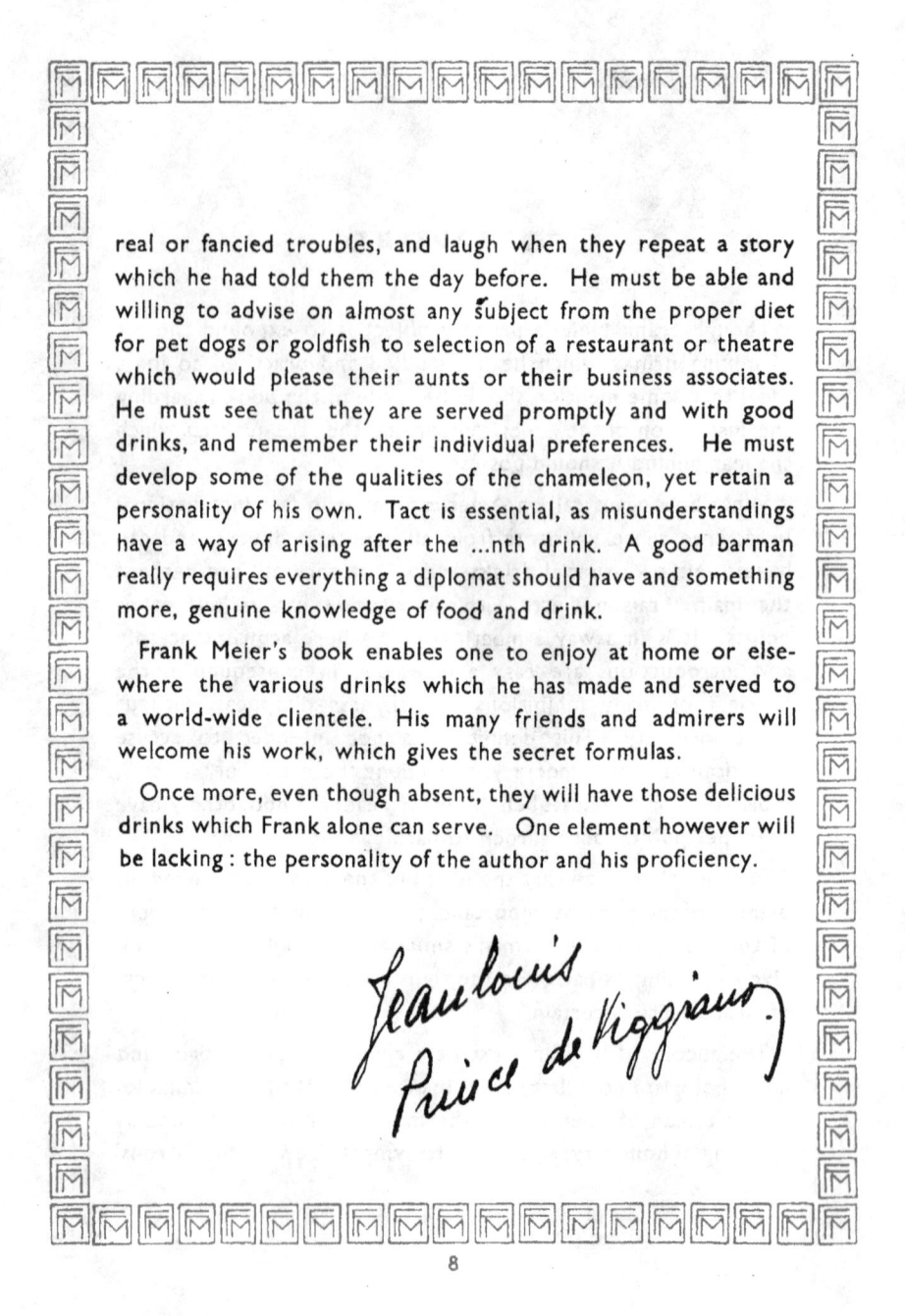

Frank Meier's book enables one to enjoy at home or elsewhere the various drinks which he has made and served to a world-wide clientele. His many friends and admirers will welcome his work, which gives the secret formulas.

Once more, even though absent, they will have those delicious drinks which Frank alone can serve. One element however will be lacking: the personality of the author and his proficiency.

*Jean louis
Prince de Viggiano*

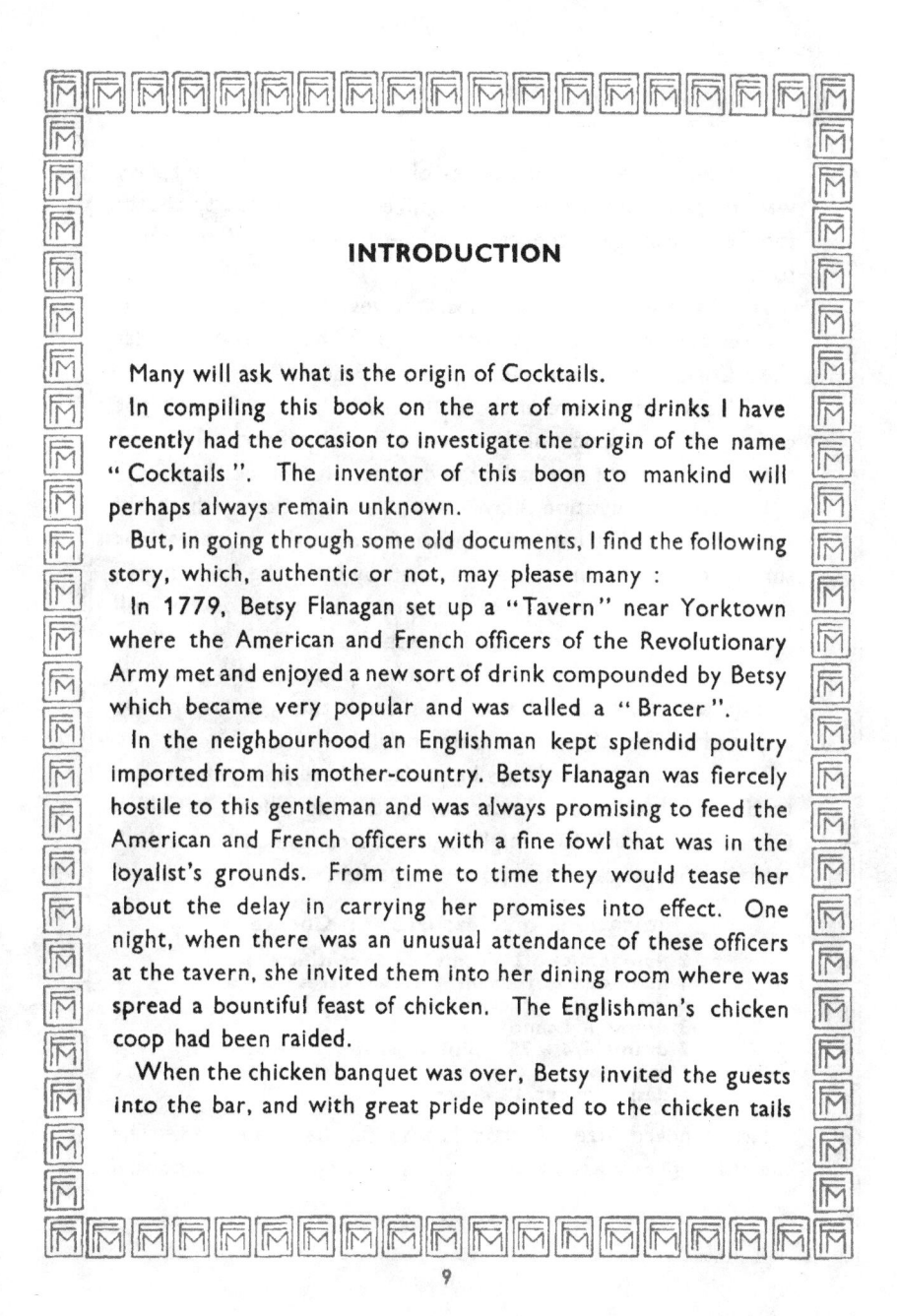

INTRODUCTION

Many will ask what is the origin of Cocktails.

In compiling this book on the art of mixing drinks I have recently had the occasion to investigate the origin of the name " Cocktails ". The inventor of this boon to mankind will perhaps always remain unknown.

But, in going through some old documents, I find the following story, which, authentic or not, may please many :

In 1779, Betsy Flanagan set up a "Tavern" near Yorktown where the American and French officers of the Revolutionary Army met and enjoyed a new sort of drink compounded by Betsy which became very popular and was called a " Bracer ".

In the neighbourhood an Englishman kept splendid poultry imported from his mother-country. Betsy Flanagan was fiercely hostile to this gentleman and was always promising to feed the American and French officers with a fine fowl that was in the loyalist's grounds. From time to time they would tease her about the delay in carrying her promises into effect. One night, when there was an unusual attendance of these officers at the tavern, she invited them into her dining room where was spread a bountiful feast of chicken. The Englishman's chicken coop had been raided.

When the chicken banquet was over, Betsy invited the guests into the bar, and with great pride pointed to the chicken tails spread gracefully around bottles of "Bracers". The surprise was complete and the event recognized by three hearty cheers for Betsy Flanagan, the cause of the Colonists and confusion to the English.

The "Bracers" came off those shelves in a great hurry and the remainder of the night was passed in the bar-room amidst the "Cocks' Tails" and the inspiring "Bracers".

"Give us some more of those 'Cocktails'," was the frequent order; "Vive la Cocktail," shouted a French officer. This was the keynote to the now celebrated name. It "stuck".

The above narration may be truth or fiction; what still remains a fact that has been known for over three generations throughout the civilized world is that, by using the finest ingredients, and mixed with care and precision, the Cocktail will always be the drink of good-fellowship.

More and more they are becoming popular, thousands of people on every part of the globe drink them, but few have acquired the art of mixing a perfect drink.

The Cocktail should always be perfect: there is no reason ever to drink a bad one. Almost any of the ingredients of which Cocktails are composed might better be consumed "straight" rather than just carelessly poured together.

Indications of Measures for Cocktails

2 fluid ounces 2 drams = 6 centilitres;
1 fluid ounce 1 dram = 3 centilitres;
4 drams 1/2 = 1 centilitre 1/2;
3 drams = 1 centilitre;
2 drams 1/4 = 75 millilitres or 1 teaspoon;
1 teaspoon = 6 dashes;
1 dash = about 12 drops.

No standard size of glass has so far been adopted. The measures given of the amount of liquid used to make a normal sized Cocktail are of six centilitres, or of two fluid ounces two drams; divided into halves, fourths, eighths, etc... One eighth equals one teaspoon or six dashes, or about seventy drops.

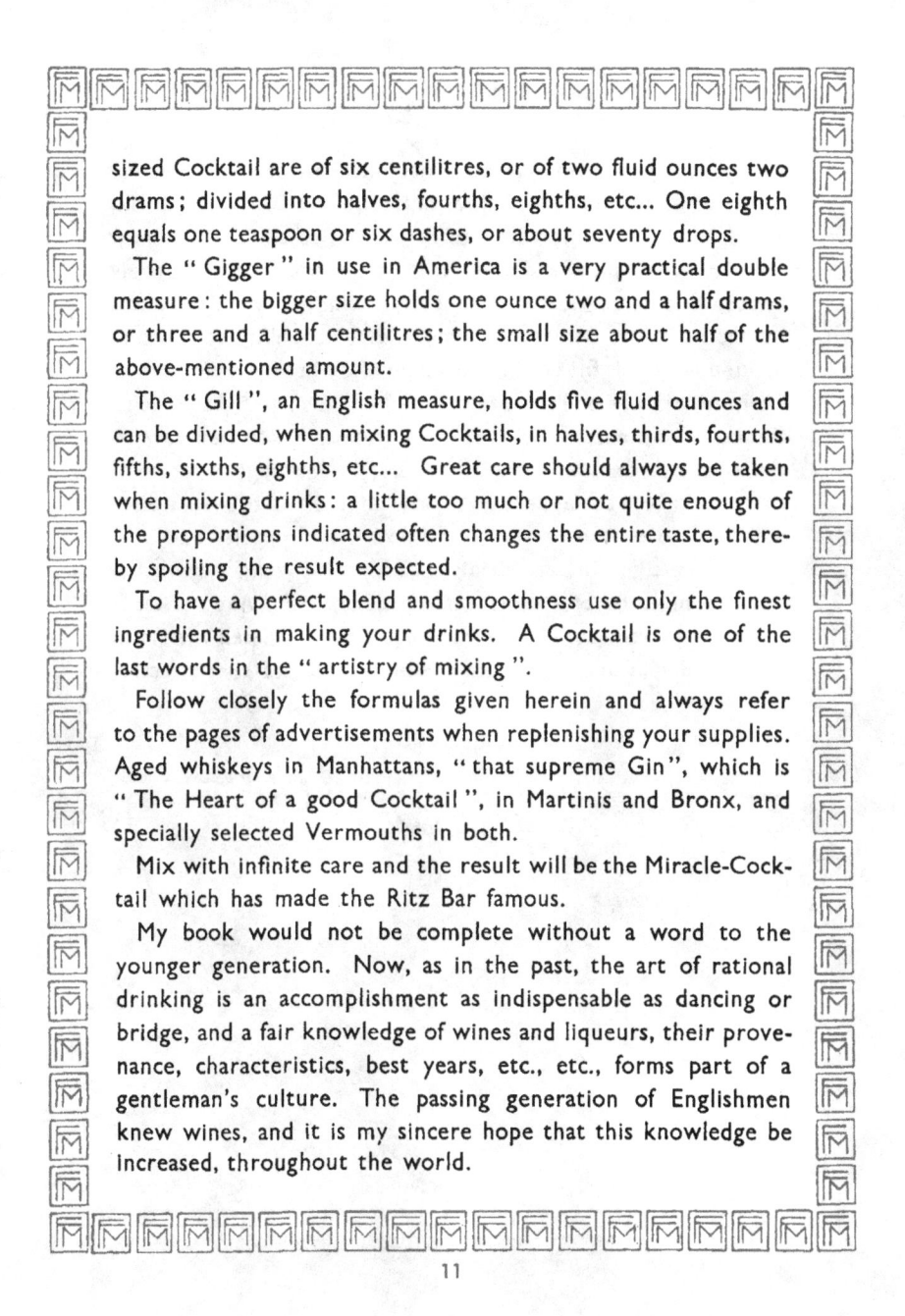

The " Gigger " in use in America is a very practical double measure: the bigger size holds one ounce two and a half drams, or three and a half centilitres; the small size about half of the above-mentioned amount.

The " Gill ", an English measure, holds five fluid ounces and can be divided, when mixing Cocktails, in halves, thirds, fourths, fifths, sixths, eighths, etc... Great care should always be taken when mixing drinks: a little too much or not quite enough of the proportions indicated often changes the entire taste, thereby spoiling the result expected.

To have a perfect blend and smoothness use only the finest ingredients in making your drinks. A Cocktail is one of the last words in the " artistry of mixing ".

Follow closely the formulas given herein and always refer to the pages of advertisements when replenishing your supplies. Aged whiskeys in Manhattans, " that supreme Gin ", which is " The Heart of a good Cocktail ", in Martinis and Bronx, and specially selected Vermouths in both.

Mix with infinite care and the result will be the Miracle-Cocktail which has made the Ritz Bar famous.

My book would not be complete without a word to the younger generation. Now, as in the past, the art of rational drinking is an accomplishment as indispensable as dancing or bridge, and a fair knowledge of wines and liqueurs, their provenance, characteristics, best years, etc., etc., forms part of a gentleman's culture. The passing generation of Englishmen knew wines, and it is my sincere hope that this knowledge be increased, throughout the world.

Any young man who can convince me that his lips will never touch alcohol need not follow my required course in drinks and drinking. To know how to drink is as essential as to know how to swim, and one should be at home in both these closely related elements. Each man reacts differently to alcohol; he should know before the time when, according to custom, he indulges in his first collegiate "binge", whether liquor affects his head, his legs or his morals; whether he sings, fights, weeps, climbs lamp-posts or behaves with excessive affection toward the opposite sex; whether, in short, it makes him a jovial companion or a social pest. A knowledge of these weaknesses will help to overcome them. "Know your capacity and stay within limits." One can drink sensibly, if one knows what a chaos a mixture of liquors can produce. "In vino veritas", so often quoted, does not mean that a man will tell the truth when in drink, but will reveal the hidden side of his character.

HOW TO ENJOY COCKTAILS AT HOME

ABOUT 300 DIFFERENT COCKTAILS AND MIXED DRINKS

FROM 12 BOTTLES

Anis Pernod fils, Bacardi Rum, Brandy, Champagne, White Curaçao, Gordon's Gin, Noilly Prat and Martini-Rossi Vermouths, Port Wine, Rye or Bourbon Whiskey, Scotch Whisky, Sherry and the following household supplies:

FRUITS : Grape Fruit, Lemons or Limes, Oranges, Pineapples, Fruit of season.

GROCERIES : Allspice, Eggs, Honey, Maraschino Cherries, Milk, Nutmeg, Rock Candy, Salt, Pepper, Celery Salt, Sugar, Tomatoes, Vinegar.

MISCELLANEOUS : Angostura Bitters, Clam Juice, Fresh Mint, Ginger Ale, Indian Tonic Water, Schweppes Soda.

SAUCES : Tabasco, Tomato Ketchup, Worcestershire.

SEA FOOD : Crab Meat, Lobster, Oysters, Shrimps

SYRUPS : Grenadine, Lemon, Pineapple, Raspberry, Strawberry.

90 COCKTAILS

Absinthe (French).	Gin.	Perfect.
Affinity.	Gin & It.	Pink Gin.
Bacardi.	Gin & Sin.	Pink Lady.
Bee's Kiss.	Gloom Chaser.	Polly's Special.
Bees' Knees.	Guards.	Port Wine.
Between the Sheets.	H. P. W.	Prairie Oyster.
Bloodhound	Happy Honey Annie.	Quaker.
Brain Duster.	Harvard.	Ray Long.
Brandy.	Hawaiian.	Rob Roy.
Bronx.	Homestead.	Rosslyn.
Buby.	Ingram.	Side Car.
Bunny Hug.	Italian Vermouth.	Soda.
Canadian.	Last Round.	S.S. Washington.
Champagne.	Leviathan.	Suissesse.
Chatterley.	Maiden's Blush.	T. N. T.
Clam Juice.	Majestic.	Temptation.
Clover Club.	Manhattan.	Tomato.
Clover Leaf.	Martini (Dry).	Trinity.
Coffee.	Martini (Medium).	Ward Eight.
Crocker.	Martini (Sweet).	Whiskey.
Daiquiri.	Mary Pickford.	White Lady.
East India.	Millionaire.	White Rose.
Edward VIII.	Monkey Gland.	White Shadow.
Elk's Own.	Old Fashion (5).	Whiz-Bang.
Fancy White Curaçao.	Olympic.	Winter Sport.
Fascinator.	Opal.	Yashmak.
Favorite.	Orange Blossom.	
Florida Yacht Club.	Oyster (Crab Meat,	
Fourth Degree.	Lobster, Shrimp).	

206 MIXED DRINKS

BLAZERS (3)
Blue, Brandy, Rye or Bourbon Whiskey.

COBBLERS (5)
Brandy, Champagne, Port Wine, Sherry, Whiskey.

COLLINS (5)
Bacardi, Brandy, Gin, Rye or Bourbon Whiskey, Scotch Whisky.

COOLERS (6)
Bacardi, Brandy, Hawaiian, Saratoga, Scotch Whisky, Zenith.

CUPS (2)
Grape Fruit, Grape Juice.

DAISIES (4)
Brandy, Gin, Rye or Bourbon Whiskey, Scotch Whisky.

EGG NOGS (5 Hot & 5 Cold)
Brandy, Gin, Sherry, Rye or Bourbon Whiskey, Scotch Whisky.

FIXES (5)
Bacardi, Brandy, Gin, Rye or Bourbon Whiskey, Scotch Whisky.

FIZZES (24)
American, Bacardi, Brandy, Bucks, Diamond, Frank's Special, Gin, Golden, Grenadine, Hoffman House, Imperial, Jubilee, Morning Glory, Nicky's, Orange, Pineapple, Royal, Seapea, Scotch Whisky, Silver, Southside, Strawberry, Texas, Violet.

FLIPS (7)
Brandy, Gin, Lemon, Porto, Sherry, Rye or Bourbon Whiskey, Scotch Whisky.

HIGHBALLS (5)
Bacardi, Brandy, Gin, Rye or Bourbon Whiskey, Scotch Whisky.

JULEPS (6)
Brandy, Champagne, Gin, Mint, Pineapple, Scotch Whisky.

LEMONADES (10)
Angostura, Brandy, Egg, Fruit, Orangeade, Plain Lemonade, Raspberry, Strawberry, Rye or Bourbon Whiskey, Scotch Whisky.

MISCELLANEOUS (33)
American Rose, Angostura & Ginger Ale, Angostura & Soda, Barman's Delight, Brandy & Honey, Brandy (Hot), Corpse Reviver, Frank's Refresher, Gin Buck, Gin & Honey, Gin (Hot), Gin Spider, Horse's Neck, King's & Queen's Peg, Magnolia, Mamy Taylor, Milk & Schweppes, Mimosa, Morning Bracer, Morning Smile, Parisette, Pick-Me-Up No. 1 & 2, Rock & Rye, Rye or Bourbon Whiskey & Honey, Sherry & Egg, Stone Wall, Rye or Bourbon Whiskey (Hot), Scotch Whisky & Honey, Summer Delight, Tomate, White Plush.

MORNING GLORY DAISIES (5)
Bacardi, Brandy, Gin, Rye or Bourbon Whiskey, Scotch Whisky.

NEGUS (Hot) (2)
Port Wine, Sherry.

PUFFS (5)
Bacardi, Brandy, Gin, Rye or Bourbon Whiskey, Scotch Whisky.

PUNCHES (7 Cold & 1 Hot)
Brandy, Champagne, Christmas (Hot), Curaçao, Gin, Rye or Bourbon Whiskey, Scotch Whisky.

RICKIES (5)
Bacardi, Brandy, Gin, Rye or Bourbon Whiskey, Scotch Whisky.

SANGAREES (6 Hot & 6 Cold)
Brandy, Gin, Port Wine, Sherry, Rye or Bourbon Whiskey, Scotch Whisky.

SKINS (4 Hot & 4 Cold)
Brandy, Gin, Rye or Bourbon Whiskey, Scotch Whisky.

SLINGS (5 Hot & 5 Cold)
Bacardi, Brandy, Gin, Rye or Bourbon Whiskey, Scotch Whisky.

SMASHES (4)
Brandy, Gin, Rye or Bourbon Whiskey, Scotch Whisky.

SOURS (5)
Bacardi, Brandy, Gin, Rye or Bourbon Whiskey, Scotch Whisky.

SQUASHES (2)
Lemon, Rosey.

TODDIES (5 Hot & 5 Cold)
Bacardi, Brandy, Gin, Rye or Bourbon Whiskey, Scotch Whisky.

ZOOMS (5)
Bacardi, Brandy, Gin, Rye or Bourbon Whiskey, Scotch Whisky.

VARIOUS SPECIALITIES AND THEIR ORIGIN

AGUARDIENTE is a strong Liquor distilled from Grapes, very popular in Spain and Mexico.

AKVAVIT is a strong white Liqueur made in Scandinavia.

ARACK, GUARUZO & KAMTCHATKA WATKY are distilled from Rice.

ARAKI & LAGBI are Liquors made from the juice of Dates.

BARACK-PALINKA is distilled from Apricots, in Hungary.

CACHIRI & PRAYA are beverages made from sweet Potatoes.

CALISAY is an excellent Magen bitter made in Freiburg.

CANA, CAXACA, GUARAPO, PARATY & TEQUILA are distilled from Sugar cane.

CHA & SINDAY are beverages made in China and India from the sap of the Palm tree.

CHICHA is distilled from Grapes, in Bolivia.

DANTZIGER WASSER is a delicious white Liqueur containing little gold flakes.

DOUZICO is Absinthe made in Turkey.

ELIXIR DE SPA is considered the best cure for indigestion.

FINKEL is inferior Gin made in Norway.

FUNDADOR is the name of a Spanish Brandy.

IVA LIQUEUR is a green Liqueur obtained from herbs grown on the highest Alps in Switzerland.

IZARRA is one of the many French Liqueurs (like Chartreuse, Bénédictine, Florestine des Alpes, Vieille Cure, etc...).

KAWA is made from certain roots in Hawaii.

KIRSCHWASSER is distilled from Cherries.

KVAS is a national beverage in Russia, made from Bread.

MARASCHINO is distilled from the Mahaleb Cherry.

MASTIC is a Liqueur made in Greece.

MAZATO is a Peruvian beverage made from Corn (Maize).

MESCAL is a Mexican Liquor made from Maquey Aloe.

MONTWIJN - Old Dutch word for Whiskey.

NALIVKA is a Liqueur very popular in Russia.

OAKULIHOU is a popular beverage in the Hawaii Islands.

PIMENTO DRAM is a sort of Rum made in Jamaica.

PINCHE SOTO is a Liqueur made in Spain.

POLYNNAIA is a sort of Whiskey made in Russia.

POTHEEN, name given to Whiskey distilled privately in Ireland.

QUETSCH or SLIVOVITZ is distilled from Prunes (very popular in Central Europe and the Balkans).

RATAFIA is a Liqueur made from different fruits or plants macerated in Alcohol.

SAKE, made from rice, is the national drink in Japan.

SBITEN is a hot drink popular in N. Russia made with Honey, Pepper and boiling water.

SCHNAPPS is Holland Gin, originally made in Schiedam; the word Schnapps is commonly used in Europe to designate potent spirits of all sorts.

SPUMANTE, Italian term for Sparkling Wines.

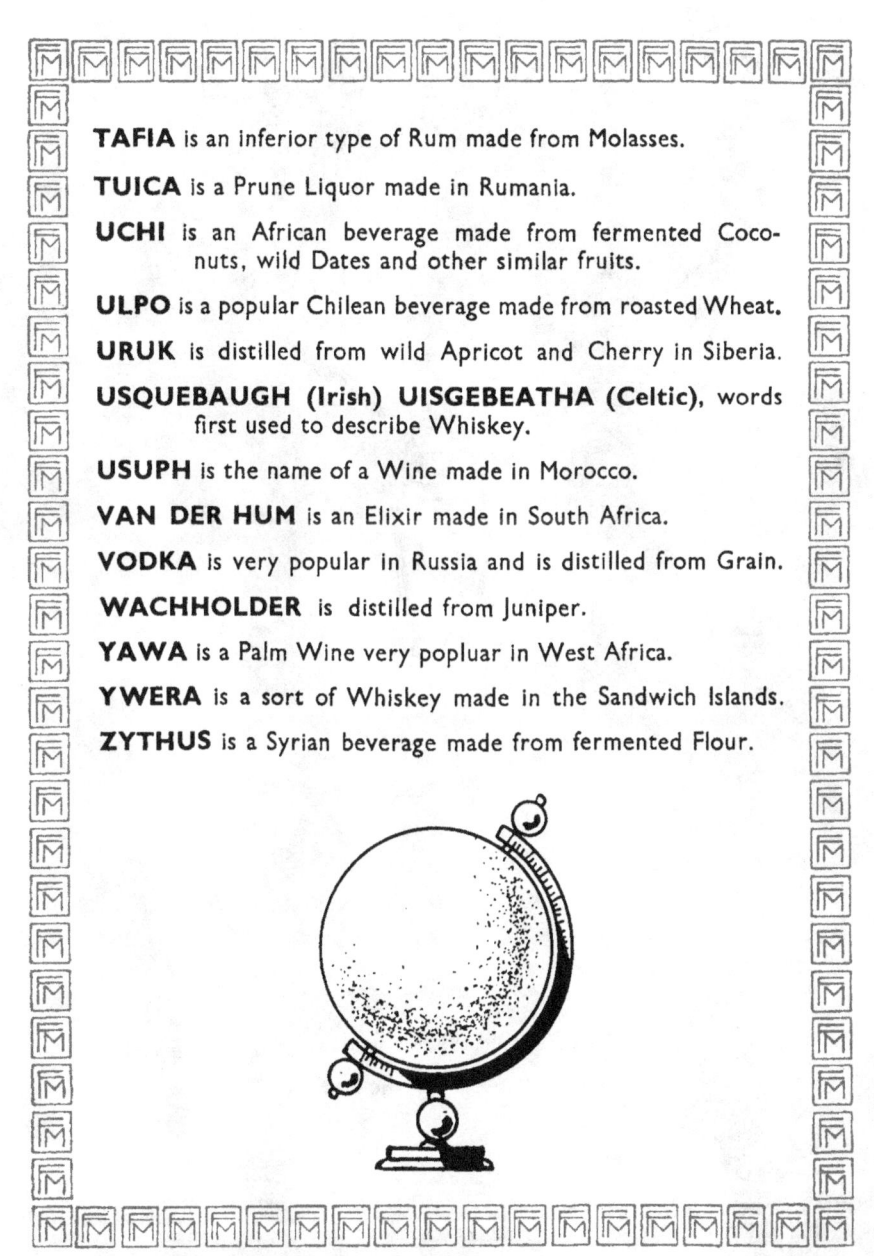

TAFIA is an inferior type of Rum made from Molasses.

TUICA is a Prune Liquor made in Rumania.

UCHI is an African beverage made from fermented Coconuts, wild Dates and other similar fruits.

ULPO is a popular Chilean beverage made from roasted Wheat.

URUK is distilled from wild Apricot and Cherry in Siberia.

USQUEBAUGH (Irish) UISGEBEATHA (Celtic), words first used to describe Whiskey.

USUPH is the name of a Wine made in Morocco.

VAN DER HUM is an Elixir made in South Africa.

VODKA is very popular in Russia and is distilled from Grain.

WACHHOLDER is distilled from Juniper.

YAWA is a Palm Wine very popluar in West Africa.

YWERA is a sort of Whiskey made in the Sandwich Islands.

ZYTHUS is a Syrian beverage made from fermented Flour.

Recipes marked ⟨F⟩
were originated by the Author.

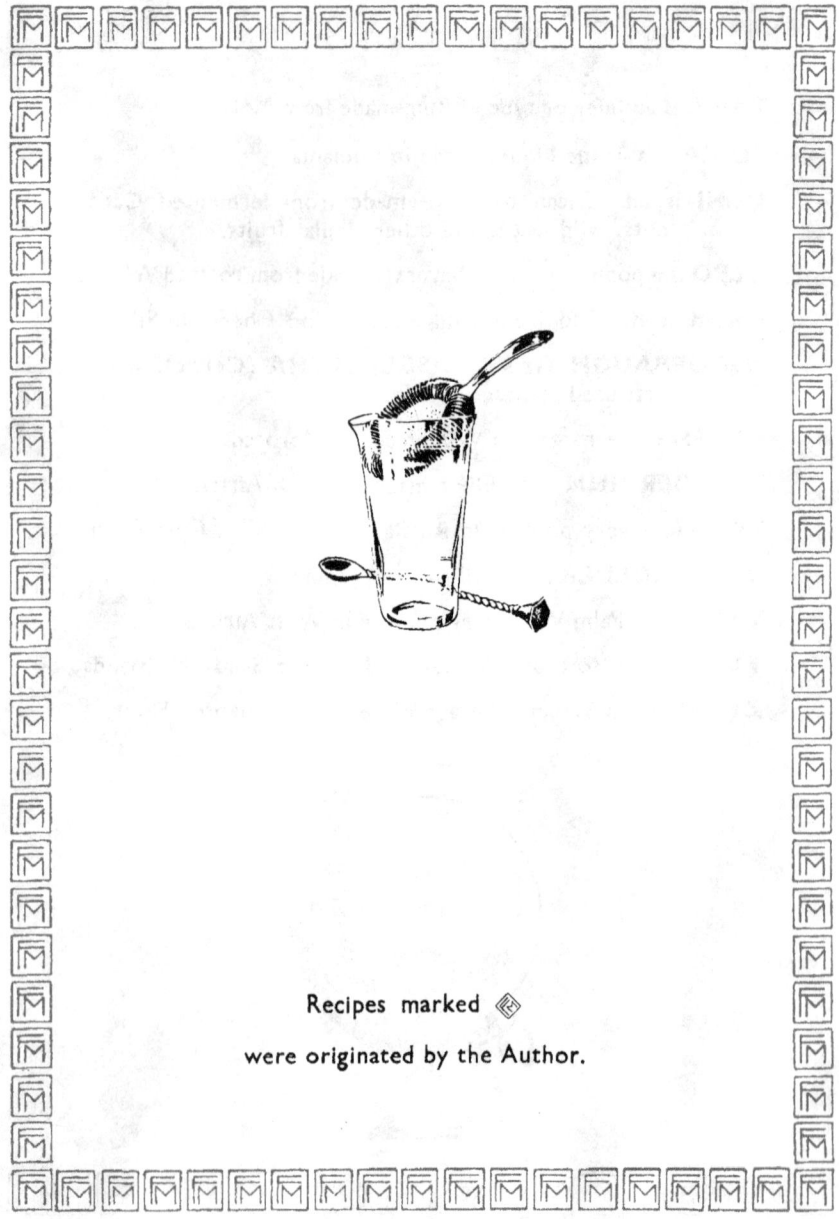

COCKTAILS

THIRSTY EARTH DRINKS UP THE RAIN,
TREES FROM EARTH DRINK THAT AGAIN;
OCEAN DRINKS THE AIR; THE SUN
DRINKS THE SEA, AND HIM THE MOON.
ANY REASON, CANST THOU THINK,
I SHOULD THIRST WHILE ALL THESE DRINK?

                    ANACREON

WHAT WOULD A DINNER BE WITHOUT A COCKTAIL?

COCKTAILS

IN MIXING COCKTAILS OR ANY OTHER DRINKS, IN SHAKER OR MIXING-GLASS, ICE ALWAYS PRECEDES OTHER CONTENTS.

THE TERM "GLASS," USED THROUGHOUT THESE RECIPES, MEANS A 2-OUNCE, 2-DRAM OR 6-CENTILITRE GLASS.

THE DESIGNATIONS "ONE-FIFTH," "ONE-SIXTH," ETC., NOT FOLLOWED BY THE WORD "GLASS," INDICATE FRACTIONAL PARTS OF THE LIQUOR OR INGREDIENT USED.

ABSINTHE Nº 1
In shaker: a dash of Anisette, one glass of Absinthe; shake well and serve very cold.

ABSINTHE Nº 2
In shaker: a dash of Orange Bitters, one-third Gin, two-thirds Absinthe; shake well and serve very cold.

Add Sugar or Syrup if Absinthe is not sweetened.

ABSINTHE (French style)
In tumbler: a large piece of Ice, one glass of Absinthe; place a lump of sugar on Absinthe-spoon or ordinary fork, pour upon it water to suit taste and serve.

ADONIS
In mixing-glass: a dash of Orange Bitters, half dry Sherry, half Italian Vermouth; stir slightly and serve.

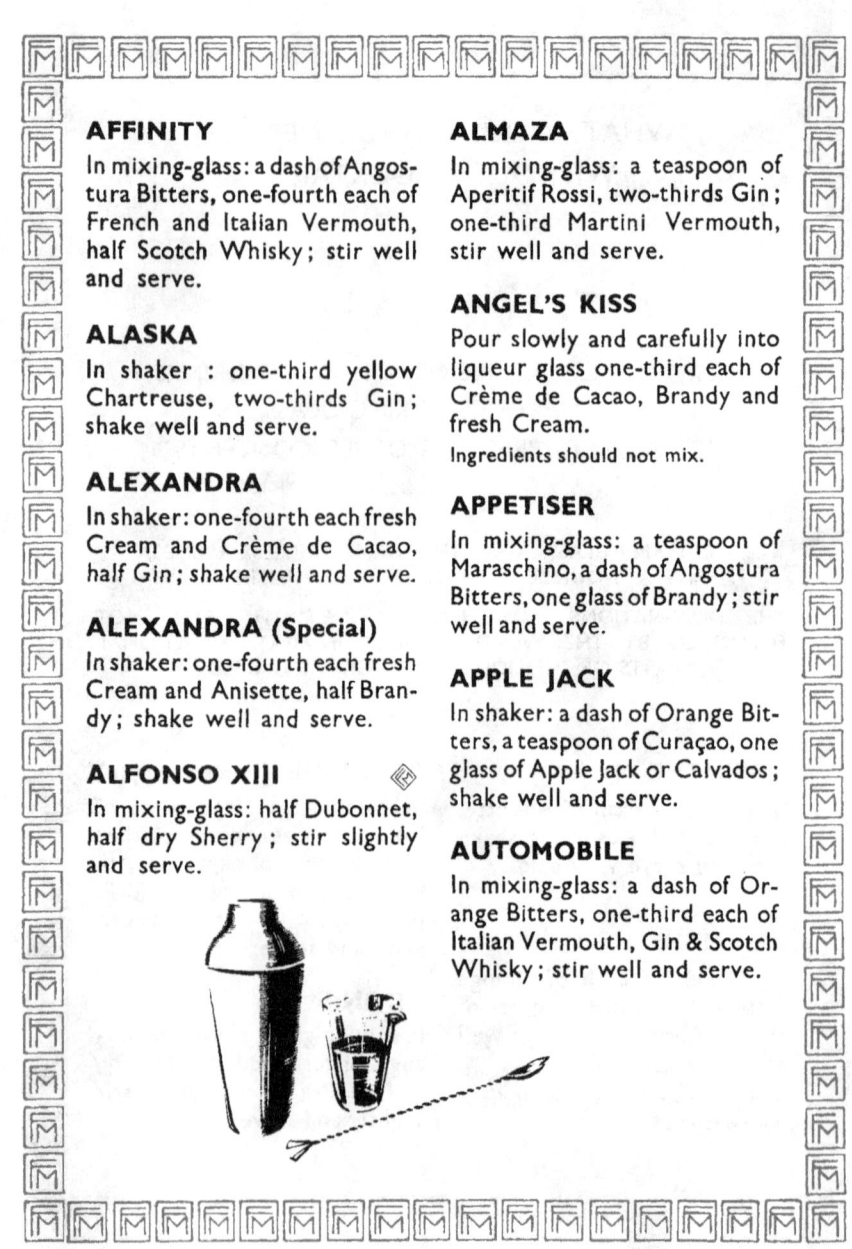

AFFINITY
In mixing-glass: a dash of Angostura Bitters, one-fourth each of French and Italian Vermouth, half Scotch Whisky; stir well and serve.

ALASKA
In shaker : one-third yellow Chartreuse, two-thirds Gin; shake well and serve.

ALEXANDRA
In shaker: one-fourth each fresh Cream and Crème de Cacao, half Gin; shake well and serve.

ALEXANDRA (Special)
In shaker: one-fourth each fresh Cream and Anisette, half Brandy; shake well and serve.

ALFONSO XIII
In mixing-glass: half Dubonnet, half dry Sherry; stir slightly and serve.

ALMAZA
In mixing-glass: a teaspoon of Aperitif Rossi, two-thirds Gin; one-third Martini Vermouth, stir well and serve.

ANGEL'S KISS
Pour slowly and carefully into liqueur glass one-third each of Crème de Cacao, Brandy and fresh Cream.
Ingredients should not mix.

APPETISER
In mixing-glass: a teaspoon of Maraschino, a dash of Angostura Bitters, one glass of Brandy; stir well and serve.

APPLE JACK
In shaker: a dash of Orange Bitters, a teaspoon of Curaçao, one glass of Apple Jack or Calvados; shake well and serve.

AUTOMOBILE
In mixing-glass: a dash of Orange Bitters, one-third each of Italian Vermouth, Gin & Scotch Whisky; stir well and serve.

BACARDI
In shaker: the juice of one-quarter Lemon, a teaspoon of French Vermouth, one-half teaspoon of Grenadine, one-half glass Bacardi Rum; shake well and serve.

B. V. D.
In mixing-glass: one-third Bacardi Rum, Vermouth (French) Dubonnet; stir well and serve.

BEE'S KISS
In shaker: a teaspoon each of Fresh Cream and Honey, one-half glass of Bacardi; shake well and serve.

BEES' KNEES
In shaker: the juice of one-quarter Lemon, a teaspoon of Honey, one-half glass of Gin; shake well and serve.

BENTLEY
In mixing-glass: half Dubonnet, half Apple Jack or Calvados; stir well and serve.

BETWEEN THE SHEETS
In shaker: a teaspoon of Lemon juice, one-third each of Brandy, Curaçao and Bacardi; shake well and serve.

BIJOU
In mixing-glass: a dash of Orange Bitters, one-third each of French Vermouth, Curaçao and Gin; stir well and serve with Maraschino Cherry.

BLACKTHORN
In mixing-glass: a dash each of Angostura Bitters and Anis "Pernod fils", half French Vermouth, half Irish Whiskey; stir well and serve.

BLOODHOUND
In shaker: crush three ripe Strawberries; a teaspoon each of French and Italian Vermouth, one-half glass of Gin; shake well and serve.

BLUE BIRD
Special for Sir Malcolm Campbell

In shaker: a teaspoon each of Lemon juice and Curaçao, one-half glass of Gin, three drops of Tincture of (Vegetable) Blue; shake well and serve.

BOBBY BURNS

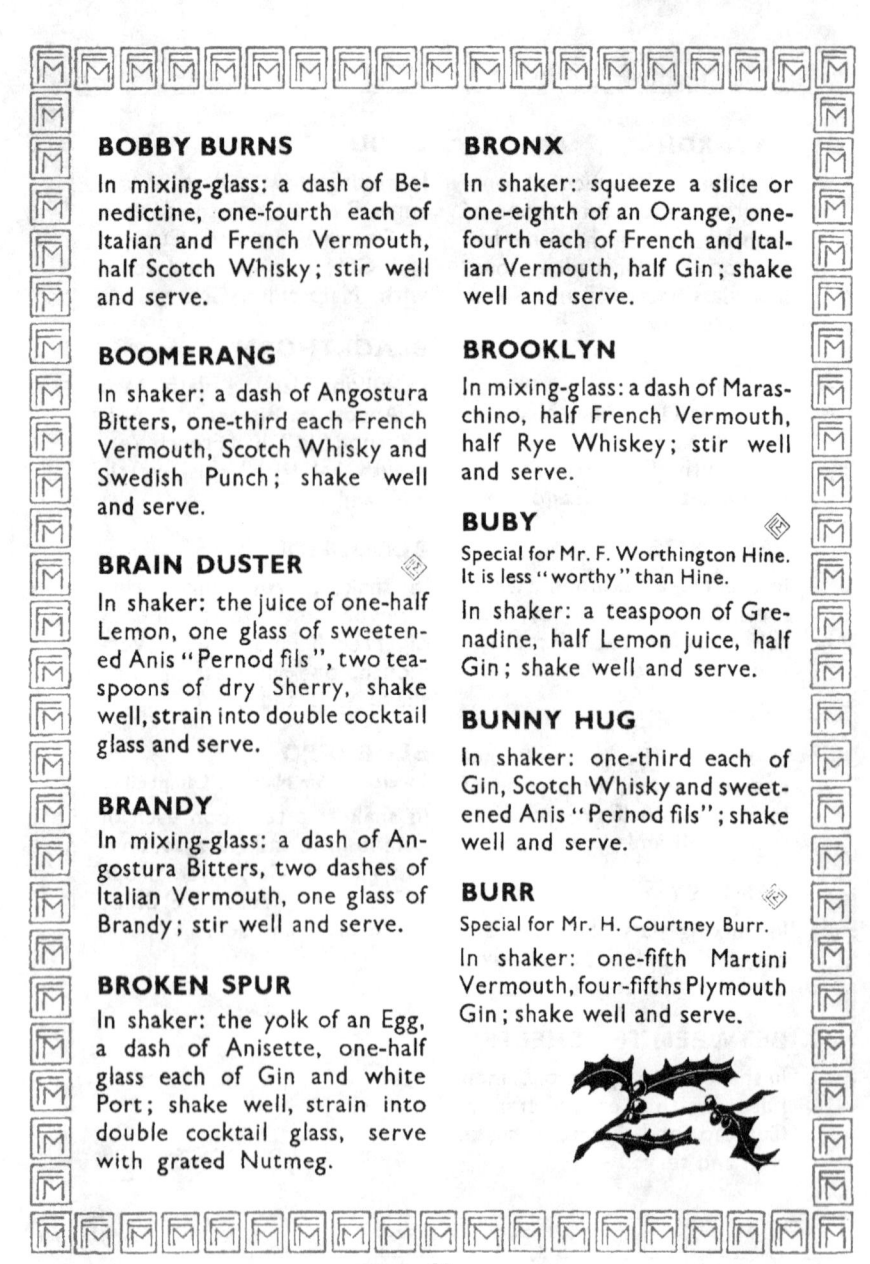

In mixing-glass: a dash of Benedictine, one-fourth each of Italian and French Vermouth, half Scotch Whisky; stir well and serve.

BOOMERANG

In shaker: a dash of Angostura Bitters, one-third each French Vermouth, Scotch Whisky and Swedish Punch; shake well and serve.

BRAIN DUSTER

In shaker: the juice of one-half Lemon, one glass of sweetened Anis "Pernod fils", two teaspoons of dry Sherry, shake well, strain into double cocktail glass and serve.

BRANDY

In mixing-glass: a dash of Angostura Bitters, two dashes of Italian Vermouth, one glass of Brandy; stir well and serve.

BROKEN SPUR

In shaker: the yolk of an Egg, a dash of Anisette, one-half glass each of Gin and white Port; shake well, strain into double cocktail glass, serve with grated Nutmeg.

BRONX

In shaker: squeeze a slice or one-eighth of an Orange, one-fourth each of French and Italian Vermouth, half Gin; shake well and serve.

BROOKLYN

In mixing-glass: a dash of Maraschino, half French Vermouth, half Rye Whiskey; stir well and serve.

BUBY

Special for Mr. F. Worthington Hine. It is less "worthy" than Hine.

In shaker: a teaspoon of Grenadine, half Lemon juice, half Gin; shake well and serve.

BUNNY HUG

In shaker: one-third each of Gin, Scotch Whisky and sweetened Anis "Pernod fils"; shake well and serve.

BURR

Special for Mr. H. Courtney Burr.

In shaker: one-fifth Martini Vermouth, four-fifths Plymouth Gin; shake well and serve.

BYRRH

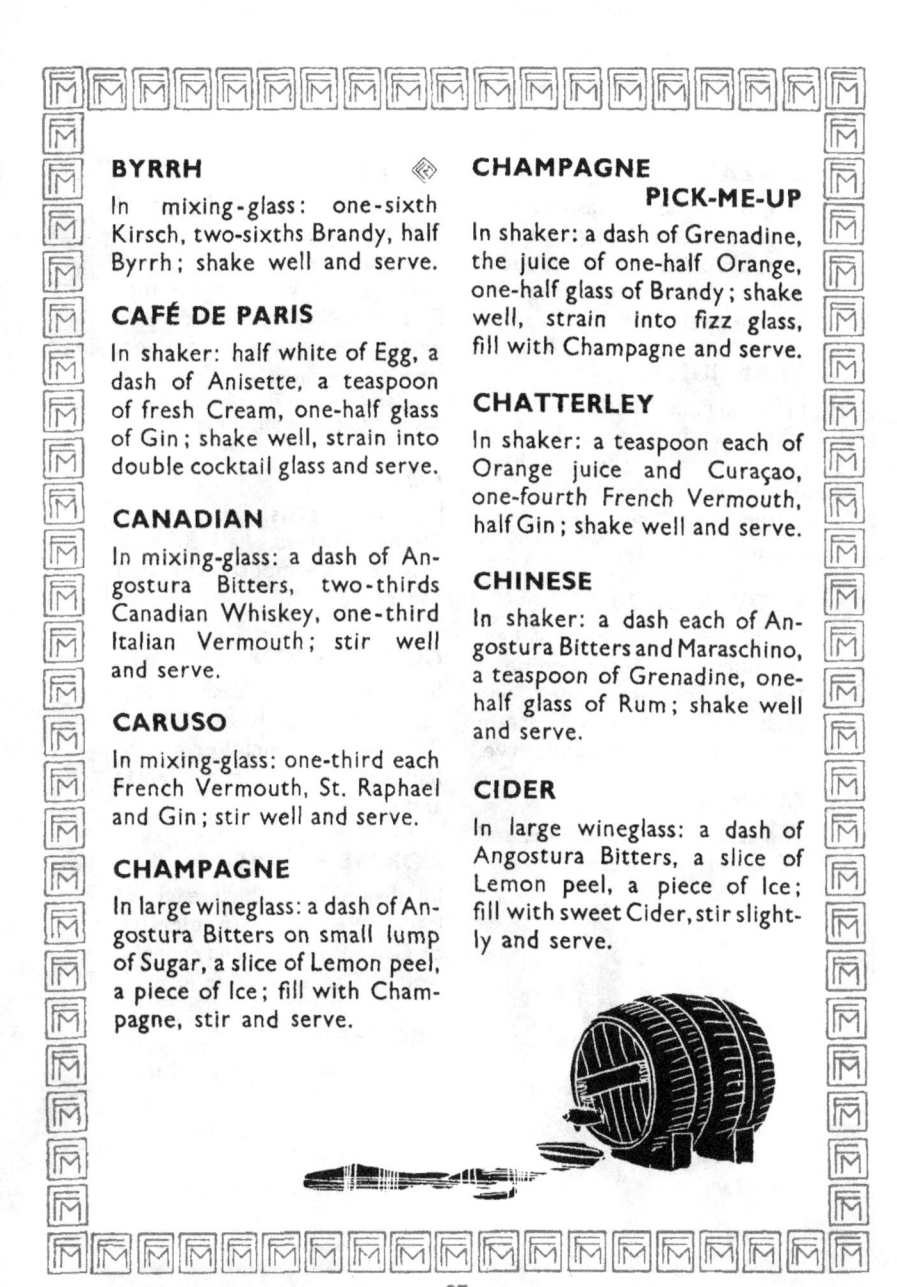

In mixing-glass: one-sixth Kirsch, two-sixths Brandy, half Byrrh; shake well and serve.

CAFÉ DE PARIS

In shaker: half white of Egg, a dash of Anisette, a teaspoon of fresh Cream, one-half glass of Gin; shake well, strain into double cocktail glass and serve.

CANADIAN

In mixing-glass: a dash of Angostura Bitters, two-thirds Canadian Whiskey, one-third Italian Vermouth; stir well and serve.

CARUSO

In mixing-glass: one-third each French Vermouth, St. Raphael and Gin; stir well and serve.

CHAMPAGNE

In large wineglass: a dash of Angostura Bitters on small lump of Sugar, a slice of Lemon peel, a piece of Ice; fill with Champagne, stir and serve.

CHAMPAGNE PICK-ME-UP

In shaker: a dash of Grenadine, the juice of one-half Orange, one-half glass of Brandy; shake well, strain into fizz glass, fill with Champagne and serve.

CHATTERLEY

In shaker: a teaspoon each of Orange juice and Curaçao, one-fourth French Vermouth, half Gin; shake well and serve.

CHINESE

In shaker: a dash each of Angostura Bitters and Maraschino, a teaspoon of Grenadine, one-half glass of Rum; shake well and serve.

CIDER

In large wineglass: a dash of Angostura Bitters, a slice of Lemon peel, a piece of Ice; fill with sweet Cider, stir slightly and serve.

CINZANO

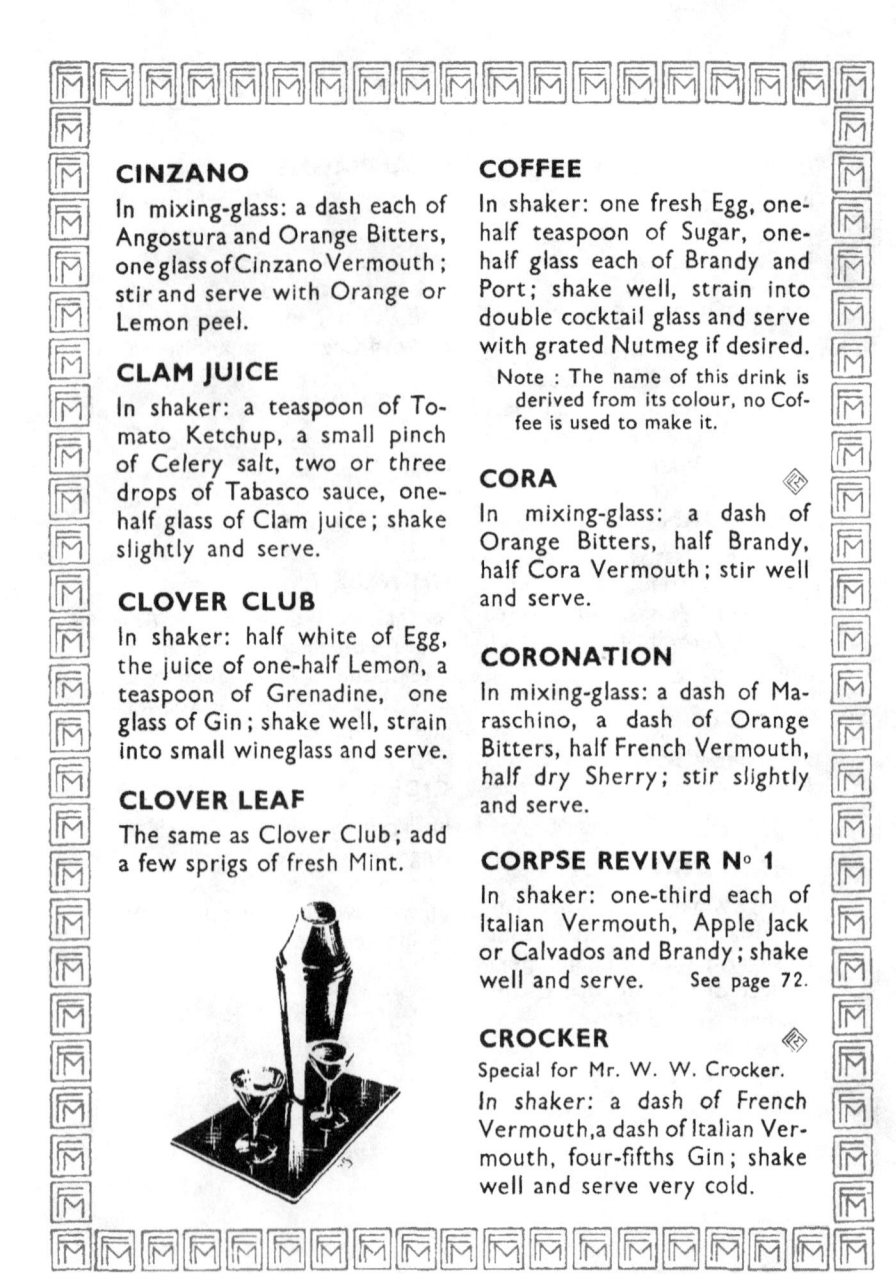

In mixing-glass: a dash each of Angostura and Orange Bitters, one glass of Cinzano Vermouth; stir and serve with Orange or Lemon peel.

CLAM JUICE

In shaker: a teaspoon of Tomato Ketchup, a small pinch of Celery salt, two or three drops of Tabasco sauce, one-half glass of Clam juice; shake slightly and serve.

CLOVER CLUB

In shaker: half white of Egg, the juice of one-half Lemon, a teaspoon of Grenadine, one glass of Gin; shake well, strain into small wineglass and serve.

CLOVER LEAF

The same as Clover Club; add a few sprigs of fresh Mint.

COFFEE

In shaker: one fresh Egg, one-half teaspoon of Sugar, one-half glass each of Brandy and Port; shake well, strain into double cocktail glass and serve with grated Nutmeg if desired.

Note : The name of this drink is derived from its colour, no Coffee is used to make it.

CORA

In mixing-glass: a dash of Orange Bitters, half Brandy, half Cora Vermouth; stir well and serve.

CORONATION

In mixing-glass: a dash of Maraschino, a dash of Orange Bitters, half French Vermouth, half dry Sherry; stir slightly and serve.

CORPSE REVIVER N° 1

In shaker: one-third each of Italian Vermouth, Apple Jack or Calvados and Brandy; shake well and serve.   See page 72.

CROCKER

Special for Mr. W. W. Crocker.

In shaker: a dash of French Vermouth, a dash of Italian Vermouth, four-fifths Gin; shake well and serve very cold.

DAIQUIRI
In shaker: the juice of one-half Lime or quarter Lemon, one-half teaspoon of Sugar, one-half glass of Bacardi; shake well and serve.

DEAUVILLE
In large wineglass: a dash of Angostura Bitters on small lump of Sugar, a dash of Anis "Pernod fils", a piece of Ice; fill with Champagne, a dash of Apple Jack or Calvados on top, and serve.

DERBY
In shaker: a dash of Peach Bitters, a sprig of fresh Mint, one glass of Gin; shake well and serve.

DIKI-DIKI
In shaker: one-sixth unsweetened Grape Fruit juice, one-sixth Swedish Punch, two-thirds Apple Jack or Calvados; shake well and serve.

DOCTOR
In shaker: a teaspoon each of Lemon and Orange juice, half Swedish Punch, half Bacardi; shake well and serve.

D. O. M.
In shaker: a teaspoon each of Orange juice and Benedictine, three-fourths Gin; shake well and serve.

DOUGLAS
In mixing-glass: one-third French Vermouth, two-thirds Old Tom Gin; stir well and serve with Orange peel.

DUBONNET
In mixing-glass: a dash of Angostura Bitters, one glass of Dubonnet; stir slightly and serve with Lemon peel.

DUNLAP
In mixing-glass: a dash of Angostura Bitters, half sweet Sherry, half Rum; stir well and serve.

EAST INDIA
In shaker: a dash of Angostura Bitters, a teaspoon of Pineapple Syrup, one glass of Brandy; shake well and serve with a piece of Pineapple.

EDWARD VIII
In small tumbler: one glass of Seagram's Rye Whiskey, a dash of Anis "Pernod fils", two teaspoons each of Italian Vermouth and plain water, a piece of Ice in long Orange peel, stir well and serve.

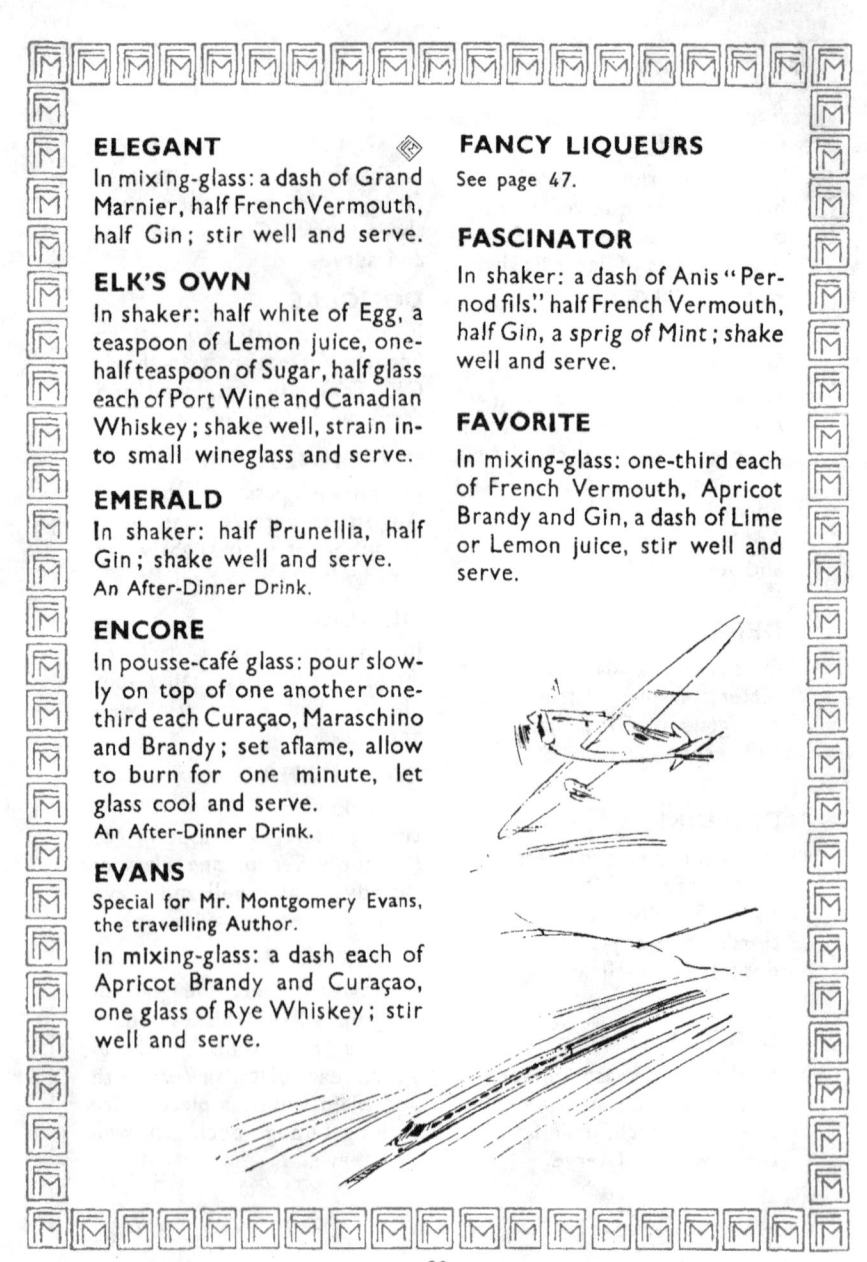

ELEGANT
In mixing-glass: a dash of Grand Marnier, half French Vermouth, half Gin; stir well and serve.

ELK'S OWN
In shaker: half white of Egg, a teaspoon of Lemon juice, one-half teaspoon of Sugar, half glass each of Port Wine and Canadian Whiskey; shake well, strain into small wineglass and serve.

EMERALD
In shaker: half Prunellia, half Gin; shake well and serve.
An After-Dinner Drink.

ENCORE
In pousse-café glass: pour slowly on top of one another one-third each Curaçao, Maraschino and Brandy; set aflame, allow to burn for one minute, let glass cool and serve.
An After-Dinner Drink.

EVANS
Special for Mr. Montgomery Evans, the travelling Author.

In mixing-glass: a dash each of Apricot Brandy and Curaçao, one glass of Rye Whiskey; stir well and serve.

FANCY LIQUEURS
See page 47.

FASCINATOR
In shaker: a dash of Anis "Pernod fils," half French Vermouth, half Gin, a sprig of Mint; shake well and serve.

FAVORITE
In mixing-glass: one-third each of French Vermouth, Apricot Brandy and Gin, a dash of Lime or Lemon juice, stir well and serve.

FERNET MINT
In cocktail glass: half Fernet Branca, half green Crème de Menthe; stir slightly and serve. May be iced if desired.

FERNET VERMOUTH
In cocktail glass: half Fernet Branca, half Italian Vermouth; stir slightly and serve. May be iced if desired.

F. Y. C. S.
Florida Yacht Club Special.
In shaker: a teaspoon each of French and Italian Vermouth, two teaspoons of unsweetened Grape Fruit juice, one-half glass of Bacardi; shake well, strain into small wineglass containing a piece of Ice and serve.

FOURTH DEGREE
In mixing-glass: two dashes of Anis "Pernod fils", one-fourth French Vermouth, one-fourth Italian Vermouth, half Gin; stir well and serve.

FRANK'S SPECIAL
In mixing-glass: a dash of Peach Brandy, half French Vermouth, half Gordon's Gin; stir well and serve.

FRENCH VERMOUTH
In mixing-glass: a dash each of Orange Bitters and Curaçao, one glass of French Vermouth; stir slightly and serve.

FUTURITY
In mixing-glass: a dash of Angostura Bitters, one-third French Vermouth, two-thirds Sloe Gin; stir well and serve.

GENEVER
In mixing-glass: a dash of Angostura Bitters, one glass of Holland Gin; stir well and serve.

GIBSON
In mixing-glass: one-fourth Italian Vermouth, three-fourths Gin; stir well and serve with small white Onion.

GIMLET
In cocktail glass: one-third Lime Juice Cordial, two-thirds Gin; stir and serve.   Do not ice.

GIN
In mixing-glass: a dash of Angostura Bitters, a dash of Italian Vermouth, one glass of Gin; stir well and serve.

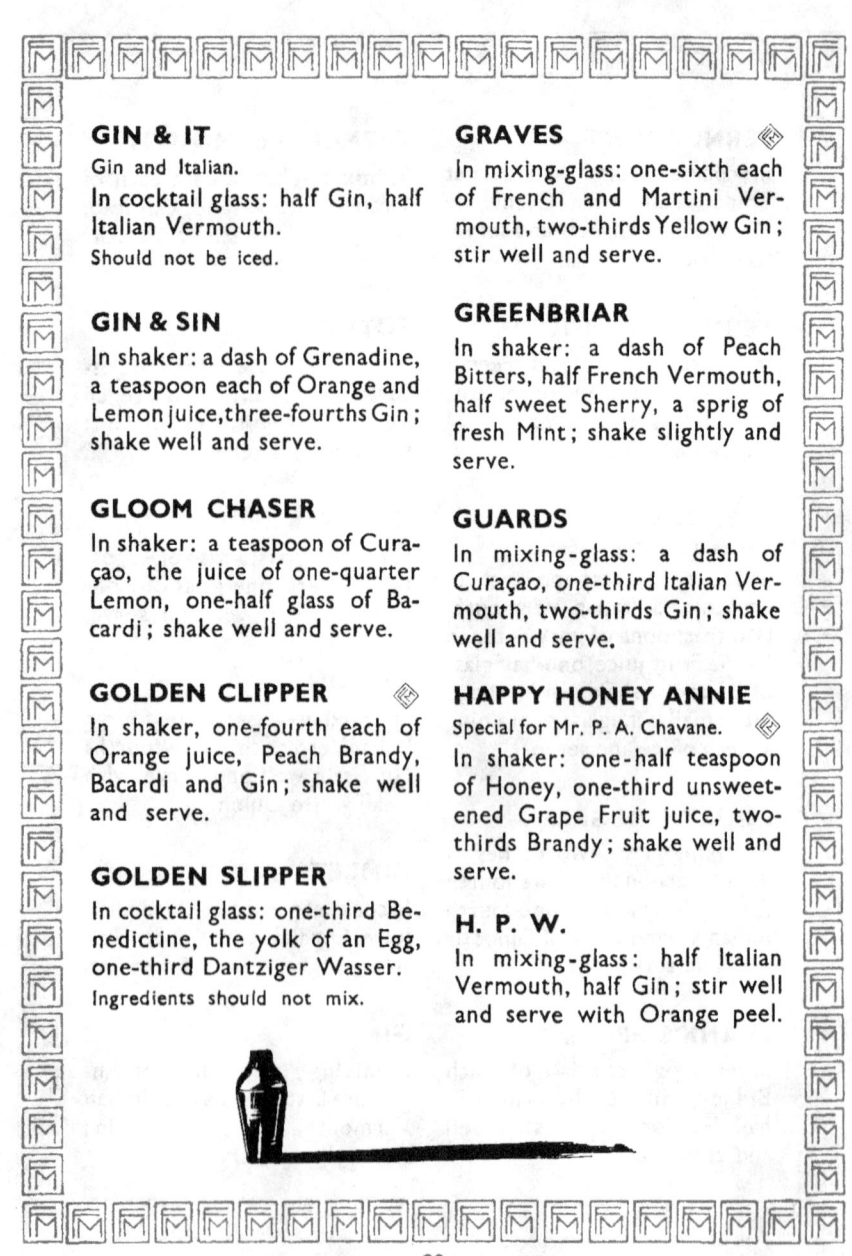

GIN & IT
Gin and Italian.
In cocktail glass: half Gin, half Italian Vermouth.
Should not be iced.

GIN & SIN
In shaker: a dash of Grenadine, a teaspoon each of Orange and Lemon juice, three-fourths Gin; shake well and serve.

GLOOM CHASER
In shaker: a teaspoon of Curaçao, the juice of one-quarter Lemon, one-half glass of Bacardi; shake well and serve.

GOLDEN CLIPPER
In shaker, one-fourth each of Orange juice, Peach Brandy, Bacardi and Gin; shake well and serve.

GOLDEN SLIPPER
In cocktail glass: one-third Benedictine, the yolk of an Egg, one-third Dantziger Wasser.
Ingredients should not mix.

GRAVES
In mixing-glass: one-sixth each of French and Martini Vermouth, two-thirds Yellow Gin; stir well and serve.

GREENBRIAR
In shaker: a dash of Peach Bitters, half French Vermouth, half sweet Sherry, a sprig of fresh Mint; shake slightly and serve.

GUARDS
In mixing-glass: a dash of Curaçao, one-third Italian Vermouth, two-thirds Gin; shake well and serve.

HAPPY HONEY ANNIE
Special for Mr. P. A. Chavane.
In shaker: one-half teaspoon of Honey, one-third unsweetened Grape Fruit juice, two-thirds Brandy; shake well and serve.

H. P. W.
In mixing-glass: half Italian Vermouth, half Gin; stir well and serve with Orange peel.

HARVARD
In mixing-glass: a dash of Angostura Bitters, half Italian Vermouth, half Brandy; stir well and serve.

HAWAIIAN
In shaker: a dash of Curaçao, the juice of one-quarter Orange, one-half glass of Gin; shake well and serve.

HIGHBINDER
In cocktail glass: half Brandy, half Blackberry Brandy; stir and serve.

HOFFMAN HOUSE
In mixing-glass: a dash of Orange Bitters, one-third of French Vermouth, two-thirds Old Tom Gin; stir well and serve with Orange peel.

HOMESTEAD
In shaker: a slice of Orange, one-third Italian Vermouth, two-thirds Gin; shake well and serve.

H.R.W.
In shaker: crush three or four very ripe Cherries, one-third French Vermouth, two-thirds Gin; shake well and serve.

INGRAM
In shaker: a dash of Grenadine, half Orange juice, half Lemon juice; shake slightly and serve.

IRISH WHISKEY
In mixing-glass: a dash each of Angostura Bitters, Curaçao, Maraschino and Anis "Pernod fils", three-fourths Irish Whiskey; stir well and serve.

ITALIAN VERMOUTH
In mixing-glass: a dash of Angostura Bitters, a glass of Martini-Rossi Vermouth; stir well and serve.

JACK ROSE
In shaker: the juice of one-quarter Lemon, one-half teaspoon of Grenadine, one-half glass of Apple Jack or Calvados; shake well and serve.

KNICKERBOCKER
In shaker: crush a small slice of ripe Pineapple, a teaspoon each of Raspberry syrup, Lemon and Orange juice, one glass of Rum; shake well, strain into small wineglass and serve.

LAST ROUND
In mixing-glass: two dashes of Anis "Pernod fils", two dashes of Brandy, half French Vermouth, half Gin; stir well and serve.

LEAVE IT TO ME
In shaker: a teaspoon of Lemon juice, a dash of Maraschino, one-fourth each of Apricot Brandy and French Vermouth, half Gin; shake well and serve.

LEVIATHAN
In shaker: one-fourth Orange juice, one-fourth Italian Vermouth, half Brandy; shake well and serve.

LONDON FOG
In shaker: a dash of Angostura Bitters, half white Crème de Menthe, half Anisette; shake well and serve.
An After-Dinner Drink.

LONE TREE
In mixing-glass: one-third Italian Vermouth, two-thirds Gin; stir well and serve with Olive.

MAIDEN'S BLUSH
In shaker: one-half teaspoon of Grenadine, one-third Anis "Pernod fils", two-thirds Gin; shake well and serve.

MAJESTIC
(OTTO'S SPECIAL)
In shaker: the juice of one-half Lemon, a teaspoon each of French and Italian Vermouth, one glass of white Rum; shake well, strain into double cocktail glass and serve.

MANHATTAN
In mixing-glass: one-fourth Italian Vermouth, one-fourth French Vermouth, half Rye Whiskey; stir well and serve.

MAPLE LEAF
In shaker: the juice of one-half Lemon, one-half glass of Bourbon Whiskey, a teaspoon of Maple syrup; shake well and serve.

MARTINI (Dry)
In mixing-glass: half French Vermouth, half Gin; stir well and serve.

MARTINI (Medium)

In mixing-glass: one-fourth French Vermouth, one-fourth Martini Vermouth, half Gin; stir well and serve.

MARTINI (Sweet)

In mixing-glass: half Martini Vermouth, half Gin; stir well and serve.

MARY PICKFORD

In shaker: one-half teaspoon of Grenadine, half unsweetened Pineapple juice, half white Rum; shake well and serve.

MILLIONAIRE

In shaker: half white of Egg, a dash of Anis "Pernod fils", a dash of Grenadine, one-half glass of Rye Whiskey; shake well, strain into double cocktail glass and serve.

MILLION DOLLAR

In shaker: half white of Egg, a dash of Grenadine, a teaspoon of Pineapple juice, one-half glass of Gin; shake well, strain into double cocktail glass and serve.

MONKEY GLAND

In shaker: a dash of Anis "Pernod fils", a dash of Grenadine, half Orange juice, half Gin; shake well and serve.

N. C. R.

Special for the National Cash Register Company.

In shaker: one-third Noilly Prat Vermouth, Crème de Cacao, Rum; shake well and serve.

OLD FASHION

In small tumbler: a dash of Angostura Bitters on small lump of Sugar, enough water to dissolve Sugar, one glass of Rye or Bourbon Whiskey, a large piece of Ice; stir, add half slice of Orange and serve with glass of water.

Note. — This is the old-fashioned way of making Cocktails. Any Liquor may be chosen to replace Whiskey.

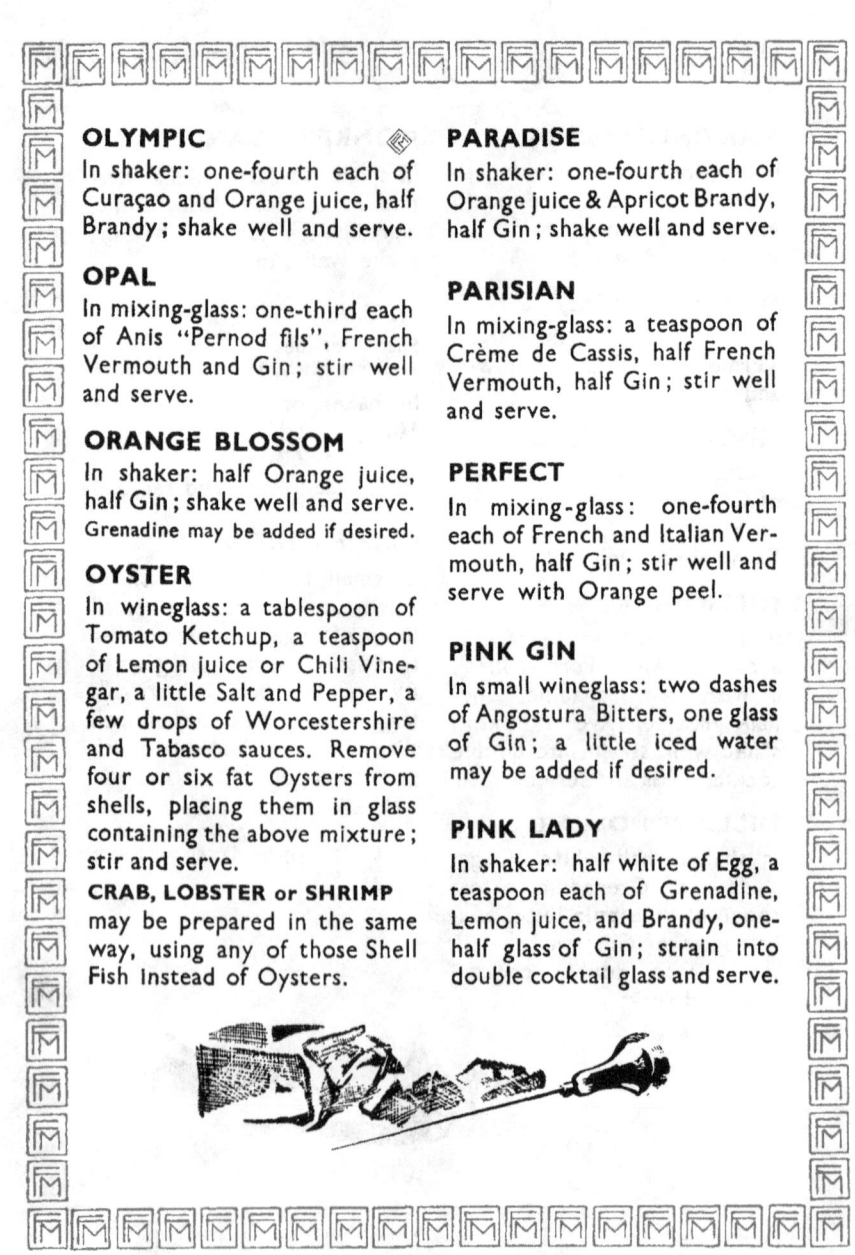

OLYMPIC
In shaker: one-fourth each of Curaçao and Orange juice, half Brandy; shake well and serve.

OPAL
In mixing-glass: one-third each of Anis "Pernod fils", French Vermouth and Gin; stir well and serve.

ORANGE BLOSSOM
In shaker: half Orange juice, half Gin; shake well and serve. Grenadine may be added if desired.

OYSTER
In wineglass: a tablespoon of Tomato Ketchup, a teaspoon of Lemon juice or Chili Vinegar, a little Salt and Pepper, a few drops of Worcestershire and Tabasco sauces. Remove four or six fat Oysters from shells, placing them in glass containing the above mixture; stir and serve.

CRAB, LOBSTER or SHRIMP
may be prepared in the same way, using any of those Shell Fish instead of Oysters.

PARADISE
In shaker: one-fourth each of Orange juice & Apricot Brandy, half Gin; shake well and serve.

PARISIAN
In mixing-glass: a teaspoon of Crème de Cassis, half French Vermouth, half Gin; stir well and serve.

PERFECT
In mixing-glass: one-fourth each of French and Italian Vermouth, half Gin; stir well and serve with Orange peel.

PINK GIN
In small wineglass: two dashes of Angostura Bitters, one glass of Gin; a little iced water may be added if desired.

PINK LADY
In shaker: half white of Egg, a teaspoon each of Grenadine, Lemon juice, and Brandy, one-half glass of Gin; strain into double cocktail glass and serve.

PIPE LINE
In shaker: one-fourth Lemon juice, one-fourth Apricot Brandy, half Bacardi; shake well and serve.

PLANTER'S
In shaker: one-fourth Lemon syrup, one-fourth Orange juice half Rum; shake well and serve.

PLUNGER
A favourite at the Casinos in Deauville and Cannes.

In shaker: one-third each of Swedish Punch, Bacardi and Apple Jack or Calvados; shake well and serve.

POLLY'S SPECIAL
By W. Pollock, Park Lane Hotel, London.

In shaker: one-fourth each of unsweetened Grapefruit juice & Curaçao, half Scotch Whisky; shake well and serve.

POMPADOUR
In shaker: the juice of one-quarter Lemon, half St. James Rum, half Pompadour; shake well and serve.

   Note. — Pompadour is a specially prepared Wine from the Pinot (Charentais) Grape and contains at least 18° of alcohol.

PORT WINE
In mixing-glass: a dash of Angostura Bitters, a teaspoon of Brandy, one glass of Port; stir slightly and serve.

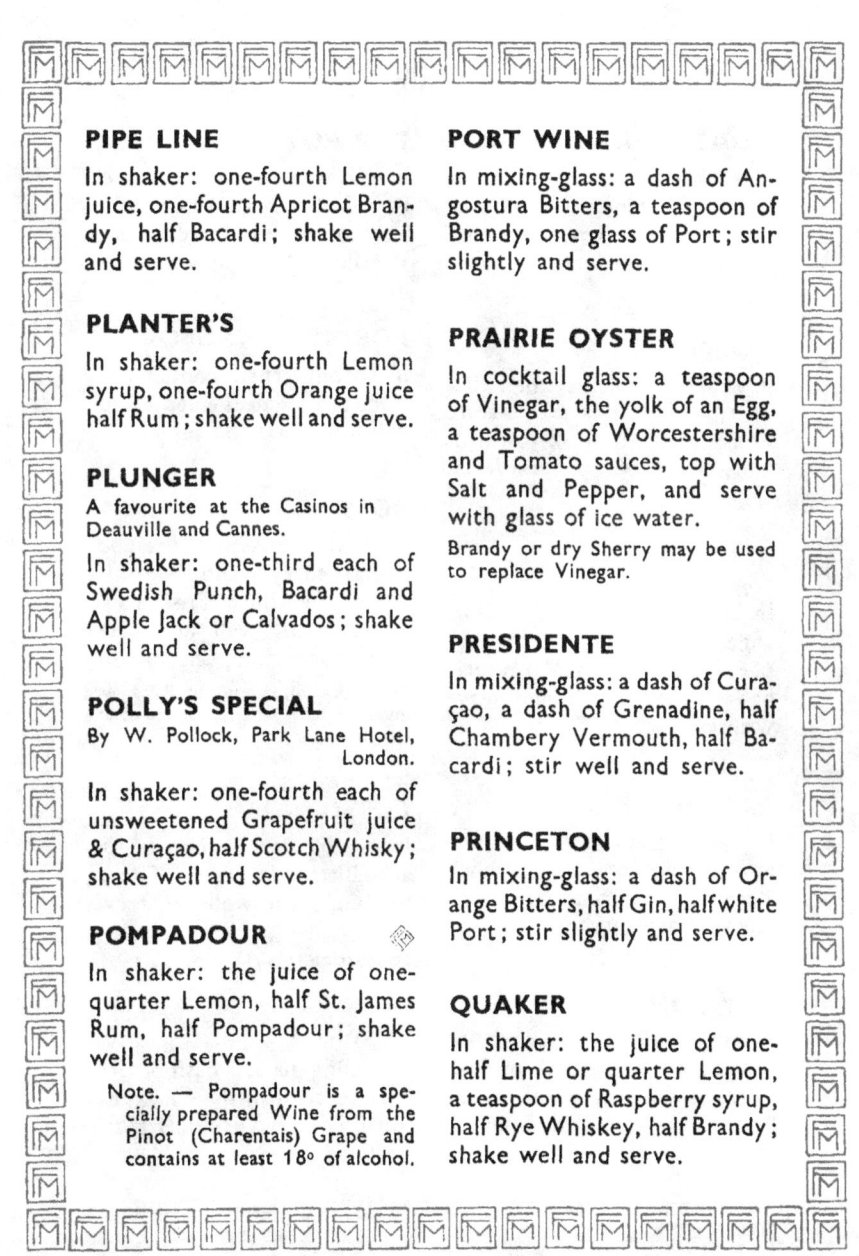

PRAIRIE OYSTER
In cocktail glass: a teaspoon of Vinegar, the yolk of an Egg, a teaspoon of Worcestershire and Tomato sauces, top with Salt and Pepper, and serve with glass of ice water.

Brandy or dry Sherry may be used to replace Vinegar.

PRESIDENTE
In mixing-glass: a dash of Curaçao, a dash of Grenadine, half Chambery Vermouth, half Bacardi; stir well and serve.

PRINCETON
In mixing-glass: a dash of Orange Bitters, half Gin, half white Port; stir slightly and serve.

QUAKER
In shaker: the juice of one-half Lime or quarter Lemon, a teaspoon of Raspberry syrup, half Rye Whiskey, half Brandy; shake well and serve.

QUATRE PAVÉS SPECIAL

In shaker: a teaspoon each of Grand Marnier, Orange and Lemon juice, two-thirds Gin; shake well and serve.

QUEEN'S

In shaker: crush a small slice of ripe Pineapple; one-third French Vermouth, two-thirds Gin; shake well and serve.

R. A. C.
Royal Automobile Club.

In mixing-glass: a dash of Orange Bitters, one-fourth each of French and Italian Vermouth, half Gin; stir well and serve with Maraschino Cherry.

RACQUET CLUB

In mixing-glass: a dash of Orange Bitters, one-third French Vermouth, two-thirds Gin; stir well and serve.

RAY LONG

In mixing-glass: a dash of Angostura Bitters, a dash of Anis "Pernod fils", one-third Italian Vermouth, two-thirds Brandy; stir well and serve.

ROB ROY

In mixing-glass: a dash of Angostura Bitters, one-third Italian Vermouth, two-thirds Scotch Whisky; stir well and serve.

ROBINSON CRUSOE

In coconut shell containing a piece of Ice: half Pineapple juice, half Rum; stir and serve.

ROSE

In mixing-glass: a teaspoon of Raspberry syrup, one-third Kirsch, two-thirds French Vermouth, stir well and serve with Maraschino Cherry.

This Cocktail, famous in Paris, was invented by "Johnny" Mitta of the Chatham Bar.

ROSSI

In mixing-glass: a dash of Orange Bitters, half Apéritif Rossi, half Gin; stir well and serve.

The Rossi Aperitif is a product of Martini-Rossi, Turin, Italy.

ROSSLYN

In mixing-glass: a dash of Grenadine, two-thirds Gin, one-third French Vermouth; stir well and serve.

ROYAL

Originated by the Author upon the opening of the Ritz Bar, Paris.

In large wineglass: a dash of Angostura Bitters on small lump of Sugar, a **large** piece of Ice, a slice of Lemon peel; fill with Ackerman-Laurance dry 'Royal' sparkling wine, stir and serve.

ROYAL ROMANCE

In shaker: one-fourth each of Passion Fruit juice and Grand Marnier, half Gin; shake well and serve.

ROYAL SMILE

In shaker: the juice of one-half Lime or quarter Lemon, a teaspoon of Grenadine, half Gin, half Apple Jack or Calvados; shake well and serve.

RUSSIAN

In shaker: a teaspoon each of Crème de Cacao and fresh Cream, three-fourths Vodka; shake well and serve.

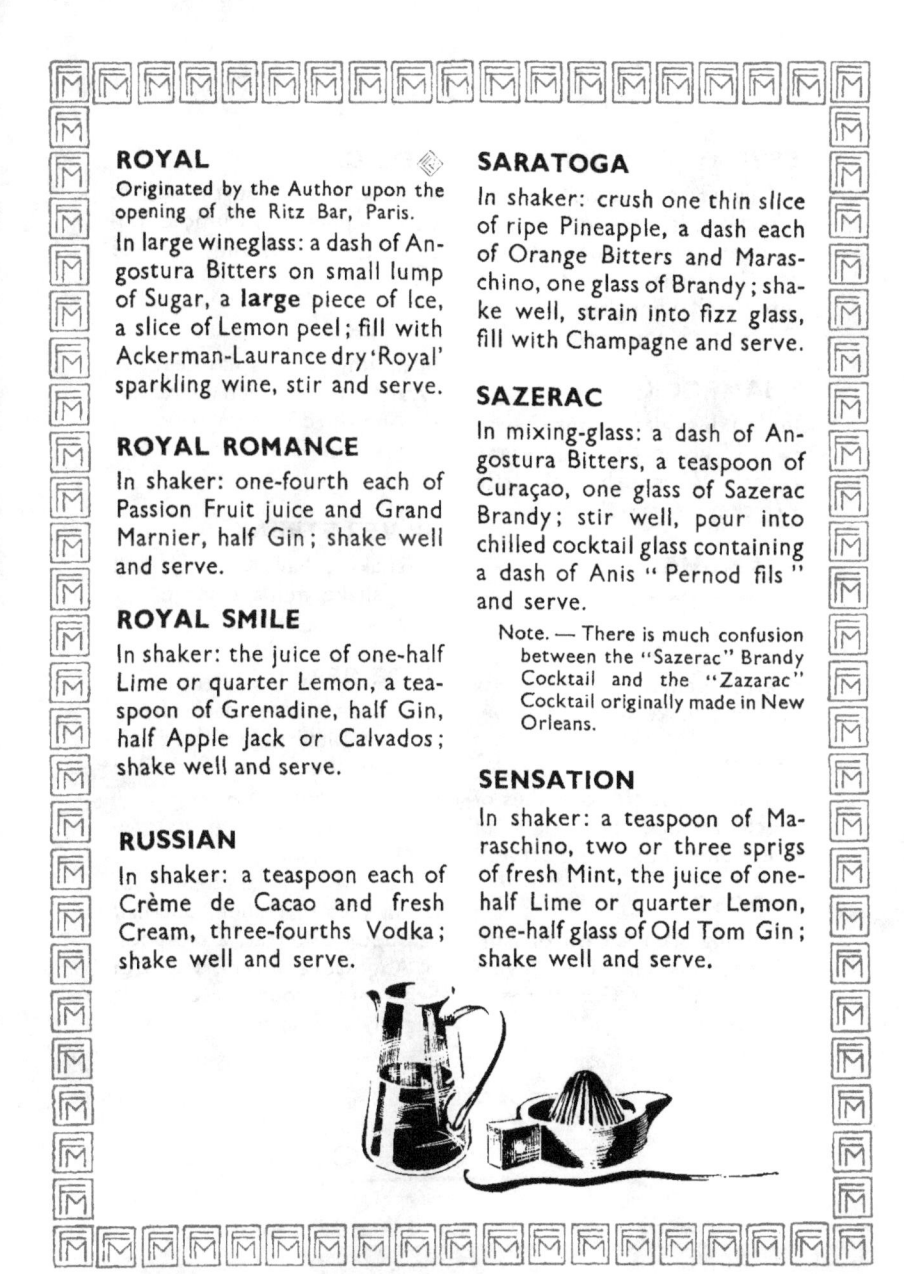

SARATOGA

In shaker: crush one thin slice of ripe Pineapple, a dash each of Orange Bitters and Maraschino, one glass of Brandy; shake well, strain into fizz glass, fill with Champagne and serve.

SAZERAC

In mixing-glass: a dash of Angostura Bitters, a teaspoon of Curaçao, one glass of Sazerac Brandy; stir well, pour into chilled cocktail glass containing a dash of Anis " Pernod fils " and serve.

> Note. — There is much confusion between the "Sazerac" Brandy Cocktail and the "Zazarac" Cocktail originally made in New Orleans.

SENSATION

In shaker: a teaspoon of Maraschino, two or three sprigs of fresh Mint, the juice of one-half Lime or quarter Lemon, one-half glass of Old Tom Gin; shake well and serve.

SEVENTY-FIVE ("75").
In shaker: a teaspoon of Anis "Pernod fils", the juice of one-quarter Lemon, one-half glass of Gin; shake well, strain into small wineglass, fill with Champagne and serve.

SHAMROCK
In mixing-glass: one-fourth each of green Chartreuse and French Vermouth, half Irish Whiskey; stir well and serve.

SHANGHAI
In shaker: a teaspoon of Grenadine, a dash of Anis "Pernod fils", the juice of one-quarter Lemon, one-half glass of Rum; shake well and serve.

SHERRY
In mixing-glass: two dashes of Peach Bitters, one glass of sweet Sherry; stir and serve.

SHROVE
In mixing-glass: a dash of Anis "Pernod fils", half French Vermouth, half Sloe Gin; stir well and serve.

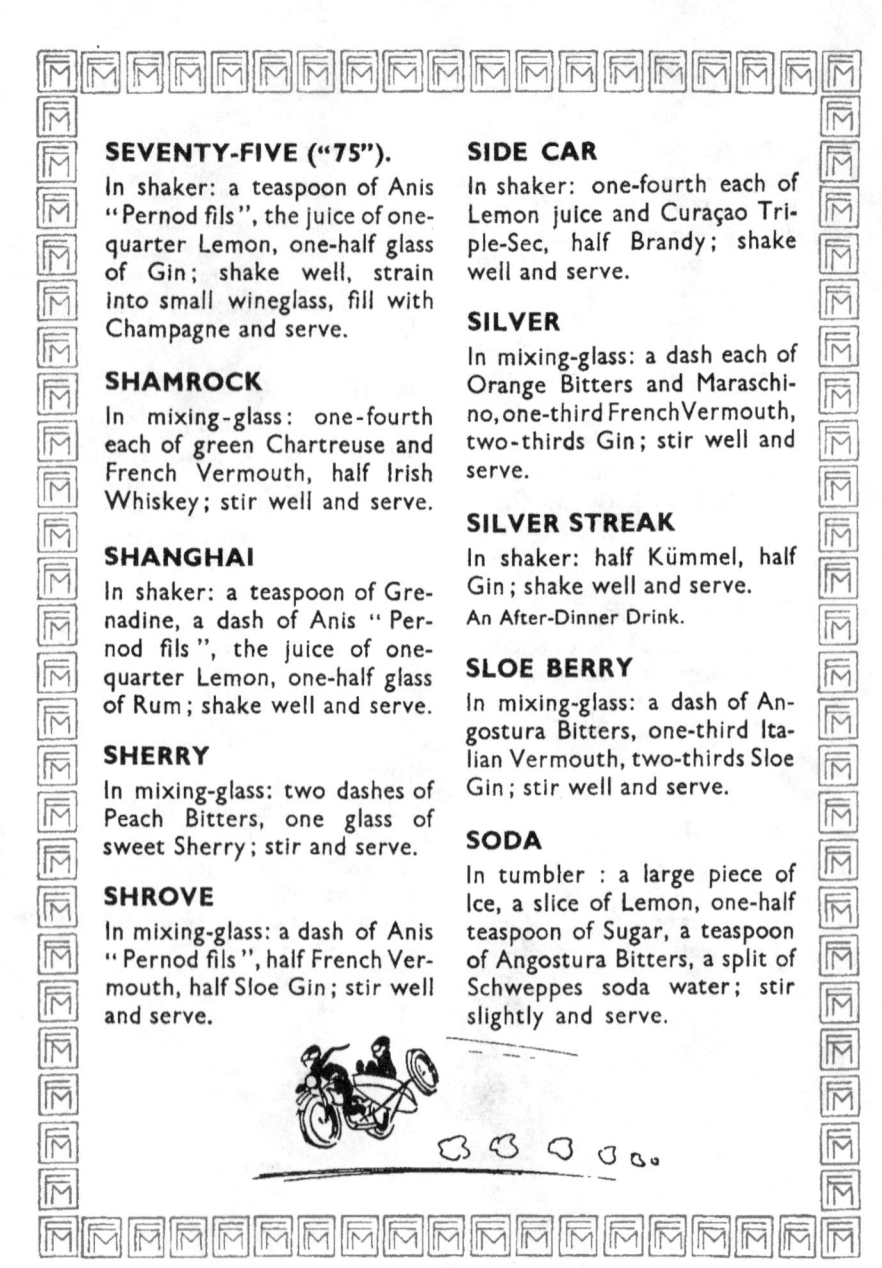

SIDE CAR
In shaker: one-fourth each of Lemon juice and Curaçao Triple-Sec, half Brandy; shake well and serve.

SILVER
In mixing-glass: a dash each of Orange Bitters and Maraschino, one-third French Vermouth, two-thirds Gin; stir well and serve.

SILVER STREAK
In shaker: half Kümmel, half Gin; shake well and serve.
An After-Dinner Drink.

SLOE BERRY
In mixing-glass: a dash of Angostura Bitters, one-third Italian Vermouth, two-thirds Sloe Gin; stir well and serve.

SODA
In tumbler : a large piece of Ice, a slice of Lemon, one-half teaspoon of Sugar, a teaspoon of Angostura Bitters, a split of Schweppes soda water; stir slightly and serve.

SOUTHERN CROSS
In shaker: the juice of one-half Lime or quarter Lemon, one-half teaspoon of Sugar, a dash of Curaçao, one-half glass each of St. Croix Rum and Brandy; shake well, strain into double cocktail glass, add squirt of Schweppes soda water or syphon and serve.

S. S. MANHATTAN
In shaker: a dash of Benedictine, half Orange juice, half Bourbon Whiskey; shake well and serve.

S. S. WASHINGTON
In shaker: a dash of Grenadine, the juice of one-quarter Lemon, half Gin; half Bacardi; shake well and serve.

STAR
In mixing-glass: a dash of Orange Bitters, one-third Italian Vermouth, two-thirds Apple Jack or Calvados; stir & serve.

STINGER
In shaker: one-third white Crème de Menthe, two-thirds Brandy; shake well and serve.
An After-Dinner Drink.

SUISSESSE
In shaker: half white of Egg, the juice of one-half Lemon, one glass of sweetened Anis " Pernod fils "; shake well, strain into fizz glass, add squirt of Schweppes soda water or syphon and serve.

SURE RELIEF
In cocktail glass: a dash of Jamaica Ginger, half white Crème de Menthe, half Brandy; stir and serve.

T. N. T.
In mixing-glass: a dash of Angostura Bitters, half Canadian Whiskey, half Anis " Pernod fils "; stir well and serve.

TEMPTATION
In shaker: two-sixths Bacardi, one-sixth Lemon juice, half Anis "Pernod fils"; shake well and serve.

THIRD DEGREE
In mixing-glass: a teaspoon of Anis " Pernod fils ", one-third French Vermouth, two-thirds Gin; stir well and serve.

TIN ROOF
This cocktail is usually on the house, but the Ritz Bar has a tile roof.

TOMATO JUICE
In shaker: crush one large ripe Tomato, add Celery salt to suit taste, one-half teaspoon of Worcestershire sauce; shake well, strain into double cocktail glass and serve.

> Note. — High grade Tomato Juice is available in tins or bottles, is uniform in character and is obtainable at very reasonable prices. It is advantageous to procure it in that form instead of from fresh Tomatoes, which in most countries can be obtained only at particular seasons. Tomato Juice in tins should, when opened, be removed to bottles or jugs, and in all cases should be kept on ice.

The first to introduce the Tomato Juice Cocktail was the College Inn Food Product Co. of Chicago.

TOM MOORE
In mixing-glass: a dash of Angostura Bitters, one-third Italian Vermouth, two-thirds Irish Whiskey; stir well and serve.

TOP SPEED
In shaker, one-fourth Anis " Pernod fils ", one-fourth French Vermouth, half Brandy; shake well and serve.

TRINITY
In mixing-glass: one-third each of Gin, French and Italian Vermouth; stir well and serve.

TROPICAL
In shaker: the juice of one-half Lime or quarter Lemon, a teaspoon of Curaçao, one-half glass of Rum; shake well and serve.

TUXEDO
In mixing-glass: a dash each of Maraschino and Anis "Pernod fils", half French Vermouth, half Gin; stir well and serve.

VALENCIA
In shaker: the juice of one-quarter Orange, one-half glass of Apricot Brandy; shake well, strain into fizz glass, fill with Champagne and serve.

WARD EIGHT
In shaker: one-half teaspoon of Grenadine, one-third each of Lemon juice, Rye Whiskey and Gin; shake well and serve.

WHISKEY
In mixing-glass: a dash of Angostura Bitters, a teaspoon of Sugar syrup, one-half glass of Whiskey; stir well and serve with Maraschino Cherry.
Any Whiskey may be used.

WHITE
In mixing-glass: a teaspoon of white Curaçao, a dash of Orange Bitters, four-fifths Gin; stir well and serve.

WHITE LADY
In shaker: one-fourth each of Lemon juice & white Curaçao, half Gin; shake well and serve.

WHITE ROSE
In shaker: half white of Egg, the juice of one-quarter Lemon, one-half teaspoon of Sugar, one glass of Gin; shake well, strain into small wineglass and serve.

WHITE SHADOW
In shaker: one-third each of fresh Cream, Anis "Pernod fils", and Rye Whiskey, very little grated Nutmeg; shake well and serve.

WHIZ-BANG
In mixing-glass: a dash of Anis "Pernod fils", a dash of Grenadine, one glass of Scotch Whisky; stir well and serve.

WINTER SPORT
In shaker: a teaspoon of fresh Cream, one-third Gin, two-thirds Anis "Pernod fils"; shake well and serve.

YALE
In shaker: a dash of Angostura Bitters, one glass of old Tom Gin; shake well, strain into double cocktail glass, add squirt of Schweppes soda water or syphon and serve.

YASHMAK
In mixing-glass: a dash of Angostura Bitters, one-third each of French Vermouth, sweetened Anis "Pernod fils" and Rye Whiskey; stir well and serve.

ZAZA
In mixing-glass: a dash of Angostura Bitters, half Dubonnet, half Gin; stir well and serve.

ZAZARAC
In tumbler: dissolve a small lump of Sugar in little water, a dash each of Angostura and Orange Bitters, a teaspoon of Anis "Pernod fils", a piece of Ice, one glass of Bourbon Whiskey; add Lemon peel & squirt of Schweppes soda or syphon, stir well and serve.

44

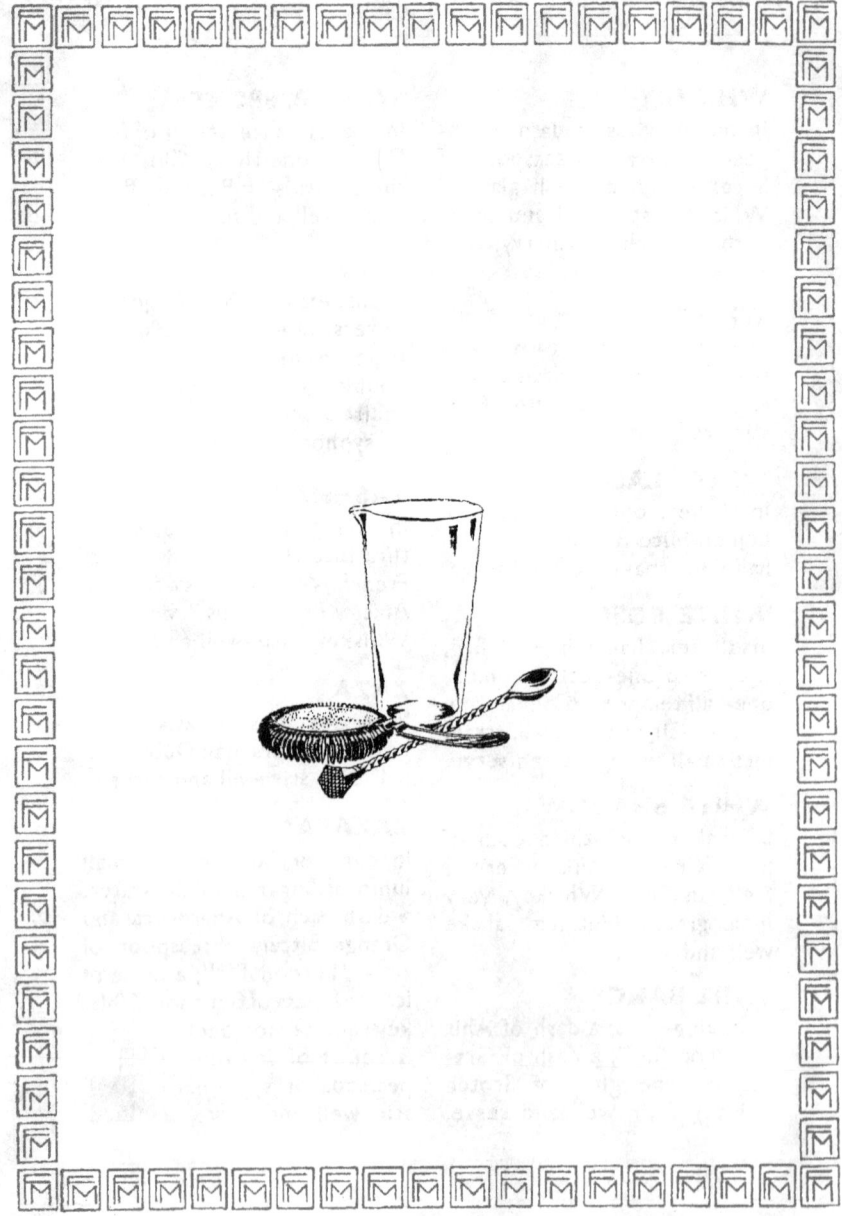

MIXED DRINKS

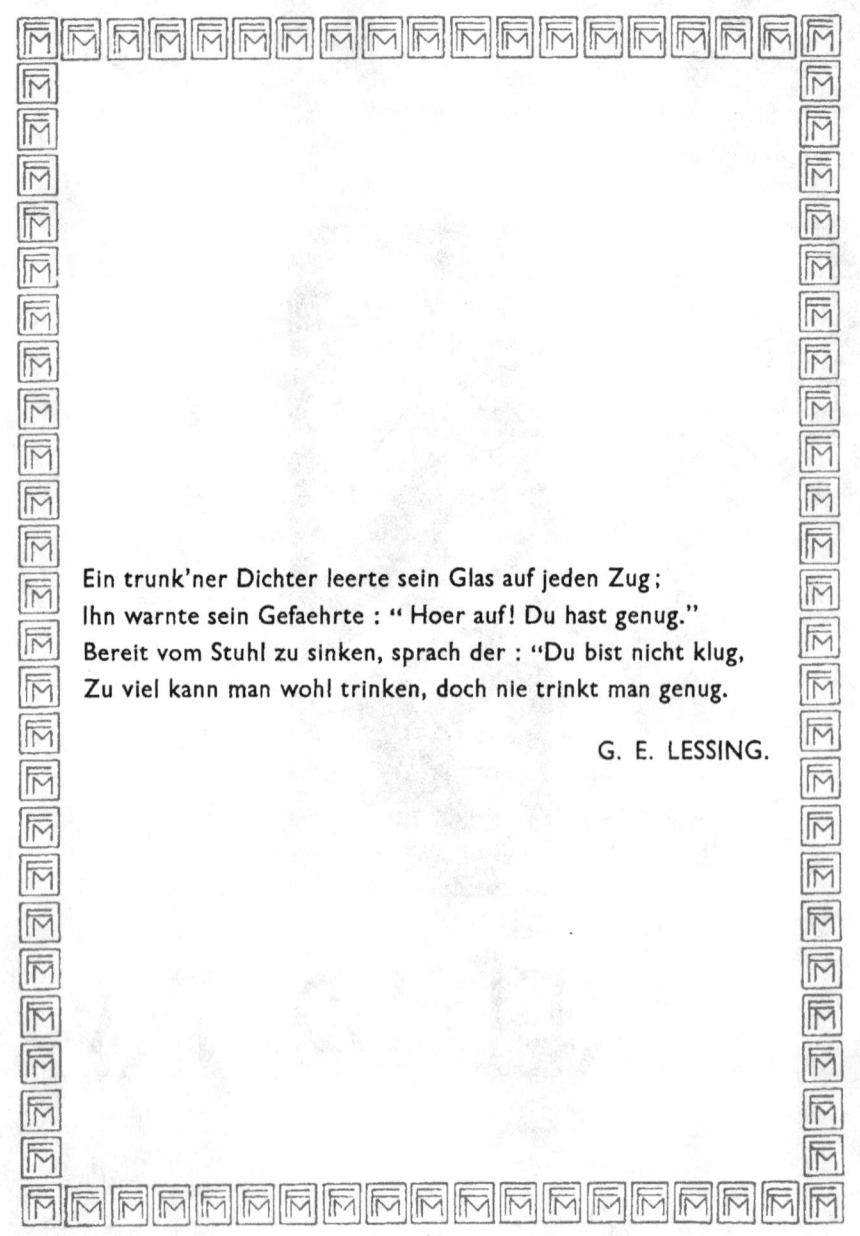

Ein trunk'ner Dichter leerte sein Glas auf jeden Zug;
Ihn warnte sein Gefaehrte : " Hoer auf! Du hast genug."
Bereit vom Stuhl zu sinken, sprach der : "Du bist nicht klug,
Zu viel kann man wohl trinken, doch nie trinkt man genug.

            G. E. LESSING.

AFTER-DINNER DRINKS

ICED LIQUEURS

BENEDICTINE COCKTAIL

Rub rim of cocktail glass with slice of Lemon, dip edge into powdered Sugar, put in Maraschino Cherry and fill with the following mixture:

In shaker, a dash of Angostura Bitters, one glass of Benedictine; shake slightly, strain into prepared glass and serve.

ANISETTE,
APRICOT BRANDY,
CHARTREUSE (yellow or green),
CHERRY BRANDY,
CORDIAL MEDOC,
CURAÇAO (red or white),
KUMMEL,
MANDARINETTE,
MARASCHINO,
PEACH BRANDY,
PRUNELLE, etc., etc.

The same as Benedictine Cocktail, using liqueur chosen.

ICED APRICOT BRANDY

In cocktail glass: three-fourths of shaved Ice; fill with Apricot Brandy and serve with straws.

ANIS DELMONO,
ANISETTE,
BENEDICTINE,
CHARTREUSE (green or yellow),
CHERRY BRANDY,
CORDIAL MEDOC,
CURAÇAO (red or white),
GRAND MARNIER,
LIQUEUR DE CASSIS,
KUMMEL,
MANDARINETTE,
MARASCHINO,
MENTHE (green or white),
PEACH BRANDY,
VIEILLE CURE, etc., etc.

The same as Iced Apricot Brandy, using liqueur chosen.

COBBLERS

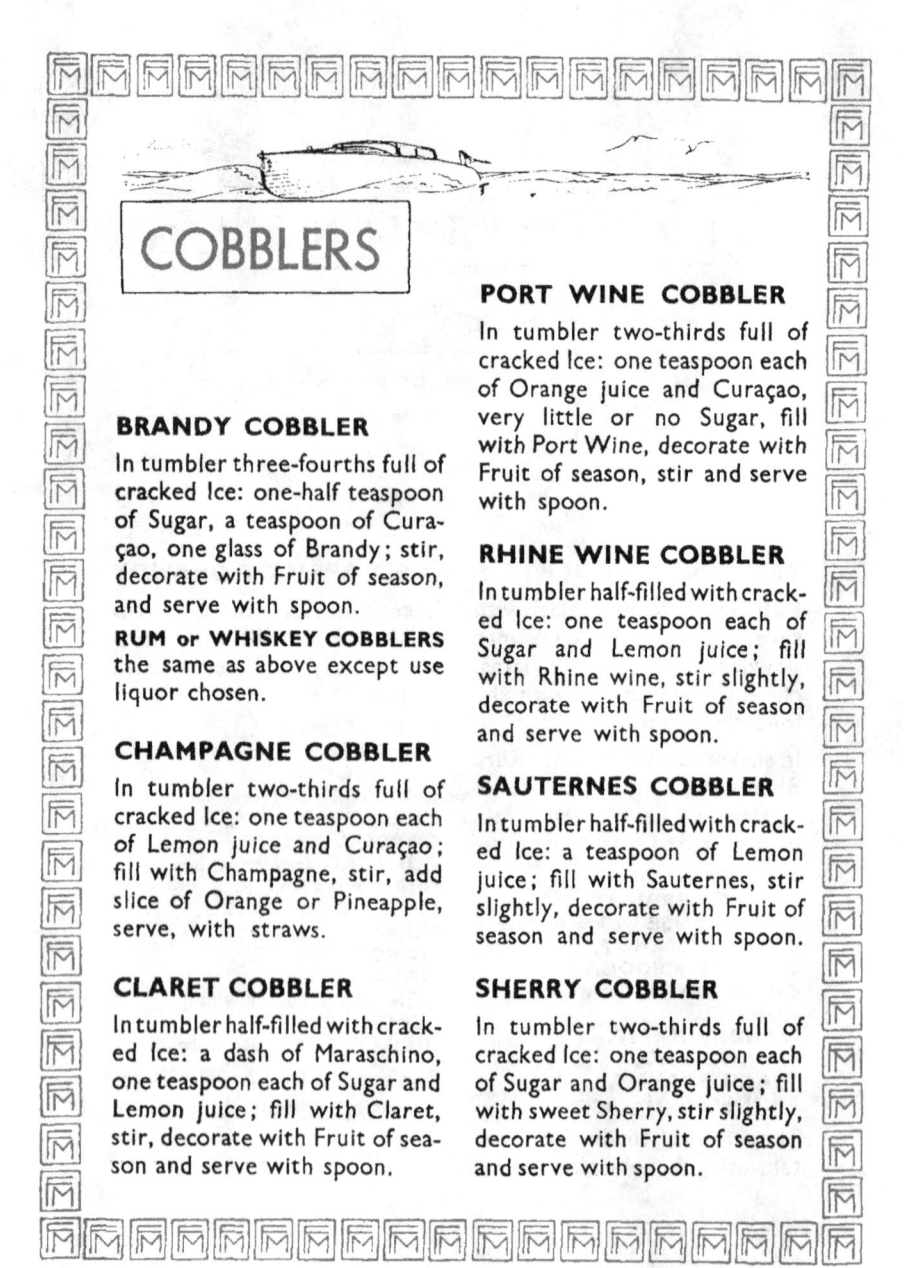

BRANDY COBBLER
In tumbler three-fourths full of cracked Ice: one-half teaspoon of Sugar, a teaspoon of Curaçao, one glass of Brandy; stir, decorate with Fruit of season, and serve with spoon.

RUM or WHISKEY COBBLERS the same as above except use liquor chosen.

CHAMPAGNE COBBLER
In tumbler two-thirds full of cracked Ice: one teaspoon each of Lemon juice and Curaçao; fill with Champagne, stir, add slice of Orange or Pineapple, serve, with straws.

CLARET COBBLER
In tumbler half-filled with cracked Ice: a dash of Maraschino, one teaspoon each of Sugar and Lemon juice; fill with Claret, stir, decorate with Fruit of season and serve with spoon.

PORT WINE COBBLER
In tumbler two-thirds full of cracked Ice: one teaspoon each of Orange juice and Curaçao, very little or no Sugar, fill with Port Wine, decorate with Fruit of season, stir and serve with spoon.

RHINE WINE COBBLER
In tumbler half-filled with cracked Ice: one teaspoon each of Sugar and Lemon juice; fill with Rhine wine, stir slightly, decorate with Fruit of season and serve with spoon.

SAUTERNES COBBLER
In tumbler half-filled with cracked Ice: a teaspoon of Lemon juice; fill with Sauternes, stir slightly, decorate with Fruit of season and serve with spoon.

SHERRY COBBLER
In tumbler two-thirds full of cracked Ice: one teaspoon each of Sugar and Orange juice; fill with sweet Sherry, stir slightly, decorate with Fruit of season and serve with spoon.

COLLINS

JOHN or TOM COLLINS
In large tumbler: two or three pieces of Ice, the juice of one-half Lemon, a teaspoon of Sugar, one glass of Gin; fill with Schweppes soda water or syphon; stir well and serve.

BRANDY, RUM or either WHISKEY COLLINS
the same as Tom Collins except use liquor chosen.

COOLERS

APRICOT BRANDY COOLER

In large tumbler: two or three pieces of Ice, a dash of Angostura Bitters, the juice of one-half Lemon, a teaspoon of Grenadine, one glass of Apricot Brandy; stir slightly while adding Schweppes soda water or syphon and serve.

BACARDI, BRANDY or RUM COOLER the same as above except use liquor chosen.

HAWAIIAN COOLER

In large tumbler: two pieces of Ice in whole Orange rind, one glass of Rye Whiskey, a split of Schweppes soda water; stir slightly and serve.

IRISH WHISKEY COOLER

In large tumbler: two pieces of Ice in whole Lemon rind, one glass of Irish Whiskey, a split of Schweppes soda water; stir slightly and serve.

REMSEN COOLER

In large tumbler: two pieces of Ice in whole Lemon rind, one glass of Old Tom Gin, a split of Schweppes soda water; stir slightly and serve.

SARATOGA COOLER

In large tumbler: three or four pieces of Ice, the juice of one Lime, one-half teaspoon of Sugar, a split of Ginger Ale; stir slightly and serve.

SCOTCH WHISKY COOLER

In large tumbler: two pieces of Ice in whole Lemon rind, one glass of Scotch Whisky, a split of Schweppes soda water; stir slightly and serve.

ZENITH COOLER

In large tumbler: three or four pieces of Ice, a tablespoon of Pineapple syrup, one glass of Gin; stir slightly while adding Schweppes soda water or syphon, and serve with slice of Pineapple.

BRANDY CRUSTA

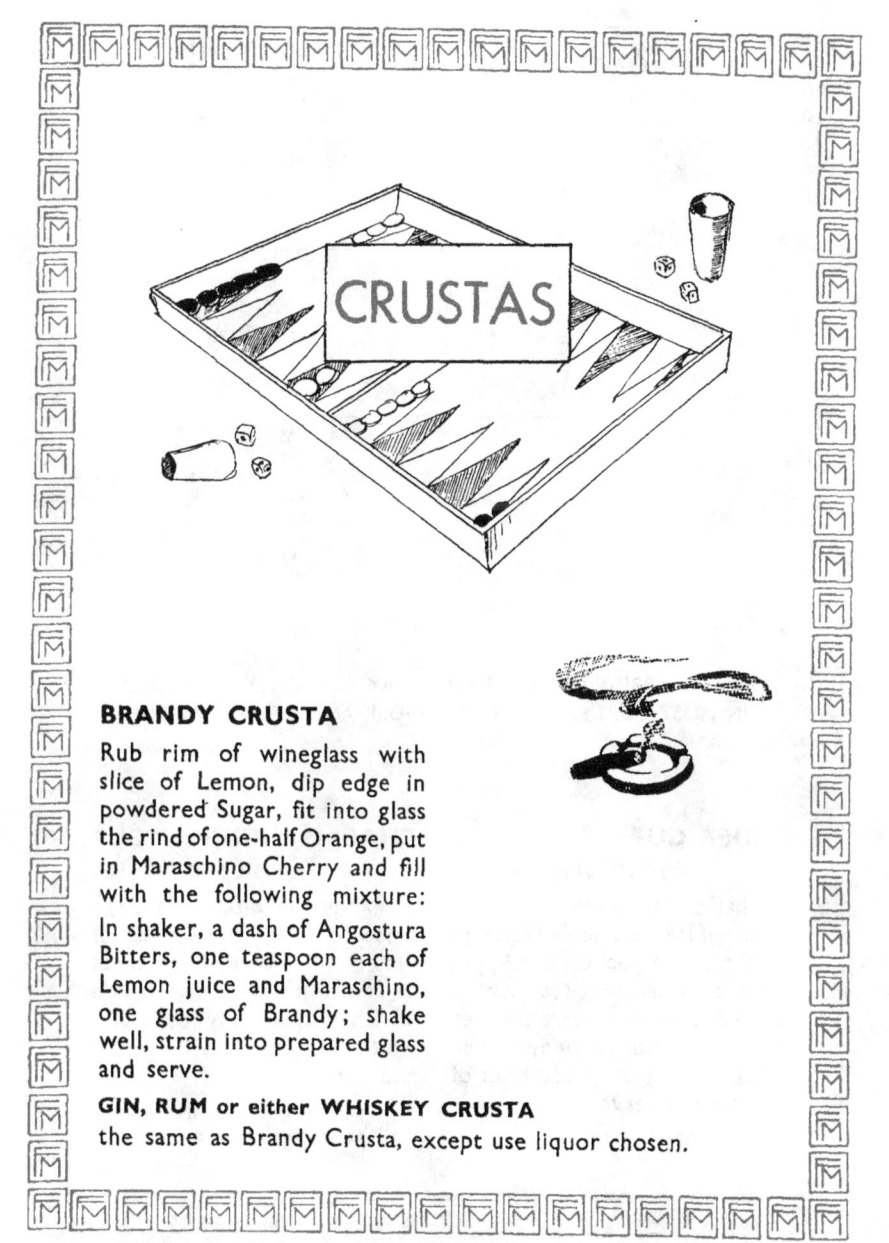

Rub rim of wineglass with slice of Lemon, dip edge in powdered Sugar, fit into glass the rind of one-half Orange, put in Maraschino Cherry and fill with the following mixture:

In shaker, a dash of Angostura Bitters, one teaspoon each of Lemon juice and Maraschino, one glass of Brandy; shake well, strain into prepared glass and serve.

GIN, RUM or either WHISKEY CRUSTA

the same as Brandy Crusta, except use liquor chosen.

CUPS

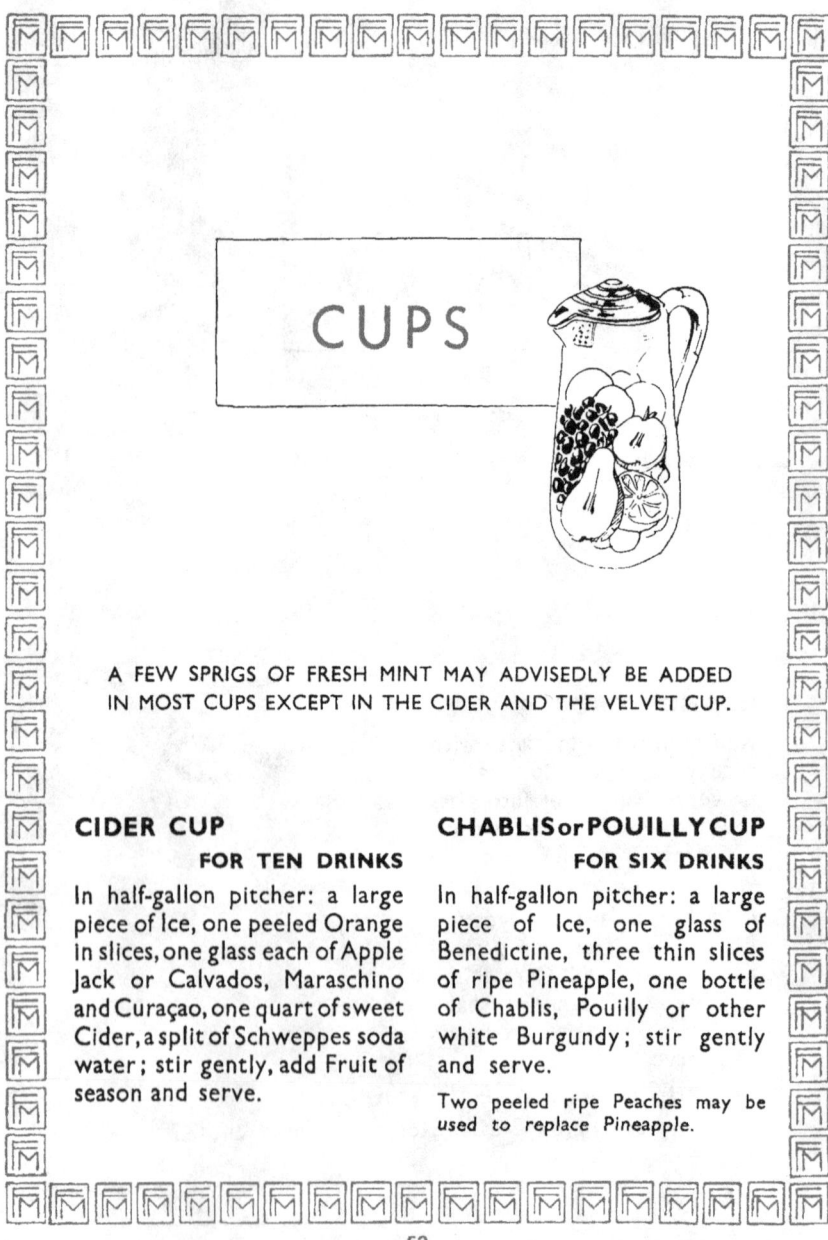

A FEW SPRIGS OF FRESH MINT MAY ADVISEDLY BE ADDED IN MOST CUPS EXCEPT IN THE CIDER AND THE VELVET CUP.

CIDER CUP
FOR TEN DRINKS

In half-gallon pitcher: a large piece of Ice, one peeled Orange in slices, one glass each of Apple Jack or Calvados, Maraschino and Curaçao, one quart of sweet Cider, a split of Schweppes soda water; stir gently, add Fruit of season and serve.

CHABLIS or POUILLY CUP
FOR SIX DRINKS

In half-gallon pitcher: a large piece of Ice, one glass of Benedictine, three thin slices of ripe Pineapple, one bottle of Chablis, Pouilly or other white Burgundy; stir gently and serve.

Two peeled ripe Peaches may be used to replace Pineapple.

CLARET or BURGUNDY CUP
FOR SIX DRINKS

In half-gallon pitcher: a large piece of Ice, three thin slices of ripe Pineapple crushed without waste of juice, one glass of Maraschino, a tablespoon of powdered Sugar, one quart of Claret or red Burgundy; stir gently and serve.

GINGER ALE CUP
FOR SIX DRINKS

In half-gallon pitcher: a large piece of Ice, one peeled Lemon in slices, the juice of one Orange, two glasses of Brandy, one glass of Maraschino, three pints of Ginger Ale; stir until very cold and serve.

GRAPE FRUIT CUP
FOR TWELVE DRINKS

In gallon pitcher or bowl: a large piece of Ice, a bottle of Brandy, one glass of Grenadine, three Grape Fruit with rinds and cells removed, a pound tin of sweetened Grape Fruit juice, one-half bottle of Schweppes soda water or syphon; stir well and serve.

KALTE ENTE
FOR TEN DRINKS

In half-gallon pitcher with whole rind of Lemon rested over brim: one glass of Curaçao, one quart of thoroughly chilled Moselle wine, one quart of thoroughly chilled sparkling Rhine wine. Unnecessary to stir before serving.

MAI-WEIN-CUP
FOR TWENTY DRINKS

In gallon pitcher with a large piece of Ice, soak a big bunch of young Waldmeister (Woodruff) in three quarts of light Moselle wine for one hour, six lumps of Sugar, one glass each of Curaçao and Brandy, add one quart of sparkling Moselle when ready to serve.

MOSELLE CUP
FOR TWELVE DRINKS

In gallon pitcher: a large piece of Ice, three peeled ripe Peaches cut into quarters, a dozen Maraschino Cherries, one glass of Benedictine, one bottle of still Moselle, one bottle of sparkling Moselle; stir gently and serve.

Powdered Sugar may be added to suit taste.

PFIRSICH BOWLE
FOR SIX DRINKS

In half-gallon pitcher: a large piece of Ice, two whole ripe Peaches pierced with fork, one quart of light Rhine wine; stir gently and serve.

Powdered Sugar may be added to suit taste.

RHINE WINE CUP
FOR SIX DRINKS

In half-gallon pitcher: a large piece of Ice, one peeled Orange in slices, one glass of Curaçao, one bottle of Rhine wine, a split of Schweppes soda water; stir gently and serve.

Powdered Sugar may be added to suit taste.

SAUTERNES CUP No 1
FOR SIX DRINKS

In half-gallon pitcher, squeeze one-half pound of Currants without waste of juice; a large piece of Ice, one bottle of Sauternes, stir gently and serve.

SAUTERNES CUP No 2
FOR TEN DRINKS

In half-gallon pitcher: a large piece of Ice, one peeled Lemon in slices, one glass of Curaçao, one glass of Brandy, a dozen Maraschino Cherries, one bottle of Sauternes, a split of Schweppes soda water, a long slice of Cucumber rind; stir gently and serve.

SPARKLING RHINE WINE CUP
FOR TEN DRINKS

In gallon pitcher: a large piece of Ice, a long slice of Cucumber rind, two ripe Pears peeled, quartered and cored; one glass each of Maraschino, Curaçao and Brandy, a bottle of sparkling Rhine wine, a split of Schweppes soda water; stir gently and serve.

VELVET CUP
FOR TEN DRINKS

In half-gallon pitcher with large piece of Ice, pour gently (to avoid overflowing) one quart of Stout and one quart of sweet Champagne; stir very gently and serve.

DAISIES

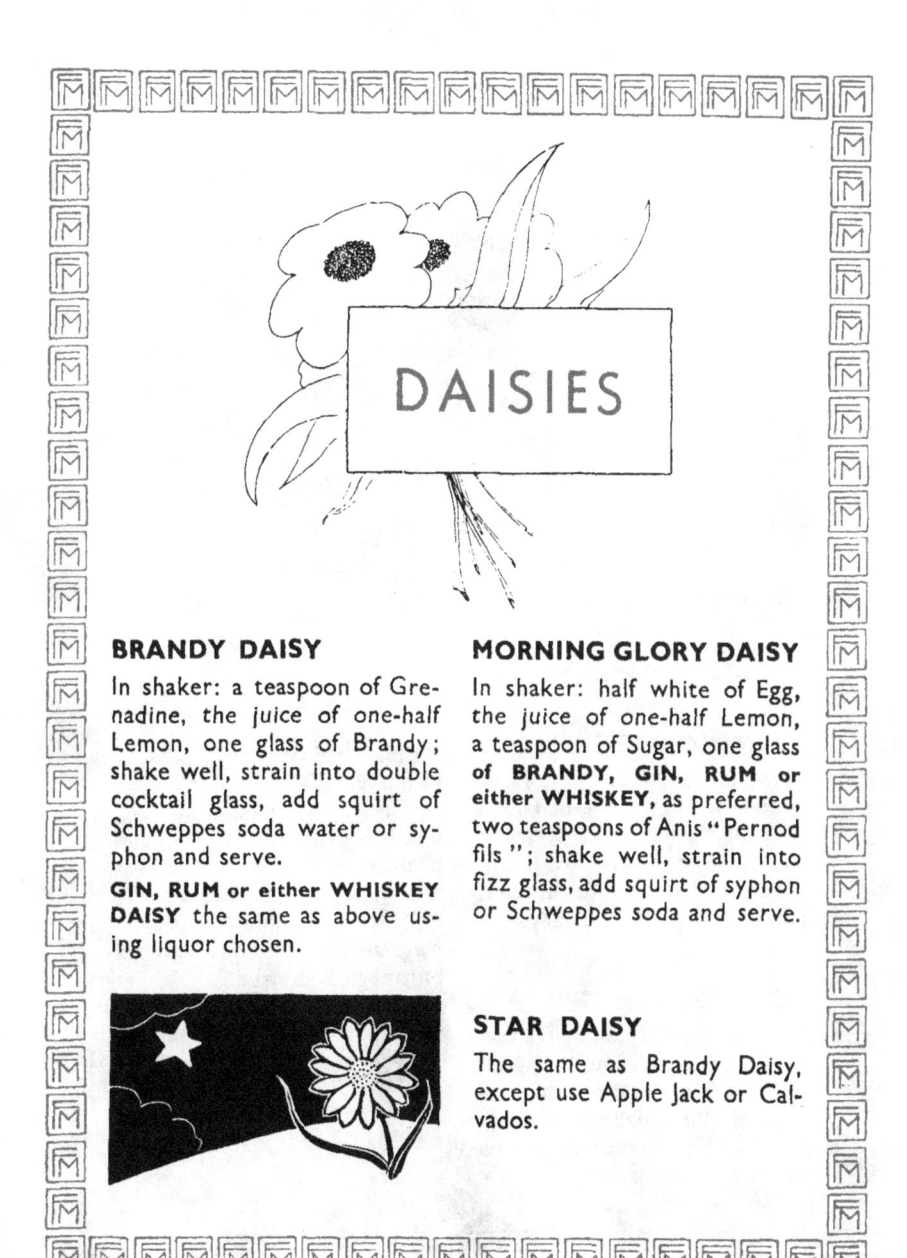

BRANDY DAISY

In shaker: a teaspoon of Grenadine, the juice of one-half Lemon, one glass of Brandy; shake well, strain into double cocktail glass, add squirt of Schweppes soda water or syphon and serve.

GIN, RUM or either **WHISKEY DAISY** the same as above using liquor chosen.

MORNING GLORY DAISY

In shaker: half white of Egg, the juice of one-half Lemon, a teaspoon of Sugar, one glass of **BRANDY, GIN, RUM or either WHISKEY,** as preferred, two teaspoons of Anis "Pernod fils"; shake well, strain into fizz glass, add squirt of syphon or Schweppes soda and serve.

STAR DAISY

The same as Brandy Daisy, except use Apple Jack or Calvados.

EGG NOGS

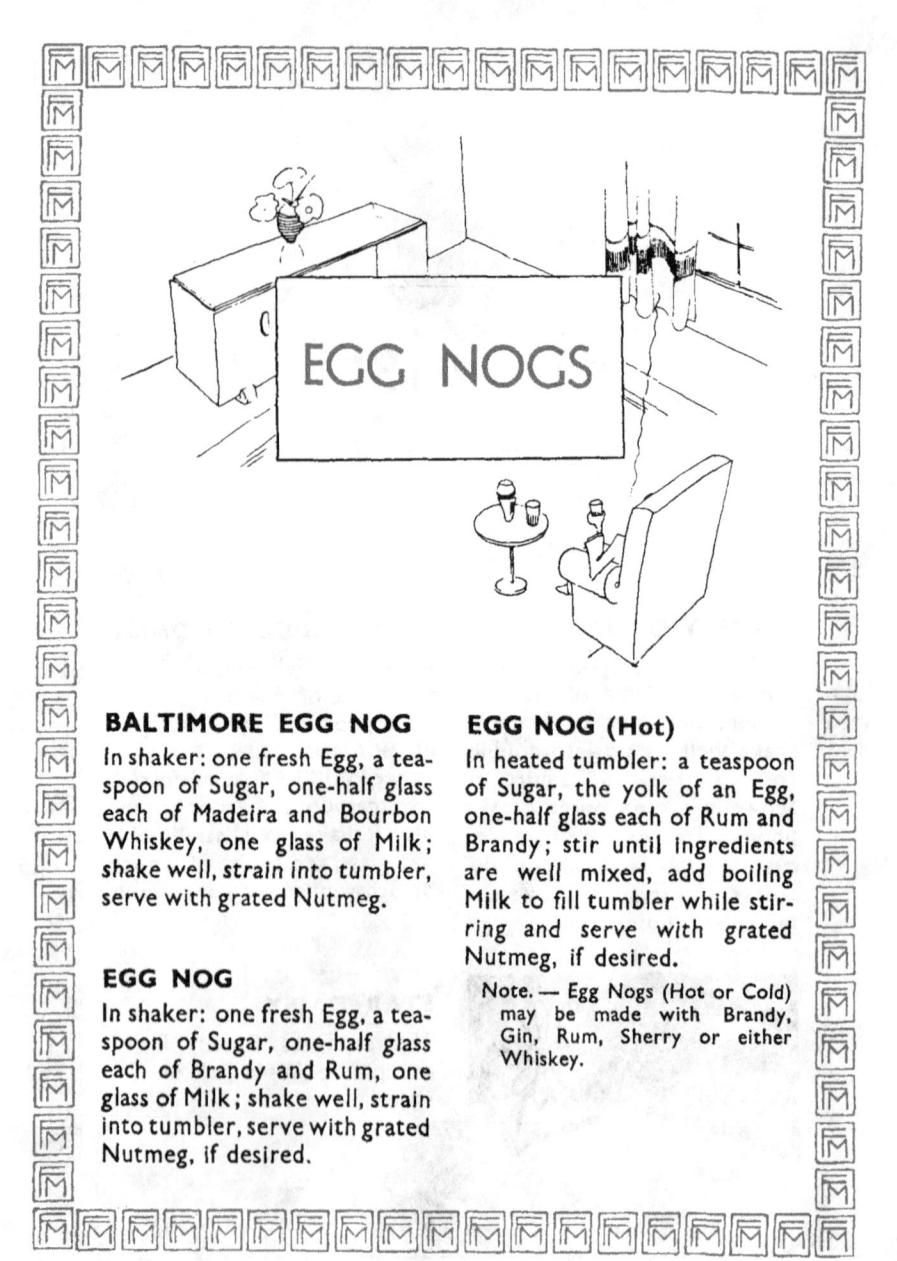

BALTIMORE EGG NOG
In shaker: one fresh Egg, a teaspoon of Sugar, one-half glass each of Madeira and Bourbon Whiskey, one glass of Milk; shake well, strain into tumbler, serve with grated Nutmeg.

EGG NOG
In shaker: one fresh Egg, a teaspoon of Sugar, one-half glass each of Brandy and Rum, one glass of Milk; shake well, strain into tumbler, serve with grated Nutmeg, if desired.

EGG NOG (Hot)
In heated tumbler: a teaspoon of Sugar, the yolk of an Egg, one-half glass each of Rum and Brandy; stir until ingredients are well mixed, add boiling Milk to fill tumbler while stirring and serve with grated Nutmeg, if desired.

Note. — Egg Nogs (Hot or Cold) may be made with Brandy, Gin, Rum, Sherry or either Whiskey.

FIXES

BRANDY FIX
In small tumbler: the juice of one-half Lemon, a teaspoon of Sugar, a dash of Curaçao, one glass of Brandy; fill with shaved Ice, stir, decorate with slice of Orange and Berries of season, serve with straws.

GIN, RUM or either WHISKEY FIX
the same as Brandy Fix, except use liquor chosen.

FIZZES

AMERICAN FIZZ
In shaker: the juice of one-half Lemon, one-half glass each of Brandy and Gin; a teaspoon of Grenadine, shake well, strain into fizz glass, add Schweppes soda water or syphon and serve.

BACARDI FIZZ
In shaker: the juice of one-half Lemon, a teaspoon of Sugar, one glass of Bacardi Rum; shake well, strain into fizz glass, add Schweppes soda water or syphon and serve.

BISMARCK FIZZ or SLOE GIN FIZZ
In shaker: the juice of one-half Lemon, one glass of Sloe Gin; shake well, strain into fizz glass, add Schweppes soda water or syphon and serve.

BRANDY FIZZ
In shaker: the juice of one-half Lemon, a teaspoon of Sugar, one glass of Brandy; shake well, strain into fizz glass, add syphon or Schweppes soda water and serve.

BUCKS FIZZ
In shaker: the juice of one-half Orange, one-half teaspoon of Sugar, one-half glass of Gin; shake well, strain into fizz glass, fill with Champagne.

DIAMOND FIZZ
In shaker: the juice of one-half Lemon, one-half teaspoon of Sugar, one-half glass of Gin; shake well, strain into fizz glass, fill with Champagne.

DUBONNET FIZZ

In shaker: the juice of one-half Orange, one glass of Dubonnet; shake slightly, strain into fizz glass, fill with Champagne and serve.

FRANK'S SPECIAL GIN FIZZ

In shaker: the juice of one-half Lemon, one-half teaspoon of Sugar, one-quarter of crushed Peach, one glass of Gin; shake well, strain into tumbler, add syphon or Schweppes soda water and serve.

GIN FIZZ

In shaker: the juice of one-half Lemon, a teaspoon of Sugar, one glass of Gin; shake well, strain into fizz glass, add Schweppes soda water or syphon and serve.

GOLDEN FIZZ

In shaker: the juice of one-half Lemon, a teaspoon of Sugar, the yolk of an Egg, one glass of Gin; shake well, strain into tumbler, add Schweppes soda water or syphon and serve.

GRENADINE GIN FIZZ

In shaker: the juice of one-half Lemon, two teaspoons of Grenadine, one glass of Gin; shake well, strain into fizz glass, add Schweppes soda water or syphon and serve.

HOFFMAN HOUSE or CREAM GIN FIZZ

In shaker: the juice of one-half Lemon, a teaspoon each of Sugar and fresh Cream, one glass of Gin; shake well, strain into tumbler, add Schweppes soda water or syphon and serve.

HOLLAND GIN FIZZ

In shaker: the juice of one-half Lemon, a teaspoon of Sugar, one glass of Holland Gin; shake well, strain into fizz glass, add Schweppes soda water or syphon and serve.

IMPERIAL FIZZ

In shaker: the juice of one-half Lemon, a teaspoon of Sugar, one-half glass of Rye or Bourbon Whiskey; shake well, strain into fizz glass, fill with Champagne and serve.

IRISH WHISKEY FIZZ

In shaker: the juice of one-half Lemon, one-half teaspoon of Sugar, a teaspoon of Curaçao, one glass of Irish Whiskey; shake well, strain into fizz glass, add Schweppes soda water or syphon and serve.

JUBILEE FIZZ

In shaker: one-half glass of unsweetened Pineapple juice, one-half glass of Gin; shake well, strain into fizz glass, fill with Champagne.

MORNING GLORY FIZZ

In shaker: the juice of one-half Lemon, a teaspoon of Sugar, half white of Egg, two dashes of Anis " Pernod fils ", one glass of Scotch Whisky; shake well, strain into tumbler, add Schweppes soda water or syphon and serve.

NEW ORLEANS FIZZ

In shaker: half white of Egg, the juice of one-half Lemon, one teaspoon each of Sugar and fresh Cream, a dash of Fleur d'Oranger, one glass of Gin; shake well, strain into tumbler, add Schweppes soda water or syphon and serve.

NICKY'S FIZZ

Special for
    Prince Nicolas Toumanoff.

In shaker: one-half glass of sweetened Grape Fruit juice, one glass of Gin; shake well, strain into fizz glass, add Schweppes soda water or syphon and serve.

ORANGE FIZZ

In shaker: the juice of one-half Orange, a dash of Grenadine, one glass of Gin; shake well, strain into fizz glass, add Schweppes soda water or syphon and serve.

PINEAPPLE FIZZ

In shaker: one-half glass of sweetened Pineapple juice, one glass of Gin; shake well, strain into fizz glass, add Schweppes soda water or syphon and serve.

ROYAL GIN FIZZ

In shaker: the juice of one-half Lemon, a teaspoon of Sugar, one fresh Egg, one-half glass of Gin; shake well, strain into tumbler, add Schweppes soda water or syphon and serve.

RUBY FIZZ

In shaker: the juice of one-half Lemon, a teaspoon of Raspberry syrup, half white of Egg, one glass of Sloe Gin; shake well, strain into tumbler, add Schweppes soda water or syphon and serve.

RUM FIZZ

In shaker: the juice of one-half Lemon, one-half teaspoon of Sugar, a teaspoon of Cherry Brandy, one-half glass of Rum; shake well, strain into fizz glass, add Schweppes soda water or syphon and serve.

SCOTCH WHISKY FIZZ

In shaker: the juice of one-half Lemon, a teaspoon of Sugar, one glass of Scotch Whisky; shake well, strain into fizz glass, add Schweppes soda water or syphon and serve.

SEAPEA "C.P."

Special for Mr. Cole Porter, famous composer of lyrics and music.

In shaker: the juice of one-half Lemon, one glass of sweetened Anis "Pernod fils"; shake well, strain into fizz glass, add Schweppes soda water or syphon and serve.

SILVER FIZZ

In shaker: the juice of one-half Lemon, a teaspoon of Sugar, half white of Egg, one glass of Gin; shake well, strain into tumbler, add Schweppes soda water or syphon and serve.

SOUR GIN FIZZ

In shaker: the juice of one-half Lemon, one glass of Old Tom Gin; shake well, strain into fizz glass, add Schweppes soda water or syphon and serve.

SOUTHSIDE FIZZ

In shaker: the juice of one-half Lemon, a teaspoon of Sugar, three sprigs of Mint, one-half glass of Gin; shake well, strain into fizz glass, add Schweppes soda water or syphon and serve.

STRAWBERRY FIZZ

In shaker: the juice of one-half Lemon, half teaspoon of Sugar, three or four crushed Strawberries, one-half glass of Gin; shake well, strain into fizz glass, add Schweppes soda water or syphon and serve.

TEXAS FIZZ

In shaker: the juices of one-quarter Lemon and quarter Orange, a dash of Grenadine, one-half glass of Gin; shake well, strain into fizz glass, fill with Champagne and serve.

VIOLET FIZZ

In shaker: the juice of one-half Lemon, a teaspoon each of Raspberry syrup and fresh Cream, one-half glass of Gin; shake well, strain into fizz glass, add Schweppes soda water or syphon and serve.

FLIPS

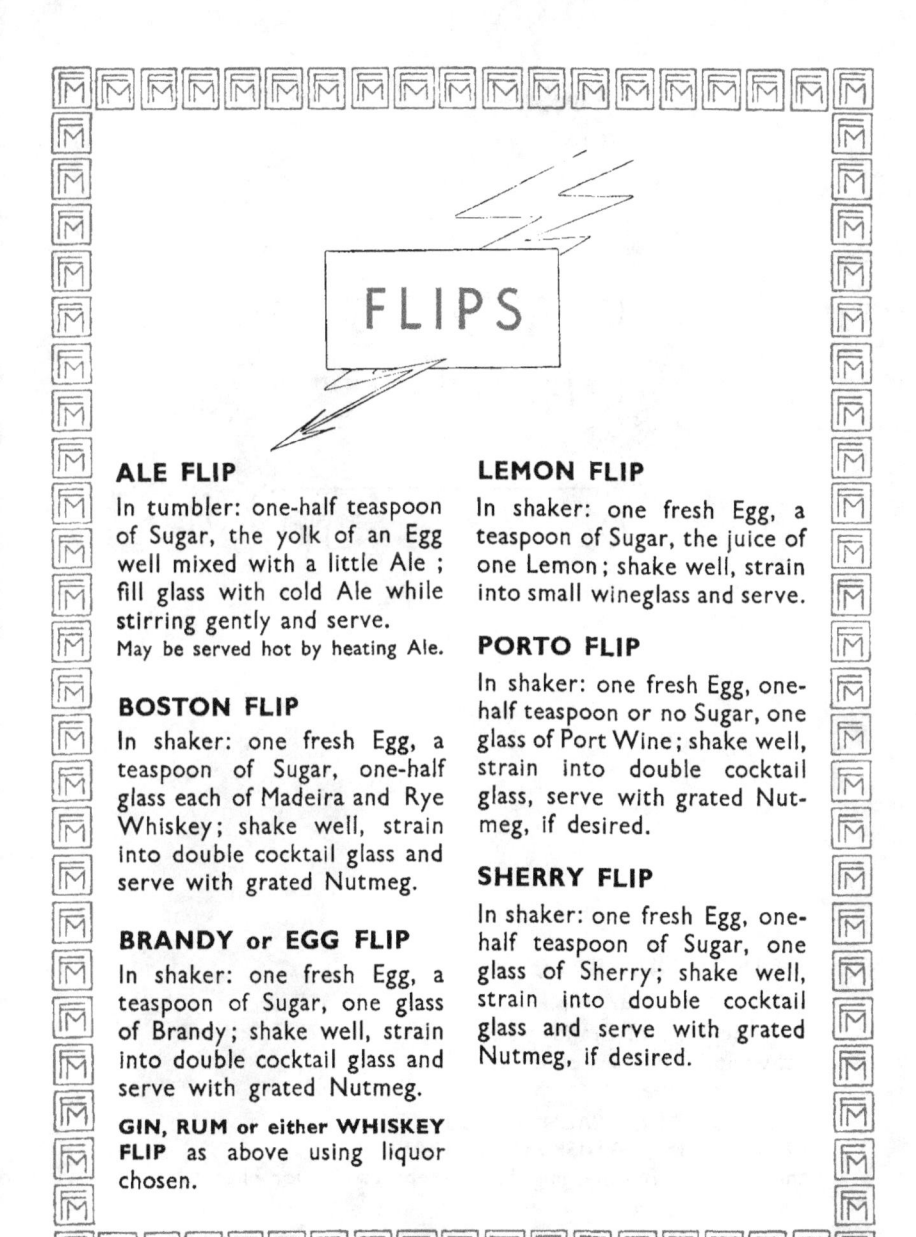

ALE FLIP
In tumbler: one-half teaspoon of Sugar, the yolk of an Egg well mixed with a little Ale; fill glass with cold Ale while stirring gently and serve.

May be served hot by heating Ale.

BOSTON FLIP
In shaker: one fresh Egg, a teaspoon of Sugar, one-half glass each of Madeira and Rye Whiskey; shake well, strain into double cocktail glass and serve with grated Nutmeg.

BRANDY or EGG FLIP
In shaker: one fresh Egg, a teaspoon of Sugar, one glass of Brandy; shake well, strain into double cocktail glass and serve with grated Nutmeg.

GIN, RUM or either WHISKEY FLIP as above using liquor chosen.

LEMON FLIP
In shaker: one fresh Egg, a teaspoon of Sugar, the juice of one Lemon; shake well, strain into small wineglass and serve.

PORTO FLIP
In shaker: one fresh Egg, one-half teaspoon or no Sugar, one glass of Port Wine; shake well, strain into double cocktail glass, serve with grated Nutmeg, if desired.

SHERRY FLIP
In shaker: one fresh Egg, one-half teaspoon of Sugar, one glass of Sherry; shake well, strain into double cocktail glass and serve with grated Nutmeg, if desired.

HIGHBALLS

BRANDY HIGHBALL
In tumbler: a large piece of Ice, one glass of Brandy; add Schweppes soda water or syphon and serve.

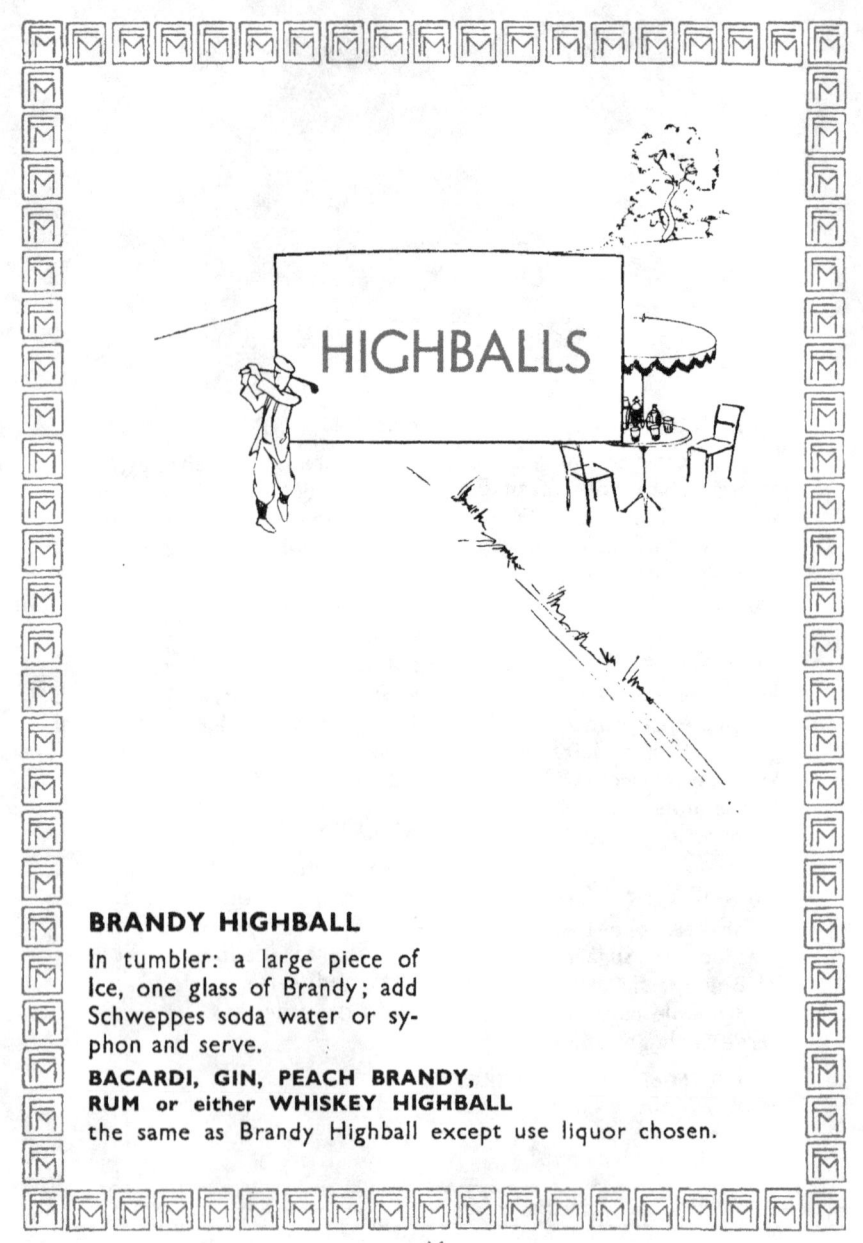

BACARDI, GIN, PEACH BRANDY, RUM or either **WHISKEY HIGHBALL**
the same as Brandy Highball except use liquor chosen.

HOT DRINKS

AMERICAN GROG
In heated tumbler: one glass of American Grog, a slice of Lemon; add boiling water to suit taste and serve.

APPLE JACK or CALVADOS TODDY
In small heated tumbler: a teaspoon or more of Sugar dissolved in little boiling water, leaving spoon in glass, one-quarter of small baked Apple, one glass of Apple Jack or Calvados; pour boiling water upon it to suit taste and serve. See page 92.

BACARDI, BRANDY, PEACH BRANDY, GIN, RUM or either **WHISKEY TODDY** as above except use liquor chosen.

Ingredients may be heated together in small saucepan, the boiling water added not being enough to heat the drink sufficiently.

BLACK STRIPE
In small heated tumbler: a teaspoon of Molasses, one glass of Rum; add boiling water to suit taste, stir and serve.
See page 71.

BLUE BLAZER
Heat two large cups; in one cup, a teaspoon of Sugar dissolved in boiling water; in the other cup, one glass of heated Scotch Whisky, set Whisky aflame, pour ingredients from one cup to the other several times, thus creating an impression of a continuous stream of fire, pour into small heated wineglass, add slice of Lemon or Lemon peel and serve.

BRANDY or RUM BLAZER
The same as Blue Blazer except use Brandy or Rum instead of Scotch Whisky.

BRANDY HOT

In small saucepan: a tablespoon of water, two lumps of Sugar, a pinch of Allspice, a small piece of Orange peel and one glass of Brandy; heat to foam, but do not boil; set aflame, allow to burn a few seconds, and strain into small heated wineglass.

GIN, RUM or either **WHISKEY HOT** as above except use liquor chosen.

BRANDY SANGAREE

In heated tumbler: a teaspoon of Sugar dissolved in little boiling water, one glass of Brandy; fill with boiling water, serve with grated Nutmeg.

GIN, PORT, RUM, SHERRY or either **WHISKEY SANGAREE** as Brandy Sangaree, using liquor chosen.   See page 86.

BRANDY SLING

In heated tumbler: two lumps of Sugar dissolved in little boiling water, a dash of Angostura Bitters, the juice of one-half Lemon, one glass of Brandy; add boiling water to suit taste and serve.

GIN, RUM or either **WHISKEY SLING** as Brandy Sling using liquor chosen.   See page 89.

COLUMBIA SKIN

In saucepan: a tablespoon of water, two lumps of Sugar, the juice of one-half Lemon, a teaspoon of Curaçao, one glass of Rum; heat to foam, but do not boil; serve in small heated wineglass.

BRANDY, GIN or either **WHISKEY SKIN** as above using liquor chosen.   See page 72.

EGG NOGS   See page 56.

GLUHWEIN or HOT CLARET

In small saucepan: two lumps of Sugar, one Clove, a small piece each of Cinnamon and Orange or Lemon peel, one-half pint of Claret; heat to foam, but do not boil; strain into heated tumbler and serve.

HOT BENEFACTOR

In heated tumbler, two lumps of Sugar dissolved in little boiling water, one glass each of Jamaica Rum and red Burgundy; fill with boiling water and serve with slice of Lemon, grated Nutmeg if desired.

Ingredients may be heated together in small saucepan, the boiling water added not being enough to heat the drink sufficiently.

MILK PUNCH

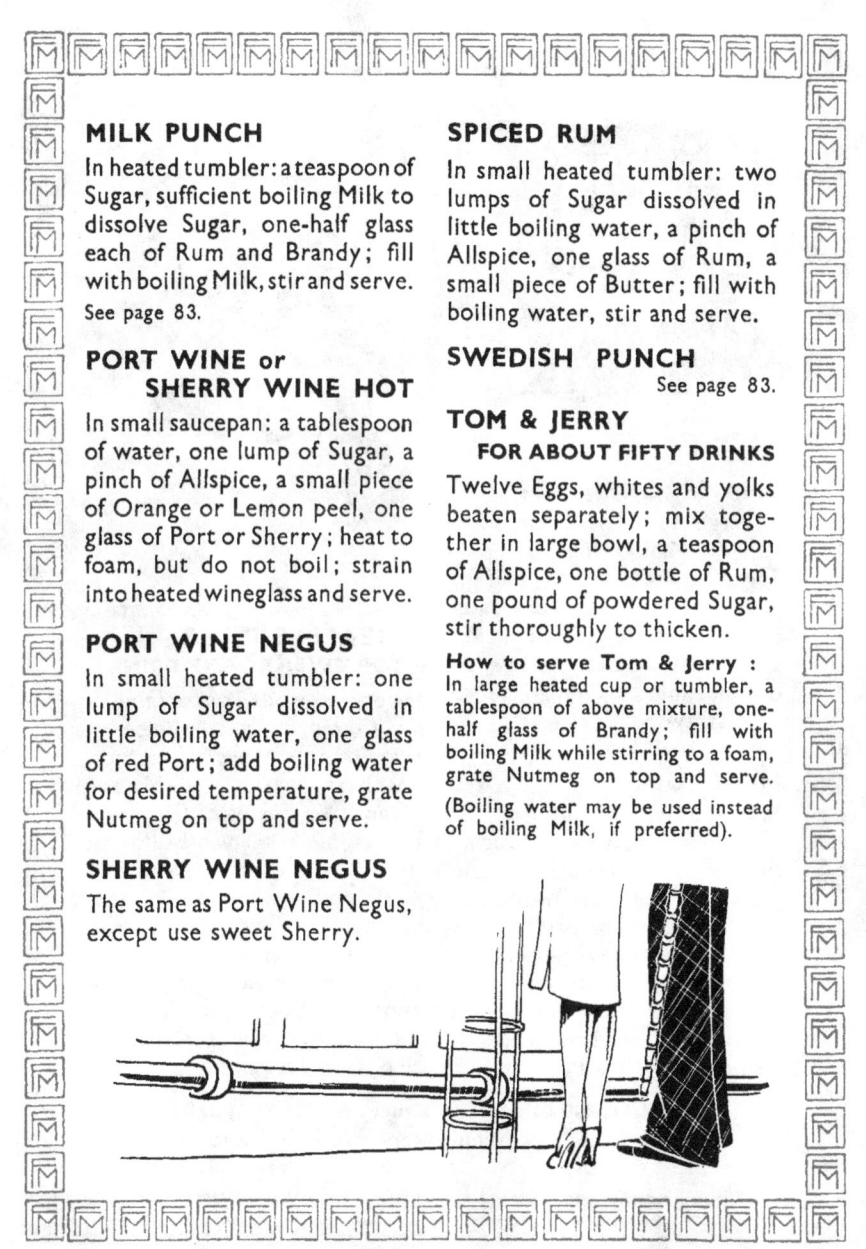

In heated tumbler: a teaspoon of Sugar, sufficient boiling Milk to dissolve Sugar, one-half glass each of Rum and Brandy; fill with boiling Milk, stir and serve. See page 83.

PORT WINE or SHERRY WINE HOT

In small saucepan: a tablespoon of water, one lump of Sugar, a pinch of Allspice, a small piece of Orange or Lemon peel, one glass of Port or Sherry; heat to foam, but do not boil; strain into heated wineglass and serve.

PORT WINE NEGUS

In small heated tumbler: one lump of Sugar dissolved in little boiling water, one glass of red Port; add boiling water for desired temperature, grate Nutmeg on top and serve.

SHERRY WINE NEGUS

The same as Port Wine Negus, except use sweet Sherry.

SPICED RUM

In small heated tumbler: two lumps of Sugar dissolved in little boiling water, a pinch of Allspice, one glass of Rum, a small piece of Butter; fill with boiling water, stir and serve.

SWEDISH PUNCH

See page 83.

TOM & JERRY

FOR ABOUT FIFTY DRINKS

Twelve Eggs, whites and yolks beaten separately; mix together in large bowl, a teaspoon of Allspice, one bottle of Rum, one pound of powdered Sugar, stir thoroughly to thicken.

How to serve Tom & Jerry:
In large heated cup or tumbler, a tablespoon of above mixture, one-half glass of Brandy; fill with boiling Milk while stirring to a foam, grate Nutmeg on top and serve.

(Boiling water may be used instead of boiling Milk, if preferred).

JULEPS

CHAMPAGNE JULEP
In large tumbler: crush four sprigs of Mint with one lump of Sugar in little water; half-fill with cracked Ice, add one glass of Brandy, pour in Champagne, stir slowly, decorate with slice of Pineapple or Orange, serve with straws.

MINT JULEP
In large tumbler half-filled with shaved Ice: a teaspoon of Sugar, five or six sprigs of Mint, one glass of Bourbon Whiskey; stir vigorously to bruise Mint and mix with Whiskey; add more shaved Ice, stir until glass is thoroughly frosted; decorate with sprig of Mint, slice of Lemon, serve with straws.

PINEAPPLE JULEP
FOR TWENTY-FIVE DRINKS
In very large bowl or container: a big lump of Ice, the juice of two Oranges, one glass each of Raspberry syrup and Maraschino, two glasses of Gin, two quarts of Ackerman-Laurance dry "Royal" sparkling Saumur, one ripe Pineapple peeled and crushed, one pound of fresh Berries; stir mixture until cold and serve in wineglass with spoon. Just before serving, add a tablespoon of Sugar to produce effervescence.

BRANDY, GIN, RUM or either WHISKEY JULEP
the same as Mint Julep except use liquor chosen.

LEMONADES

LEMONADE (Plain)
In tumbler: two or three pieces of Ice, the juice of one Lemon, a teaspoon of Sugar; fill with plain water, stir and serve.

ANGOSTURA LEMONADE
Plain Lemonade with a teaspoon of Angostura Bitters.

EGG LEMONADE
In shaker: the juice of one-half Lemon, a teaspoon of Sugar, one fresh Egg; shake well, pour into tumbler, add plain water or Schweppes soda and serve.

FRUIT LEMONADE
Plain Lemonade with slice of Pineapple and Fruit of season; serve with spoon.

BRANDY, CLARET, WHISKEY, RUM LEMONADES as plain Lemonade, float on top one-half glass of the liquor chosen.

LEMON SQUASH
Plain Lemonade use Schweppes soda water or syphon instead of plain water.

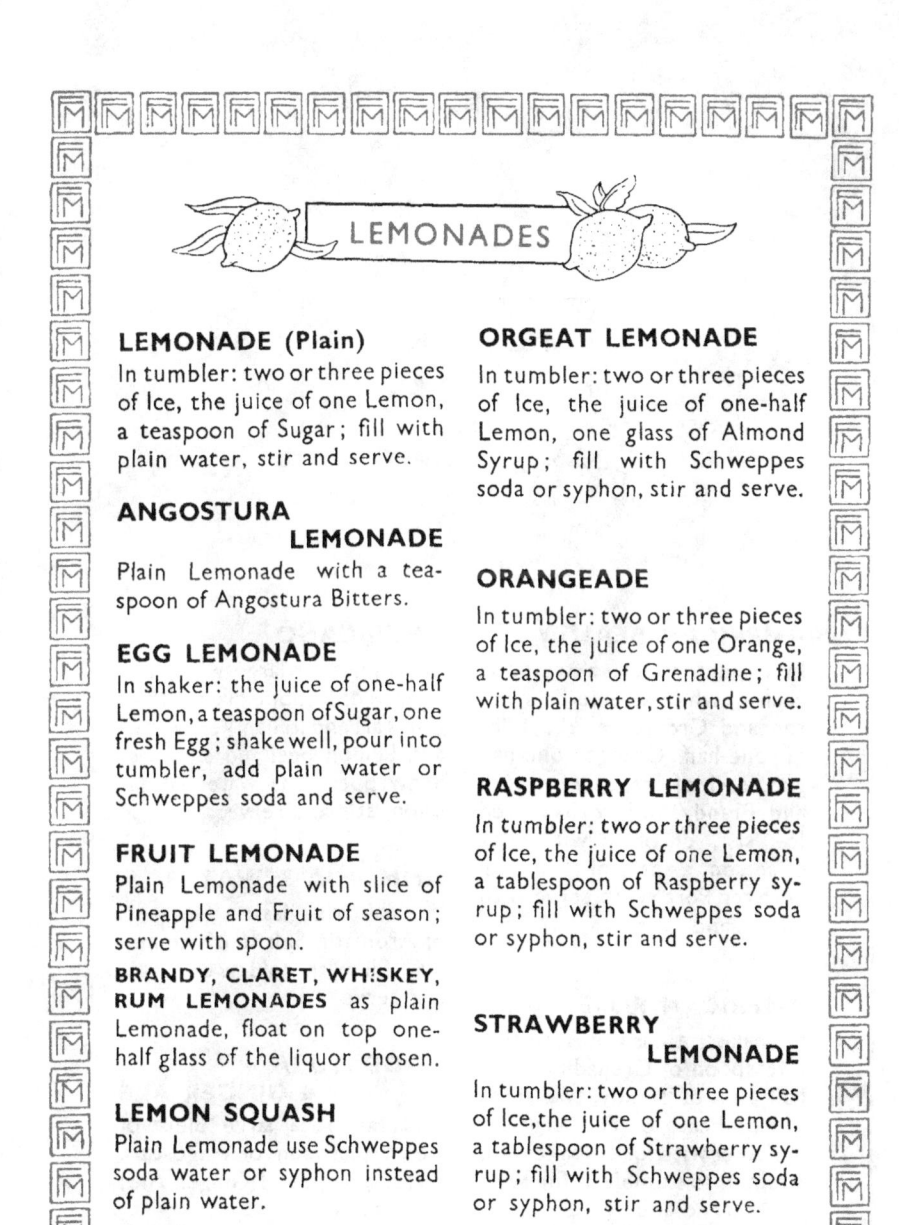

ORGEAT LEMONADE
In tumbler: two or three pieces of Ice, the juice of one-half Lemon, one glass of Almond Syrup; fill with Schweppes soda or syphon, stir and serve.

ORANGEADE
In tumbler: two or three pieces of Ice, the juice of one Orange, a teaspoon of Grenadine; fill with plain water, stir and serve.

RASPBERRY LEMONADE
In tumbler: two or three pieces of Ice, the juice of one Lemon, a tablespoon of Raspberry syrup; fill with Schweppes soda or syphon, stir and serve.

STRAWBERRY LEMONADE
In tumbler: two or three pieces of Ice, the juice of one Lemon, a tablespoon of Strawberry syrup; fill with Schweppes soda or syphon, stir and serve.

MISCELLANEOUS DRINKS

AMERICAN BEAUTY
In large tumbler: a teaspoon each of white Crème de Menthe and Grenadine, the juice of one-half Orange, one-half glass each of French Vermouth and Brandy; fill with shaved Ice, stir, decorate with Fruit of season, a sprig of Mint, top with red Port Wine, serve with straws and spoon.

AMERICAN ROSE
In shaker: a dash of Absinthe, a teaspoon of Grenadine, one-half glass of Brandy, two slices of ripe Peach or Pear crushed in shaker with fork; shake well, strain into tumbler, fill with Champagne and serve.

AMERICANO
In tumbler, or large wineglass: a piece of Ice, one glass each of Campari and Italian Vermouth; add Lemon peel and squirt of Schweppes soda water or syphon, stir and serve.

AMMONIA & WATER
In small wineglass: a teaspoon of Aromatic Spirits of Ammonia; fill with cold water, stir and serve.

ANGOSTURA & GINGER ALE
In tumbler: a large piece of Ice, a teaspoon of Angostura Bitters, a split of Ginger Ale; stir and serve.

ANGOSTURA & SODA
In tumbler: a large piece of Ice, a teaspoon of Angostura Bitters, one-half teaspoon of Sugar; fill with Schweppes soda water, stir and serve.

BARBOTAGE OF CHAMPAGNE
In tumbler half-filled with cracked Ice: a dash of Angostura Bitters, a teaspoon each of Lemon juice, and Sugar syrup; fill with Champagne, stir, add slice of Orange and serve.

BARMEN'S DELIGHT
" Just a little Whiskey, straight if you please."
(From "The World's Drinks and How to Mix Them.")

BISHOP
In tumbler half-filled with cracked Ice: a teaspoon of Sugar, the juices of one-half Lemon and half Orange; fill with red Burgundy or Claret, stir, add slice of Orange, a dash of Rum and serve.

BISMARCK or BLACK VELVET
Into large tumbler with a piece of Ice, pour slowly a split bottle of Guinness's Stout add an equal amount of Champagne; stir gently and serve.

BLACK ROSE
In tumbler: a large piece of Ice, a teaspoon of Sugar, one-half glass of St. James Rum, fill with cold black Coffee, stir and serve.

BLACK STRIPE
In cocktail glass: a teaspoon of Molasses; fill with Rum, stir and serve.   See page 65.

BORDEAUX CHAMPAGNE
In tumbler: a piece of Ice, half Claret, half Champagne; stir and serve.

BOSOM CARESSER
In shaker: the yolk of an Egg, a dash of Grenadine, a dash of Curaçao, one-half glass each of Brandy and Madeira; shake well, strain into double cocktail glass and serve.

BRANDY & HONEY
In small tumbler: a piece of Ice, a teaspoon of Honey, leaving spoon in tumbler, one glass of Brandy; stir and serve with glass of water.
PEACH BRANDY & HONEY, RUM & HONEY or either **WHISKEY & HONEY** as above except use liquor chosen.

BYRRH CASSIS
In tumbler or large wineglass: a piece of Ice, a teaspoon of Crème de Cassis, one glass of Byrrh; add Schweppes soda water or syphon and serve.

CAFÉ & KIRSCH (Cold)
In tumbler: two or three pieces of Ice, one-half glass of Kirsch; fill with cold black Coffee, stir, and serve with powdered Sugar if desired.

CASSISCO
A popular French Drink.
In tumbler or large wineglass: a piece of Ice, a tablespoon of Crème de Cassis, one-half glass of Brandy; add Schweppes soda water or syphon, stir and serve.

CHAMBERY FRAISE
In tumbler or large wineglass: a piece of Ice, a teaspoon of Strawberry syrup, one glass of Chambery Vermouth; add syphon or Schweppes soda water, stir and serve.

COLUMBIA SKIN
In shaker: a teaspoon of Sugar, the juice of one-half Lemon, a teaspoon of Curaçao, one glass of Rum; shake well, strain into small wineglass and serve.
BRANDY, GIN or either **WHISKEY SKIN** as above using liquor chosen.   See page 66.

CORPSE REVIVER N° 2
In tumbler: a piece of Ice, the juice of one-quarter Lemon, one glass of Anis "Pernod fils"; fill with Champagne, stir and serve.   See page 28.

DOG'S NOSE
In tumbler: one-half bottle of Stout; a dash of Gin and serve.

DUBONNET CITRON
In tumbler or large wineglass: a piece of Ice, a tablespoon of Lemon syrup, one glass of Dubonnet; add Schweppes soda water or syphon and serve.

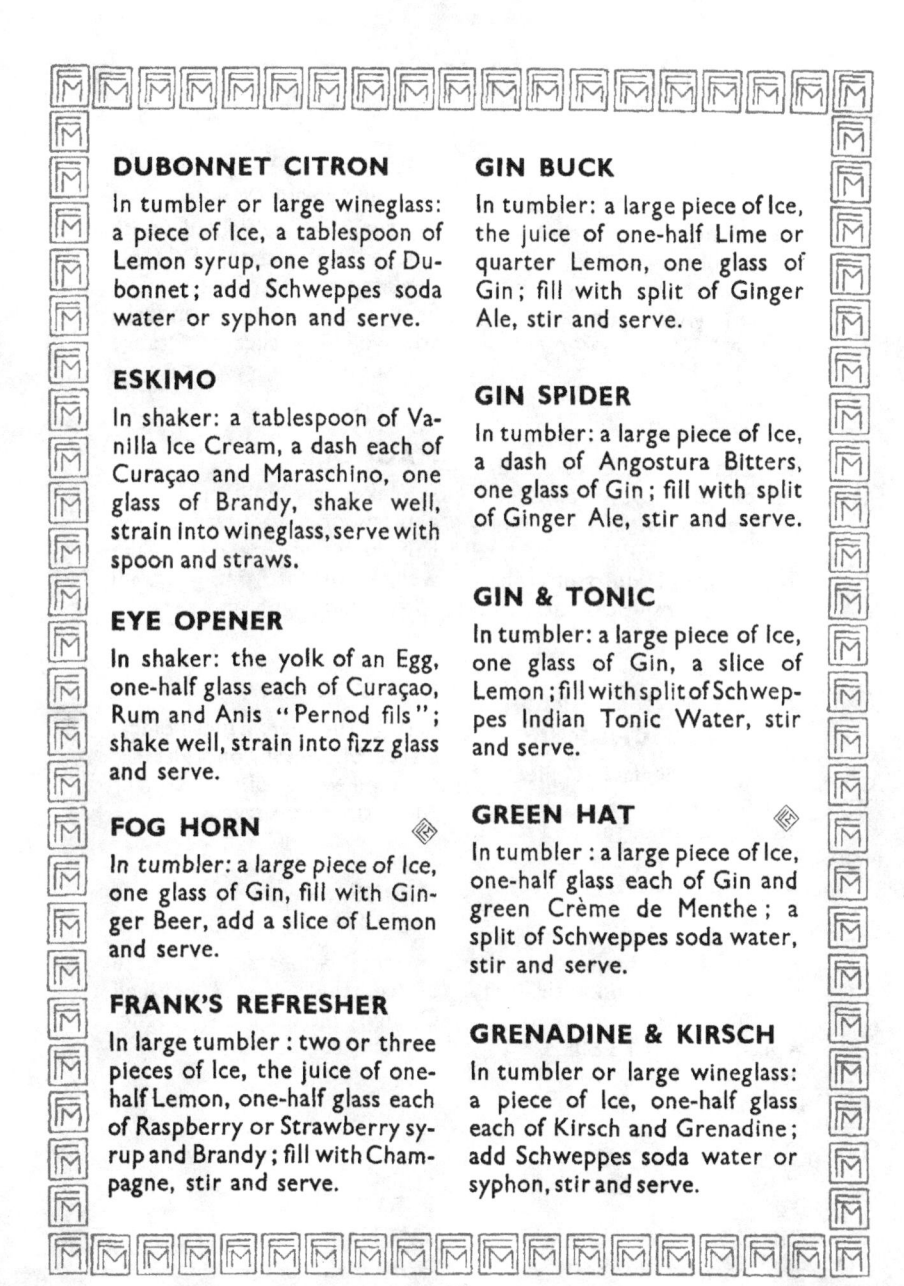

ESKIMO
In shaker: a tablespoon of Vanilla Ice Cream, a dash each of Curaçao and Maraschino, one glass of Brandy, shake well, strain into wineglass, serve with spoon and straws.

EYE OPENER
In shaker: the yolk of an Egg, one-half glass each of Curaçao, Rum and Anis "Pernod fils"; shake well, strain into fizz glass and serve.

FOG HORN
In tumbler: a large piece of Ice, one glass of Gin, fill with Ginger Beer, add a slice of Lemon and serve.

FRANK'S REFRESHER
In large tumbler: two or three pieces of Ice, the juice of one-half Lemon, one-half glass each of Raspberry or Strawberry syrup and Brandy; fill with Champagne, stir and serve.

GIN BUCK
In tumbler: a large piece of Ice, the juice of one-half Lime or quarter Lemon, one glass of Gin; fill with split of Ginger Ale, stir and serve.

GIN SPIDER
In tumbler: a large piece of Ice, a dash of Angostura Bitters, one glass of Gin; fill with split of Ginger Ale, stir and serve.

GIN & TONIC
In tumbler: a large piece of Ice, one glass of Gin, a slice of Lemon; fill with split of Schweppes Indian Tonic Water, stir and serve.

GREEN HAT
In tumbler: a large piece of Ice, one-half glass each of Gin and green Crème de Menthe; a split of Schweppes soda water, stir and serve.

GRENADINE & KIRSCH
In tumbler or large wineglass: a piece of Ice, one-half glass each of Kirsch and Grenadine; add Schweppes soda water or syphon, stir and serve.

HORSE'S NECK

In large tumbler: two pieces of Ice in whole Lemon rind, pour in split of Ginger Ale, stir and serve.

One-half glass of Brandy, Gin, Rum, or either Whiskey may be added if desired.

IRISH ROSE

In shaker: the juice of one-half Lemon, a teaspoon of Grenadine, one glass of Irish Whiskey; shake well, strain into fizz glass, add squirt of syphon or Schweppes soda water and serve.

KING'S PEG or BRANDY AND CHAMPAGNE

In large wineglass: a piece of Ice, one-half glass of Brandy; fill with Champagne, and serve.

KOLDKURE

In cocktail glass: a teaspoon of Grenadine, the juice of one-quarter Lemon, fill with Rum; stir and serve.

A good remedy for a cold.

MACKA

A popular French Drink.

In tumbler half-filled with cracked Ice: a dash of Crème de Cassis, one-third each of Gin, French and Italian Vermouth; stir well, add slice of Orange and serve.

MAGNOLIA

In shaker: the yolk of an Egg, a teaspoon of Curaçao, one-half glass of Brandy; shake well, strain into fizz glass, fill with Champagne and serve.

MAMY TAYLOR

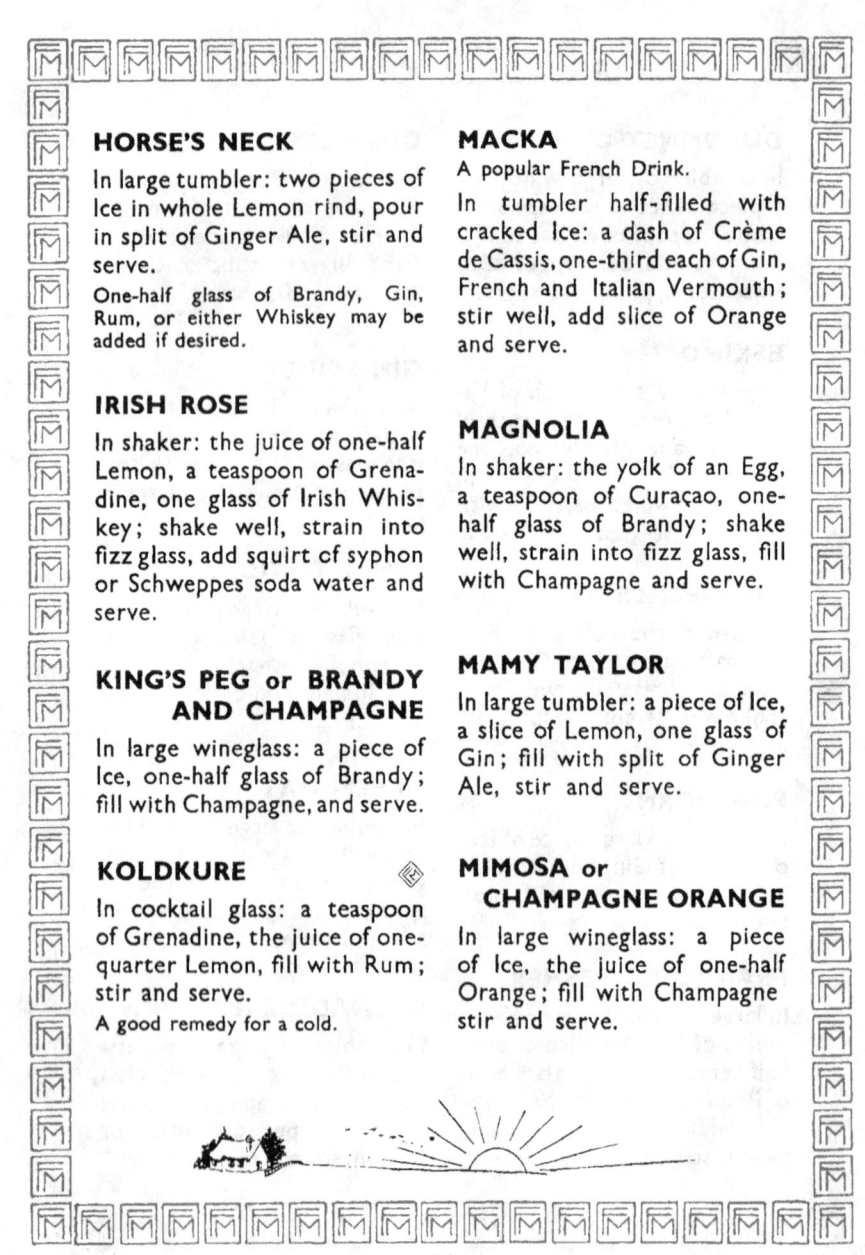

In large tumbler: a piece of Ice, a slice of Lemon, one glass of Gin; fill with split of Ginger Ale, stir and serve.

MIMOSA or CHAMPAGNE ORANGE

In large wineglass: a piece of Ice, the juice of one-half Orange; fill with Champagne stir and serve.

MORNING BRACER
In shaker: a dash of Angostura Bitters, one-half glass each of Anis "Pernod fils" and French Vermouth; shake well, strain into double cocktail glass, add squirt of Schweppes soda water or syphon and serve.

MORNING SMILE
In shaker: one fresh Egg, one-half teaspoon of Sugar, one glass of Bourbon Whiskey, one glass of fresh Milk; shake well, strain into tumbler and serve.

PICON-GRENADINE
In tumbler or large wineglass: a piece of Ice, one glass of Amer Picon, a teaspoon of Grenadine; add Schweppes soda water or syphon, stir and serve.

PICK-ME-UP
In shaker: a dash of Angostura Bitters, a teaspoon of Sugar, one glass of Brandy, one glass of fresh Milk; shake well, strain into tumbler, add squirt of syphon or Schweppes soda water and serve.

PRINCE OF WALES
In shaker: a dash of Angostura Bitters, a teaspoon of Curaçao, one-half glass each of Madeira and Brandy; shake well, strain into large wineglass, fill with Champagne, add slice of Orange and serve.

QUEEN'S PEG
or GIN & CHAMPAGNE
In large wineglass: a piece of Ice, one-half glass of Gin; fill with Champagne and serve.

RAINBOW
Into tall liqueur or pousse-café glass, pour slowly and carefully using bar or round teaspoon, holding spoon against inside of glass, the following ingredients on top of one another:

Anisette	pink
Mint	green
Chartreuse	yellow
Cherry Brandy	red
Kummel	white
Chartreuse	green
Cognac Brandy	brown

Use quantities of Liqueurs according to size and shape of glass, so that all stripes of colour are of equal height. Wynand Fockink Roode Anisette (Pink) is the best foundation for this artistic drink.

RHINE WINE or MOSELLE & SELTZER

In tumbler: two-thirds of chilled Rhine or Moselle wine, one-third of cold Schweppes soda water or syphon and serve.

ROCK & RYE

In small tumbler: a piece of crushed Rock Candy or one teaspoon of Rock Candy syrup, leaving spoon in tumbler, one glass of Rye Whiskey; a few drops of Lemon Juice, if desired, serve with glass of Ice water.

SHANDY GAFF

In large tumbler: half cold Pale Ale, half cold Ginger Ale; stir gently and serve.

SHERRY & EGG

In cocktail glass: a dash of Sherry, the yolk of an Egg; fill with Sherry and serve;
or
in cocktail glass half-filled with Sherry, drop the yolk of an Egg and serve.

SOYER AU CHAMPAGNE

In tumbler half-filled with cracked Ice: a tablespoon of Orange juice, a teaspoon each of Maraschino and Brandy; fill with Champagne, stir, add slice of Orange, Fruit of season and serve with spoon.

STONE FENCE

In tumbler: a large piece of Ice, one glass of Bourbon or Rye Whiskey; fill with sweet Cider, stir and serve.

STONE WALL

In tumbler: a large piece of Ice, one-half teaspoon of Sugar, one glass of Scotch Whisky, fill with Schweppes soda water, stir and serve.

TOISON D'OR

In cocktail glass half-filled with shaved Ice: half yellow Chartreuse, half Danziger Wasser.

An After-Dinner Drink.

TOMATE
A popular French Drink.

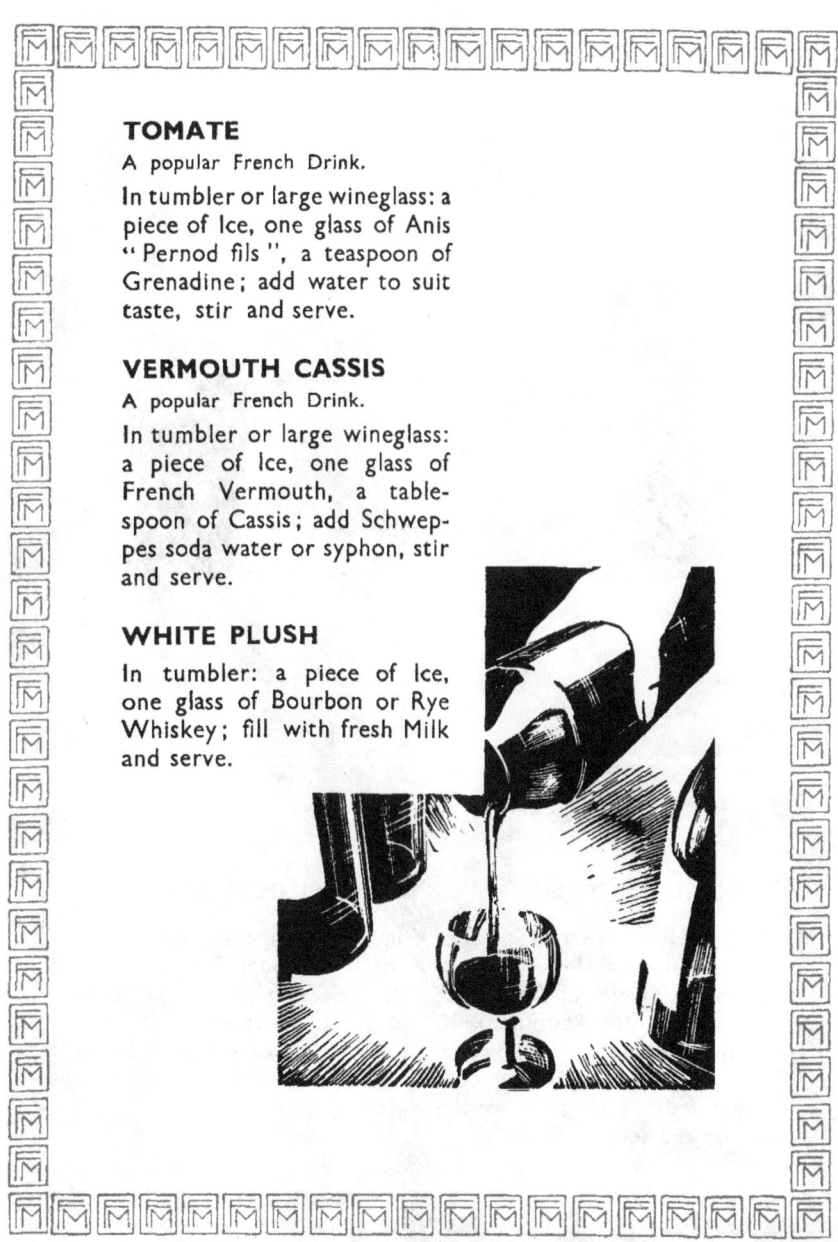

In tumbler or large wineglass: a piece of Ice, one glass of Anis "Pernod fils", a teaspoon of Grenadine; add water to suit taste, stir and serve.

VERMOUTH CASSIS
A popular French Drink.

In tumbler or large wineglass: a piece of Ice, one glass of French Vermouth, a tablespoon of Cassis; add Schweppes soda water or syphon, stir and serve.

WHITE PLUSH
In tumbler: a piece of Ice, one glass of Bourbon or Rye Whiskey; fill with fresh Milk and serve.

NON-ALCOHOLIC DRINKS

BROMO SELTZER

In tumbler: two teaspoons of Bromo Seltzer, three drops of aromatic Spirits of Ammonia; a second tumbler half-filled with Schweppes soda or plain water, mix quickly by pouring contents from one glass to the other and serve.

CLAM JUICE COCKTAIL

In shaker: a teaspoon of Tomato Ketchup, a small pinch of Celery salt, two or three drops of Tabasco sauce, one glass of Clam juice; shake slightly and serve.

GRAPE JUICE CUP
FOR TEN DRINKS

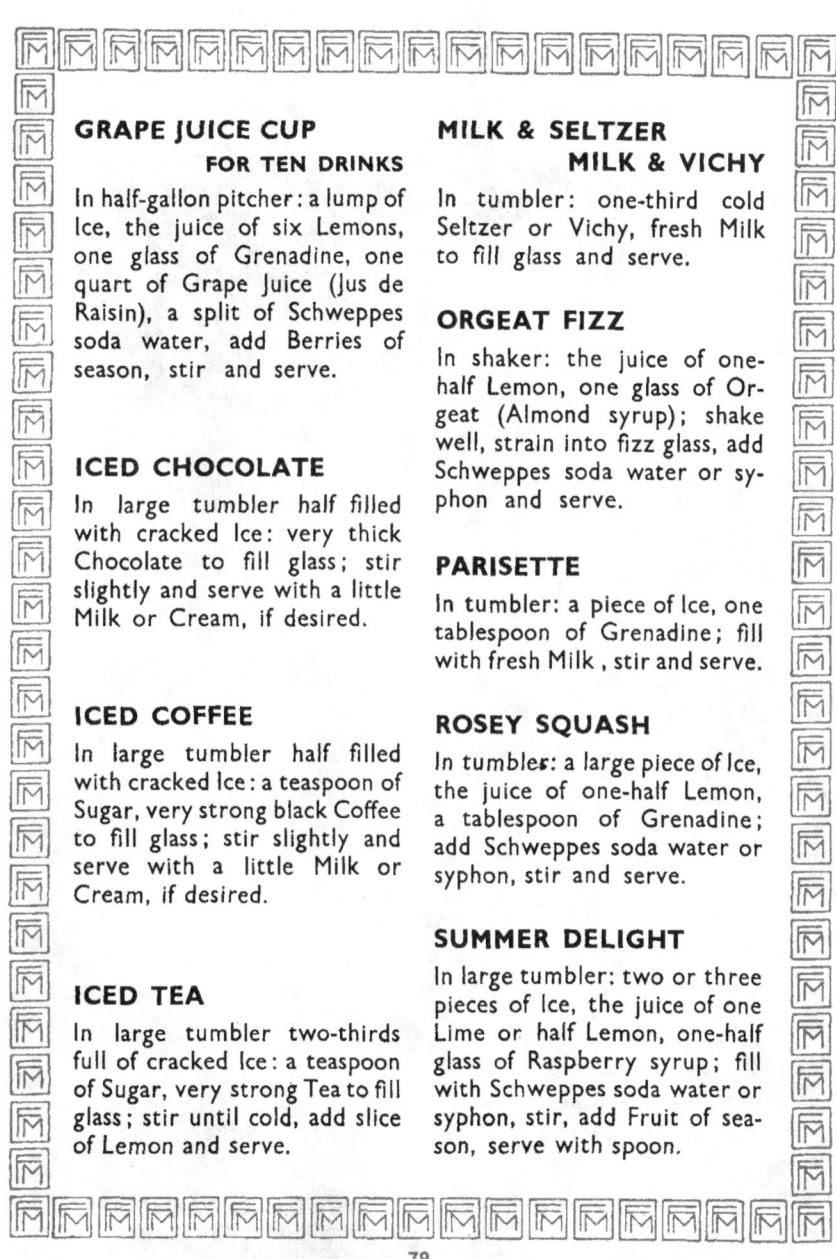

In half-gallon pitcher: a lump of Ice, the juice of six Lemons, one glass of Grenadine, one quart of Grape Juice (Jus de Raisin), a split of Schweppes soda water, add Berries of season, stir and serve.

ICED CHOCOLATE

In large tumbler half filled with cracked Ice: very thick Chocolate to fill glass; stir slightly and serve with a little Milk or Cream, if desired.

ICED COFFEE

In large tumbler half filled with cracked Ice: a teaspoon of Sugar, very strong black Coffee to fill glass; stir slightly and serve with a little Milk or Cream, if desired.

ICED TEA

In large tumbler two-thirds full of cracked Ice: a teaspoon of Sugar, very strong Tea to fill glass; stir until cold, add slice of Lemon and serve.

MILK & SELTZER
MILK & VICHY

In tumbler: one-third cold Seltzer or Vichy, fresh Milk to fill glass and serve.

ORGEAT FIZZ

In shaker: the juice of one-half Lemon, one glass of Orgeat (Almond syrup); shake well, strain into fizz glass, add Schweppes soda water or syphon and serve.

PARISETTE

In tumbler: a piece of Ice, one tablespoon of Grenadine; fill with fresh Milk, stir and serve.

ROSEY SQUASH

In tumbler: a large piece of Ice, the juice of one-half Lemon, a tablespoon of Grenadine; add Schweppes soda water or syphon, stir and serve.

SUMMER DELIGHT

In large tumbler: two or three pieces of Ice, the juice of one Lime or half Lemon, one-half glass of Raspberry syrup; fill with Schweppes soda water or syphon, stir, add Fruit of season, serve with spoon.

PUFFS

BRANDY PUFF
In tumbler: a piece of Ice, one glass of Brandy, one glass of fresh Milk; fill with Schweppes soda water or syphon, stir slightly and serve.

GIN, RUM or either WHISKEY PUFF
the same as Brandy Puff, except use liquor chosen.

PUNCHES

FRANK'S SPECIAL FOR HOME ENTERTAINMENT
CHAMPAGNE PUNCH
FOR ABOUT FIFTY DRINKS

Put into large bowl or tureen, without waste of juices, two pounds of ripe Pineapple cut in cubes and crushed, one pound of ripe Cherries with stones removed, six peeled Grape Fruit with seeds and cells removed, one pound of powdered Sugar, one-half bottle of Benedictine, one bottle of Brandy; mix well and put into Frigidaire until very cold. When ready to serve, put two tablespoons of mixture (fruits, juices and liqueurs) in large wineglass, fill with thoroughly chilled dry Champagne, serve with spoon.

Second Fruit Combination for Champagne Punch

Two pounds of ripe Strawberries, twelve sliced Bananas, and twelve peeled and sliced Peaches.

Third Fruit Combination for Champagne Punch

Twelve peeled Oranges with seeds and cells removed, ten or twelve peeled, sliced and cored Pears and one pint of Maraschino Cherries.

Hard and soft fruits should not be put together in either fruit combination.

BRANDY PUNCH

In tumbler: one-half teaspoon of Sugar dissolved in little water, a teaspoon of Raspberry syrup, the juice of one-half Lemon, one glass of Brandy; fill with shaved Ice, stir well, decorate with Berries of season, slice of Orange, serve with spoon and straws.

APRICOT and PEACH BRANDY, GIN, RUM or either **WHISKEY PUNCH** the same as above except use liquor chosen.

CHAMPAGNE PUNCH

In tumbler half-filled with cracked Ice: the juice of one-half Lemon, one-half glass of Strawberry or Raspberry syrup; fill with Champagne, stir slightly, add slice of Orange, serve with straws.

CLARET or BURGUNDY PUNCH N° 1

In tumbler half-filled with cracked Ice: a teaspoon each of Lemon juice, Sugar and Maraschino; fill with Claret or red Burgundy, stir, add slice of Orange, Fruit of season, serve with spoon.

CLARET or BURGUNDY PUNCH N° 2

In tumbler half-filled with cracked Ice: a teaspoon each of Lemon juice, Grenadine and Curaçao; fill with red Burgundy or Claret, stir, add slice of Orange, serve with straws.

CURAÇAO PUNCH

In tumbler: one-half teaspoon of Sugar, the juice of one-half Lemon, one-half glass each of Curaçao, Brandy or Rum; fill with shaved Ice, stir slightly, decorate with small slice of Pineapple and Berries of season, serve with spoon and straws.

FISH HOUSE PUNCH
In tumbler: two or three pieces of Ice, the juice of one-half Lemon, a teaspoon of Sugar, one-half glass each of Rum, Brandy, Benedictine and Peach Brandy; add squirt of syphon or Schweppes soda water, stir and serve.

MILK PUNCH
In shaker: a teaspoon of Sugar, one-half glass each Brandy and Rum, one glass of Milk; shake, allow foam to settle, strain into tumbler, grate Nutmeg on top and serve.   See page 67.

PISCO PUNCH
In large wineglass: a piece of Ice, a teaspoon each of Pineapple and Lemon juice, one glass of "Peru" Brandy; add plain water, a small slice of Pineapple, stir and serve.

PLANTER'S PUNCH
In tumbler: two or three pieces of Ice, a dash of Angostura Bitters, the juice of one-half Lime or quarter Lemon, a teaspoon of Grenadine, one glass of Rum; add squirt of Schweppes soda water or syphon, stir and serve.

ROMAN PUNCH
In tumbler: the juice of one-half Lemon, one-half glass each of Raspberry syrup, Rum, and Brandy; fill with shaved Ice, stir well, add Berries of season, a dash of Port Wine, serve with spoon and straws.

SAUTERNES PUNCH
In tumbler half-filled with cracked Ice: one-half teaspoon of Sugar, the juice of one-half Lemon, a teaspoon of Curaçao; fill with Sauternes, stir well, decorate with Fruit of season, serve with spoon and straws.

STRAWBERRY PUNCH
In tumbler : one-half teaspoon of Sugar dissolved in little water, the juice of one-half Lemon, a teaspoon of Strawberry syrup, one glass of Brandy; fill with shaved Ice, stir, add Strawberries, serve with spoon and straws.

SWEDISH PUNCH HOT
In small heated tumbler : one glass of Caloric Punch; fill with boiling water, serve with slice of Lemon.

CHRISTMAS PUNCH
FOR ABOUT FIFTY DRINKS

In three-gallon tureen or other container: a quart of strong Tea, a bottle each of Rum, Rye Whiskey and Brandy, one-half bottle of Benedictine; a tablespoon of Angostura Bitters, peel and grate into mixture a two or three-pound ripe Pineapple; add the juice of twelve Oranges, a pound or more of Sugar dissolved in ample water; mix well and put into Frigidaire until very cold. Have two quarts of thoroughly chilled Champagne ready to add, serve in wineglass with spoon.

CHRISTMAS PUNCH HOT
FOR TWENTY DRINKS

In gallon or bigger saucepan or tureen: two bottles of Brandy, two bottles of Champagne, one pound of Sugar, one pound of ripe Pineapple cut in cubes and crushed; heat to foam, but do not boil; pour on top a little Brandy, set aflame, allow to burn one minute and serve in heated wineglass with spoon.

RICKEYS

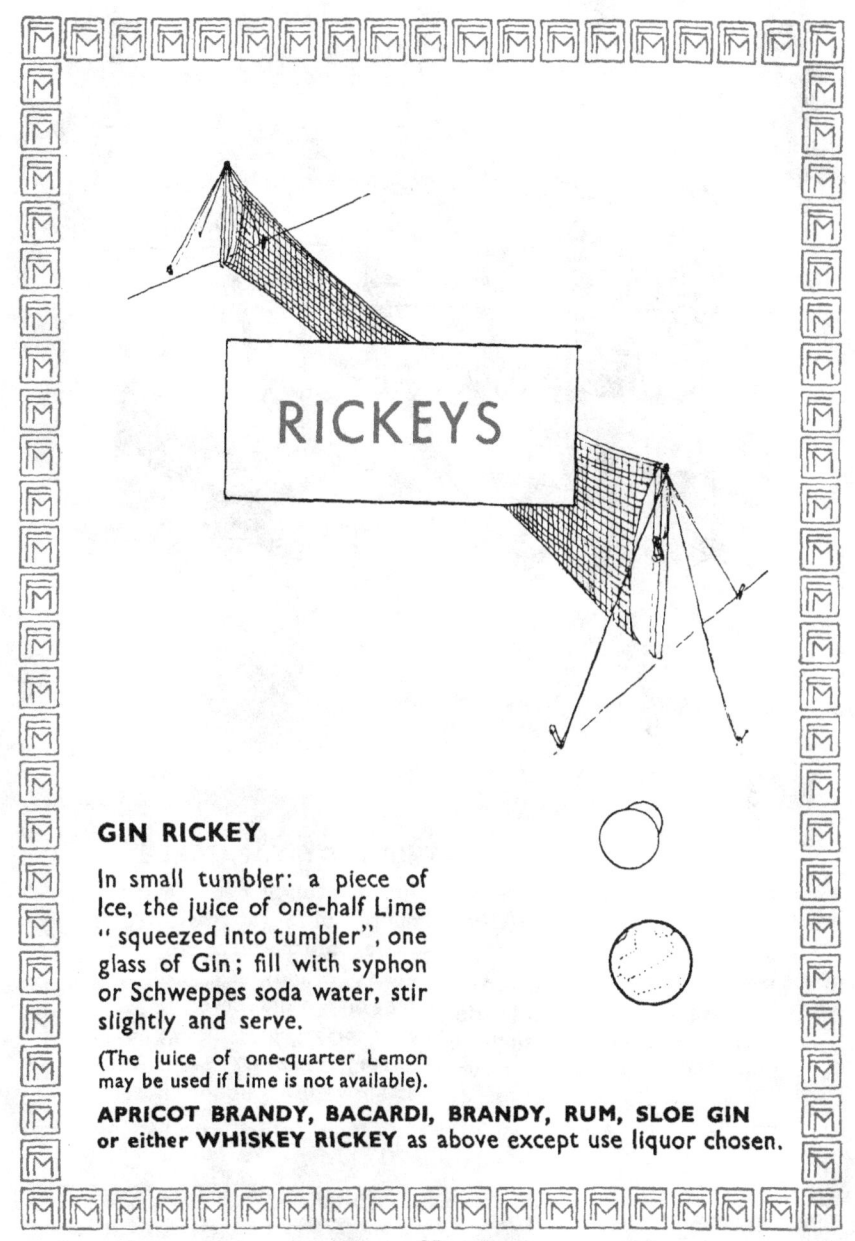

GIN RICKEY

In small tumbler: a piece of Ice, the juice of one-half Lime "squeezed into tumbler", one glass of Gin; fill with syphon or Schweppes soda water, stir slightly and serve.

(The juice of one-quarter Lemon may be used if Lime is not available).

APRICOT BRANDY, BACARDI, BRANDY, RUM, SLOE GIN or either **WHISKEY RICKEY** as above except use liquor chosen.

SANGAREES

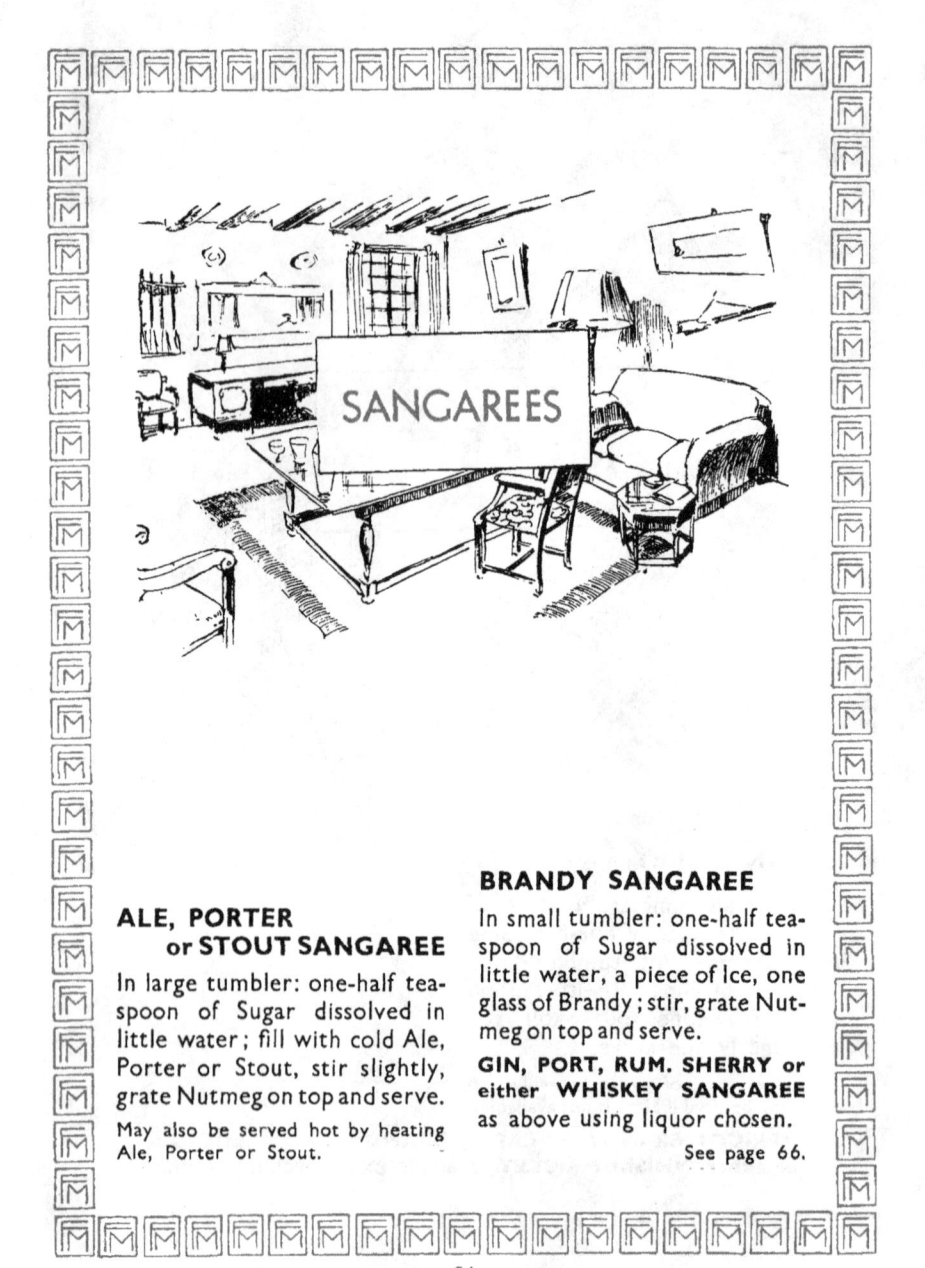

ALE, PORTER or STOUT SANGAREE

In large tumbler: one-half teaspoon of Sugar dissolved in little water; fill with cold Ale, Porter or Stout, stir slightly, grate Nutmeg on top and serve.

May also be served hot by heating Ale, Porter or Stout.

BRANDY SANGAREE

In small tumbler: one-half teaspoon of Sugar dissolved in little water, a piece of Ice, one glass of Brandy; stir, grate Nutmeg on top and serve.

GIN, PORT, RUM. SHERRY or either **WHISKEY SANGAREE** as above using liquor chosen.

See page 66.

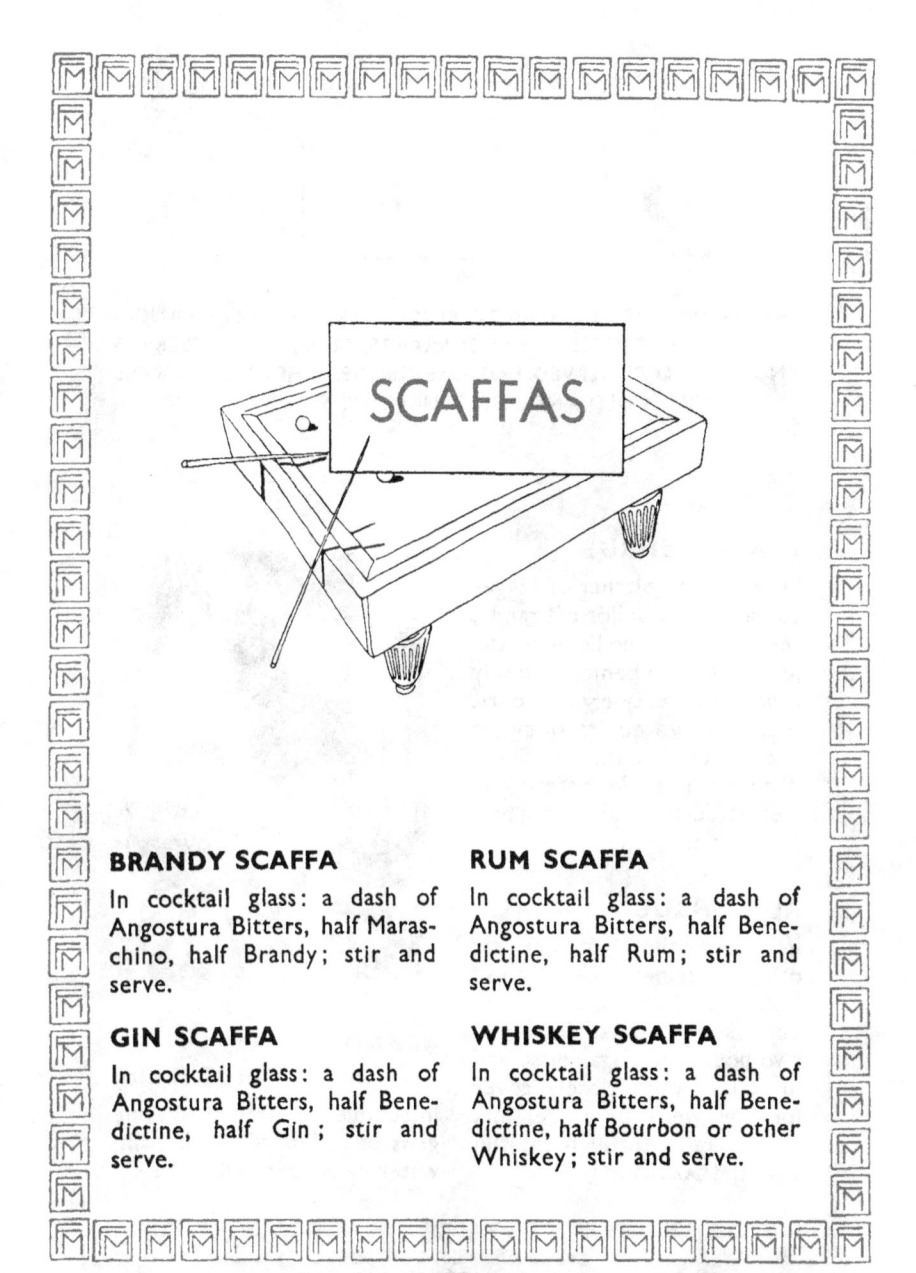

BRANDY SCAFFA
In cocktail glass: a dash of Angostura Bitters, half Maraschino, half Brandy; stir and serve.

GIN SCAFFA
In cocktail glass: a dash of Angostura Bitters, half Benedictine, half Gin; stir and serve.

RUM SCAFFA
In cocktail glass: a dash of Angostura Bitters, half Benedictine, half Rum; stir and serve.

WHISKEY SCAFFA
In cocktail glass: a dash of Angostura Bitters, half Benedictine, half Bourbon or other Whiskey; stir and serve.

SHRUBS

SHRUBS ARE MADE OF BRANDY, RUM, SHERRY, LEMONS, ORANGES AND COOKED FRUIT SUCH AS CURRANTS, CHERRIES, RASPBERRIES AND SHOULD BE SERVED HOT LIKE GROGS. THEY CAN ALSO BE PREPARED COLD AND ARE DELIGHTFUL SUMMER DRINKS.

BRANDY SHRUB

In two-gallon pitcher or bigger container: one gallon of Brandy, the rinds of three Lemons, the juice of twelve Lemons, closely cover for forty-eight hours, then add two quarts of sweet Sherry, two pounds of Sugar dissolved in little water; mix well, strain through muslin bag, and bottle.

RUM SHRUB

In three-gallon pitcher or other container: one gallon of Rum, the juice of about ten pounds of cooked Currants, two pounds of Sugar dissolved in little water; closely cover for one week or more, mix well, strain through muslin bag, and bottle.

BRANDY or RUM SHRUB (Cold)

In tumbler: a piece of Ice, one glass of Shrub, fill with plain water or seltzer and serve.

SLINGS

BRANDY SLING

In tumbler: three or four pieces of Ice, a dash of Angostura Bitters, the juice of one-half Lemon, a teaspoon of Sugar, one glass of Brandy; fill with plain water, shake well and serve.

SINGAPORE SLING

In tumbler: three or four pieces of Ice, the juice of one-half Lemon, one-half glass of Cherry Brandy, one-half glass of Gin; fill with plain water, shake well and serve.

GIN, RUM or either WHISKEY SLING See page 66.
the same as Brandy Sling except use liquor chosen.

SMASHES

BRANDY SMASH
"Actually a miniature Julep."

In small tumbler: dissolve one-half teaspoon of Sugar in little water, add two or three sprigs of Mint, one glass of Brandy; fill with shaved Ice, stir until very cold, add slice of Lemon and serve with straws.

GIN, RUM or either **WHISKEY SMASH** the same as Brandy Smash except use liquor chosen.

BRANDY SOUR

In shaker: the juice of one-half Lemon, one-half teaspoon of Sugar, one glass of Brandy; shake well, strain into double cocktail glass, add squirt of Schweppes soda water or syphon and serve.

APPLE JACK or **CALVADOS, BACARDI, GIN, RUM** or either **WHISKEY SOUR** as Brandy Sour, except use liquor chosen.

TODDIES

APPLE JACK or CALVADOS TODDY

In small tumbler: one teaspoon of Sugar dissolved in little water, leaving spoon in tumbler, a piece of Ice, one glass of Apple Jack or Calvados; stir and serve with glass of water.

BACARDI, BRANDY, PEACH BRANDY, GIN, RUM or either **WHISKEY TODDY** as Apple Jack or Calvados Toddy using liquor chosen. See page 65.

ZOOMS

BACARDI ZOOM
Special for Comte Jean de Limur.

Dissolve in small cup a teaspoon of Honey in very little boiling water, pour into shaker, add a teaspoon of fresh Cream and one glass of Bacardi, shake well, strain into small wineglass and serve.

BRANDY, GIN or either WHISKEY ZOOM
the same as Bacardi Zoom, except use liquor chosen.

SANDWICHES

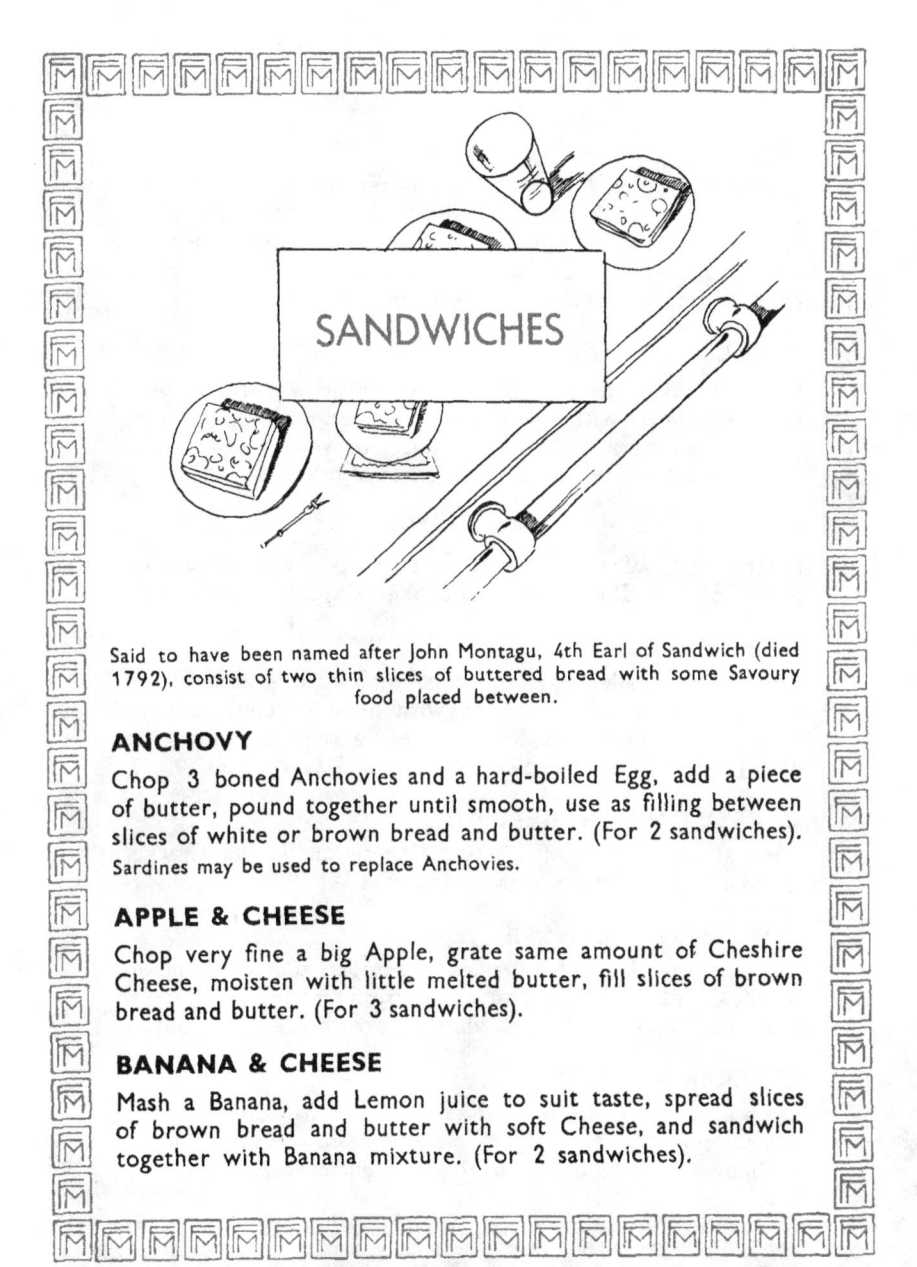

SANDWICHES

Said to have been named after John Montagu, 4th Earl of Sandwich (died 1792), consist of two thin slices of buttered bread with some Savoury food placed between.

ANCHOVY

Chop 3 boned Anchovies and a hard-boiled Egg, add a piece of butter, pound together until smooth, use as filling between slices of white or brown bread and butter. (For 2 sandwiches).

Sardines may be used to replace Anchovies.

APPLE & CHEESE

Chop very fine a big Apple, grate same amount of Cheshire Cheese, moisten with little melted butter, fill slices of brown bread and butter. (For 3 sandwiches).

BANANA & CHEESE

Mash a Banana, add Lemon juice to suit taste, spread slices of brown bread and butter with soft Cheese, and sandwich together with Banana mixture. (For 2 sandwiches).

BEEF
Spread white bread or rolls with butter mixed with very little grated horse-radish, lay thin slices of roast, pressed, salted, corned, spiced, chipped Beef or Beef Tongue on half of the prepared bread or rolls, add mustard, salt and pepper, to suit taste, cover with remaining pieces of bread or rolls.

CAVIAR
Cut and butter thin slices of white or brown bread, spread half the number with a thin layer of Caviar, sprinkle with very little Cayenne, or little Lemon juice, or very finely chopped onion, and cover with remaining slices of bread.

CHEESE
Butter toast, saltine, water biscuits or any bread; cover with grated or soft Cheese, salt and pepper, Cayenne or mustard.

CHEESE & EGG
Chop a hard-boiled Egg, add equal amount of grated Cheese, enough melted butter, season with little Cayenne, salt and dash of Worcestershire Sauce, spread a layer between slices of buttered white or brown bread. (For 2 sandwiches).

CHEESE ON CRACKERS
Place a square slice of Chester Cheese on Saltine Cracker, sprinkle with a little Cayenne, and grill.

CHESTNUT & CHEESE
Chop up very fine a few grilled Chestnuts, add equal amount of soft Cheese, moisten with a little fresh Cream and season to taste, use between slices of white or brown bread and butter.

CHICKEN & CELERY
Chop up cooked Chicken (white meat) and half the amount of raw Celery, moisten with Mayonnaise, season to taste and use as filling for white buttered bread or buttered rolls.

CHICKEN & HAM
Chop up cooked Chicken and half the amount of cooked Ham, add a little very finely chopped parsley, moisten with a little fresh cream, season to taste and spread between buttered slices of white or brown bread.

CLUB
Split a thick hot toast, butter, fill with four small slices of grilled Bacon, white Chicken meat, chopped Lettuce à la mayonnaise, slices of Tomatoes, salt and pepper and sandwich, heat slightly in oven or under grill.

CRAB
Mash up some Crab meat, moisten with salad dressing, season to taste and put between buttered slices of white or brown bread, adding a few very thin slices of Cucumber.
Lobster or Shrimp may be used to replace Crab meat.

CRAB & EGG : see Shrimp & Egg.

DEVILLED TOAST
Mix a tablespoon of butter with a teaspoon of English and French mustard, Chutney, Curry powder, Cayenne, Lemon juice and a little salt, spread on toast and heat in oven or under grill.

EGG & LETTUCE
Chop up a hard-boiled Egg, enough Lettuce for 2 sandwiches, moisten with Mayonnaise, season to taste and use between buttered slices of white bread.

EGG & WATERCRESS
Chop up a hard-boiled Egg and enough Cress for 2 sandwiches, moisten with salad dressing, add salt to suit taste and use between buttered slices of white or brown bread.
Cucumber sliced, or chopped Tomato may replace Watercress.

FISH SAVOURY

Heat slightly left over cooked Fish, mince with very finely chopped parsley, season with appropriate piquant sauce, spread on thin fried or buttered toast, put under grill, sprinkle with a little Lemon juice, and serve very hot.

FOIE GRAS

Pound together Foie Gras and half the quantity of butter, a few drops of Worcestershire Sauce, salt & pepper, use between saltine or water biscuits, sliced bread, rolls or muffins.

GAME

Chop up cooked Game, moisten with piquant brown sauce, add very little Currant or other sweet jelly, and use between buttered white bread.

GORGONZOLA or ROQUEFORT CHEESE

Pound together with tablefork Gorgonzola or Roquefort with butter and very finely chopped Celery, add a few drops of Worcestershire Sauce and a little Cayenne, spread a thickish layer on slices of white or brown bread.

HAM & CELERY

Chop up cooked Ham and half the amount of Celery, moisten with a little Cream, add Tomato Ketchup and very little Cayenne, use between small buttered rolls.

Can be served hot by placing filled rolls in oven till thoroughly heated.

HAM & CHEESE

Use toast or any sliced bread; butter, lay thin slices of cooked Ham, cover with thin slices of Gruyère or Swiss Cheese, add mustard, Chutney or Tomato Ketchup and sandwich.

LOBSTER & EGG : see Shrimp & Egg.

MUSHROOM (Hot)

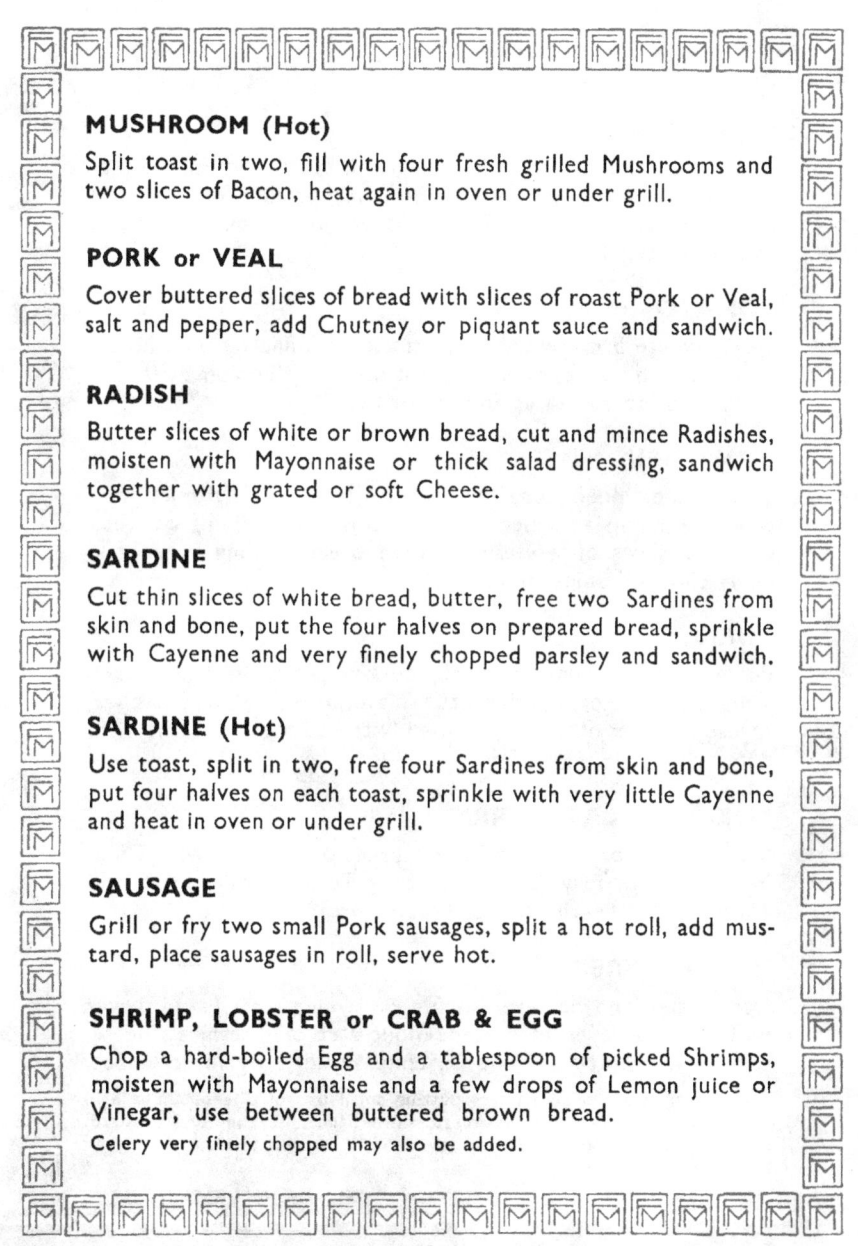

Split toast in two, fill with four fresh grilled Mushrooms and two slices of Bacon, heat again in oven or under grill.

PORK or VEAL

Cover buttered slices of bread with slices of roast Pork or Veal, salt and pepper, add Chutney or piquant sauce and sandwich.

RADISH

Butter slices of white or brown bread, cut and mince Radishes, moisten with Mayonnaise or thick salad dressing, sandwich together with grated or soft Cheese.

SARDINE

Cut thin slices of white bread, butter, free two Sardines from skin and bone, put the four halves on prepared bread, sprinkle with Cayenne and very finely chopped parsley and sandwich.

SARDINE (Hot)

Use toast, split in two, free four Sardines from skin and bone, put four halves on each toast, sprinkle with very little Cayenne and heat in oven or under grill.

SAUSAGE

Grill or fry two small Pork sausages, split a hot roll, add mustard, place sausages in roll, serve hot.

SHRIMP, LOBSTER or CRAB & EGG

Chop a hard-boiled Egg and a tablespoon of picked Shrimps, moisten with Mayonnaise and a few drops of Lemon juice or Vinegar, use between buttered brown bread.

Celery very finely chopped may also be added.

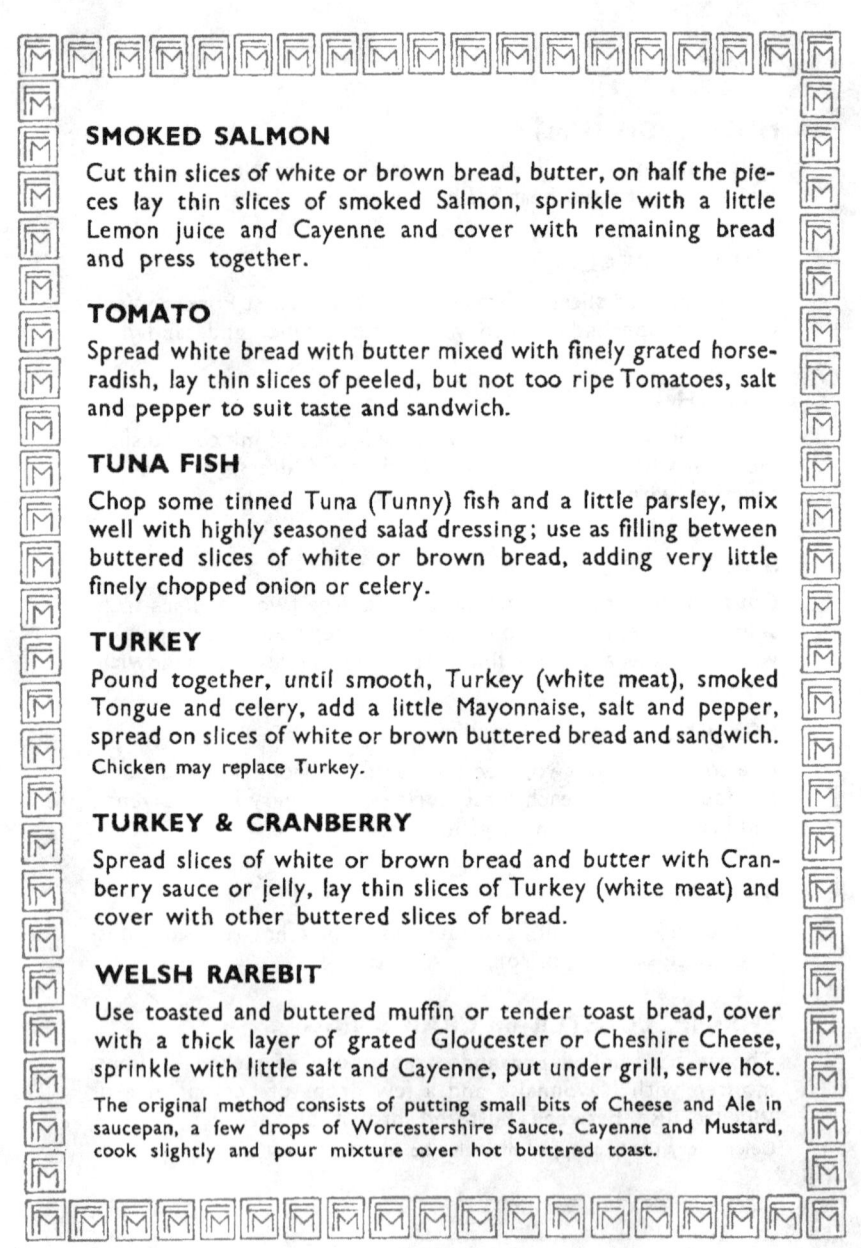

SMOKED SALMON
Cut thin slices of white or brown bread, butter, on half the pieces lay thin slices of smoked Salmon, sprinkle with a little Lemon juice and Cayenne and cover with remaining bread and press together.

TOMATO
Spread white bread with butter mixed with finely grated horseradish, lay thin slices of peeled, but not too ripe Tomatoes, salt and pepper to suit taste and sandwich.

TUNA FISH
Chop some tinned Tuna (Tunny) fish and a little parsley, mix well with highly seasoned salad dressing; use as filling between buttered slices of white or brown bread, adding very little finely chopped onion or celery.

TURKEY
Pound together, until smooth, Turkey (white meat), smoked Tongue and celery, add a little Mayonnaise, salt and pepper, spread on slices of white or brown buttered bread and sandwich.
Chicken may replace Turkey.

TURKEY & CRANBERRY
Spread slices of white or brown bread and butter with Cranberry sauce or jelly, lay thin slices of Turkey (white meat) and cover with other buttered slices of bread.

WELSH RAREBIT
Use toasted and buttered muffin or tender toast bread, cover with a thick layer of grated Gloucester or Cheshire Cheese, sprinkle with little salt and Cayenne, put under grill, serve hot.

The original method consists of putting small bits of Cheese and Ale in saucepan, a few drops of Worcestershire Sauce, Cayenne and Mustard, cook slightly and pour mixture over hot buttered toast.

WINES

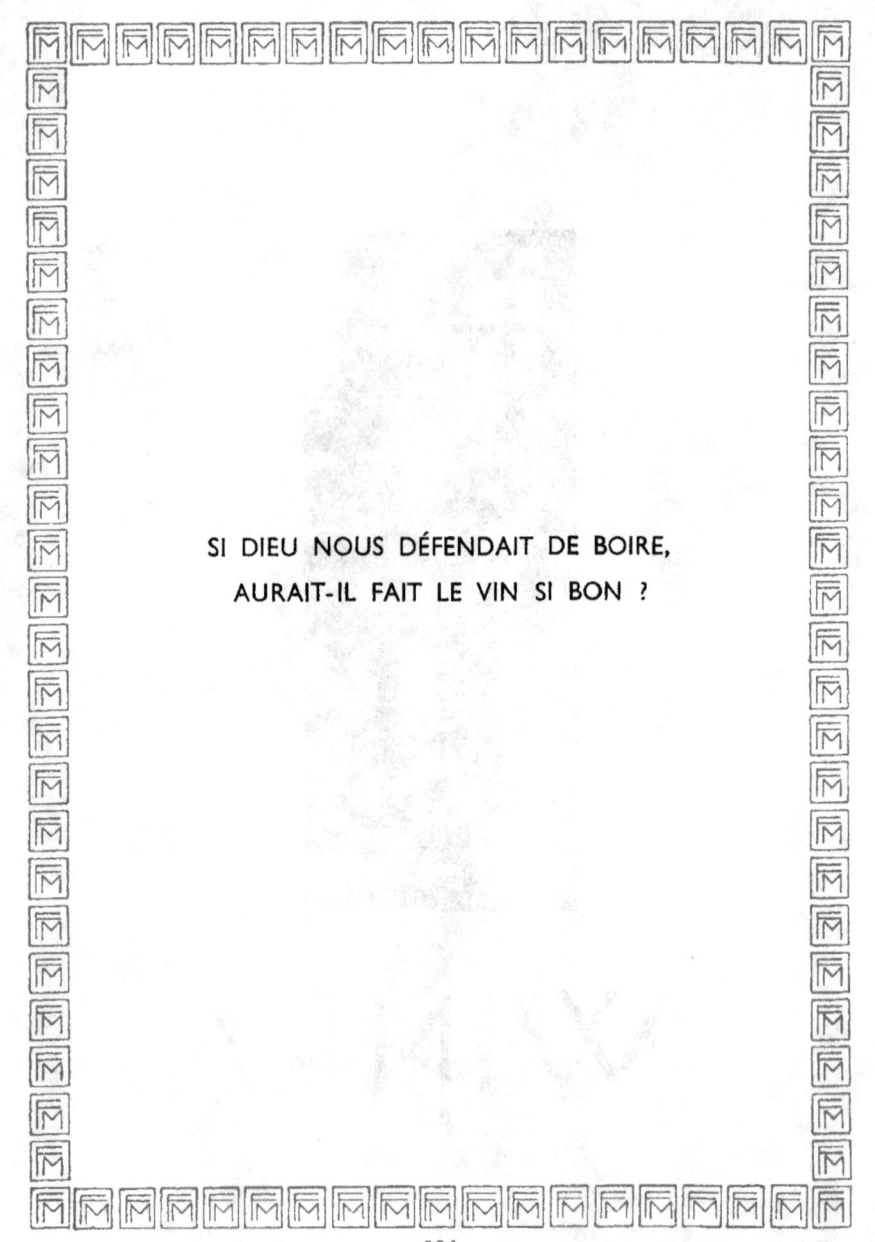

SI DIEU NOUS DÉFENDAIT DE BOIRE,
AURAIT-IL FAIT LE VIN SI BON ?

WINES

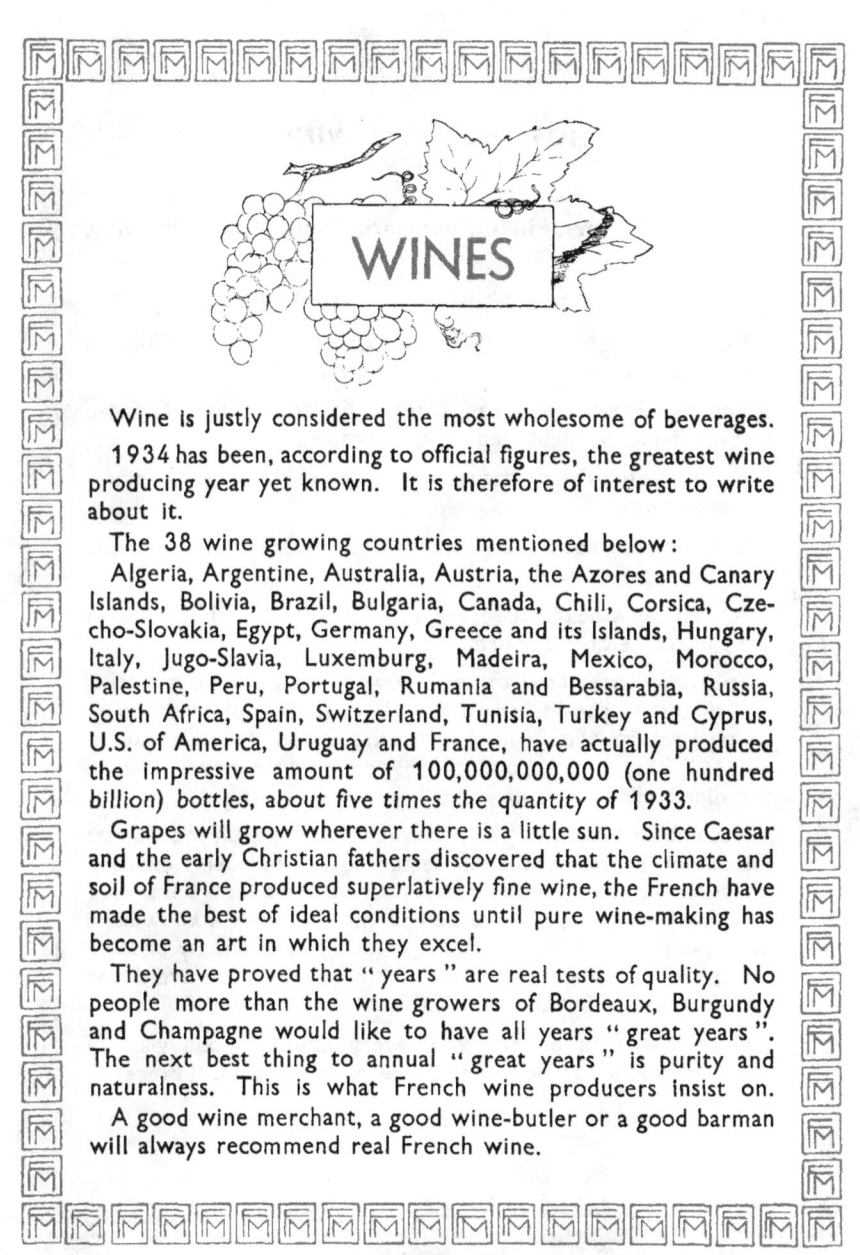

Wine is justly considered the most wholesome of beverages.

1934 has been, according to official figures, the greatest wine producing year yet known. It is therefore of interest to write about it.

The 38 wine growing countries mentioned below:

Algeria, Argentine, Australia, Austria, the Azores and Canary Islands, Bolivia, Brazil, Bulgaria, Canada, Chili, Corsica, Czecho-Slovakia, Egypt, Germany, Greece and its Islands, Hungary, Italy, Jugo-Slavia, Luxemburg, Madeira, Mexico, Morocco, Palestine, Peru, Portugal, Rumania and Bessarabia, Russia, South Africa, Spain, Switzerland, Tunisia, Turkey and Cyprus, U.S. of America, Uruguay and France, have actually produced the impressive amount of 100,000,000,000 (one hundred billion) bottles, about five times the quantity of 1933.

Grapes will grow wherever there is a little sun. Since Caesar and the early Christian fathers discovered that the climate and soil of France produced superlatively fine wine, the French have made the best of ideal conditions until pure wine-making has become an art in which they excel.

They have proved that " years " are real tests of quality. No people more than the wine growers of Bordeaux, Burgundy and Champagne would like to have all years " great years ". The next best thing to annual " great years " is purity and naturalness. This is what French wine producers insist on.

A good wine merchant, a good wine-butler or a good barman will always recommend real French wine.

HOW TO SERVE WINES

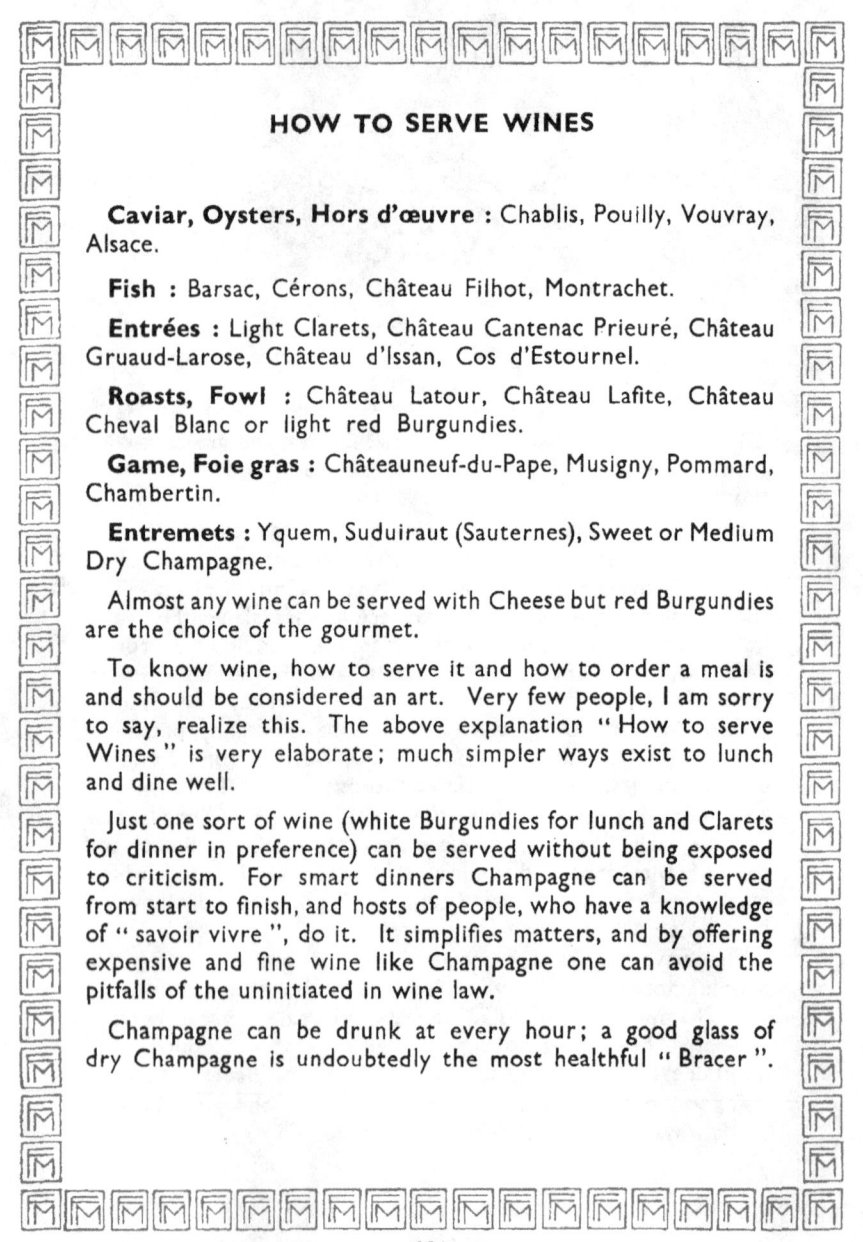

Caviar, Oysters, Hors d'œuvre : Chablis, Pouilly, Vouvray, Alsace.

Fish : Barsac, Cérons, Château Filhot, Montrachet.

Entrées : Light Clarets, Château Cantenac Prieuré, Château Gruaud-Larose, Château d'Issan, Cos d'Estournel.

Roasts, Fowl : Château Latour, Château Lafite, Château Cheval Blanc or light red Burgundies.

Game, Foie gras : Châteauneuf-du-Pape, Musigny, Pommard, Chambertin.

Entremets : Yquem, Suduiraut (Sauternes), Sweet or Medium Dry Champagne.

Almost any wine can be served with Cheese but red Burgundies are the choice of the gourmet.

To know wine, how to serve it and how to order a meal is and should be considered an art. Very few people, I am sorry to say, realize this. The above explanation " How to serve Wines " is very elaborate; much simpler ways exist to lunch and dine well.

Just one sort of wine (white Burgundies for lunch and Clarets for dinner in preference) can be served without being exposed to criticism. For smart dinners Champagne can be served from start to finish, and hosts of people, who have a knowledge of " savoir vivre ", do it. It simplifies matters, and by offering expensive and fine wine like Champagne one can avoid the pitfalls of the uninitiated in wine law.

Champagne can be drunk at every hour; a good glass of dry Champagne is undoubtedly the most healthful " Bracer ".

ALSACE

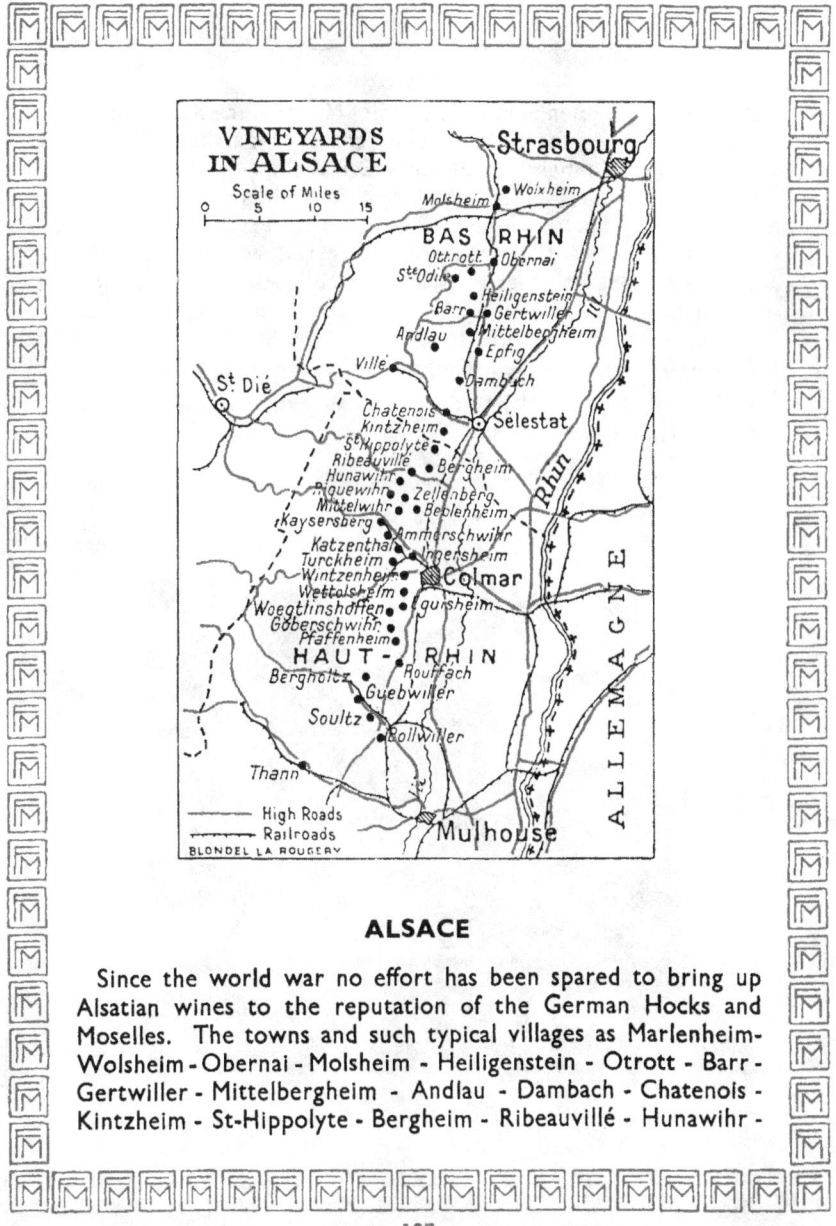

Since the world war no effort has been spared to bring up Alsatian wines to the reputation of the German Hocks and Moselles. The towns and such typical villages as Marlenheim - Wolsheim - Obernai - Molsheim - Heiligenstein - Otrott - Barr - Gertwiller - Mittelbergheim - Andlau - Dambach - Chatenois - Kintzheim - St-Hippolyte - Bergheim - Ribeauvillé - Hunawihr -

Zellenberg - Beblenheim - Riquewihr - Mittelwihr - Kientzheim - Kaysersberg - Ammerschwihr - Katzenthal - Ingersheim - Türckheim - Wintzenheim - Colmar - Eguisheim - Wettolsheim - Woegtlinshoffen - Goberschwihr - Pfaffenheim - Rouffach - Guebwiller - Soultz - Thann - and many others, surrounded as they are by beautiful vineyards along the wide Rhine valley from Strasburg up as far as Thann and Mulhouse, produce those excellent and characteristic wines called Riesling, Traminer, Gewürz-Traminer, Knitterlé, Sporen, Clos Ste-Odile, Klevner, Gentil, Sylvaner, Rangen, Knipperlé, Chasselas, Zwicker, etc...

Most of them are fairly dry, with an exquisite and peculiar bouquet, and are very popular luncheon wines.

Kindly contributed by Pierre Freyburger.

BORDEAUX

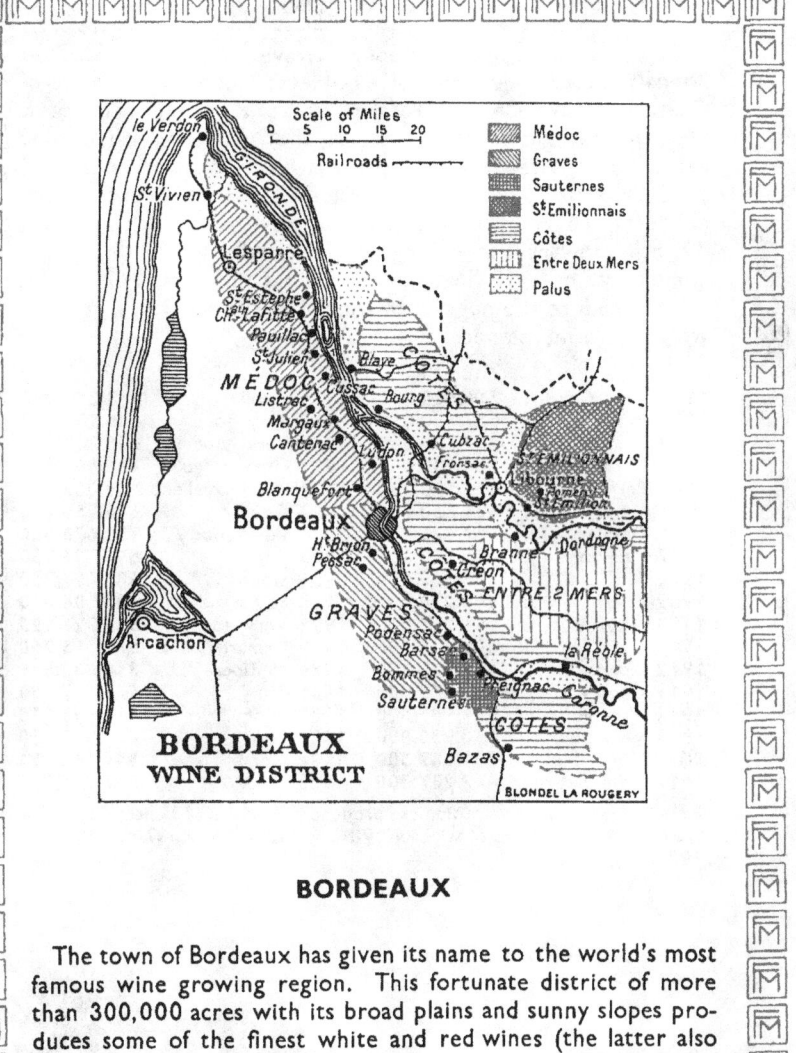

The town of Bordeaux has given its name to the world's most famous wine growing region. This fortunate district of more than 300,000 acres with its broad plains and sunny slopes produces some of the finest white and red wines (the latter also known as clarets), which can be called, without fear of contradiction, the aristocrats of the dinner table.

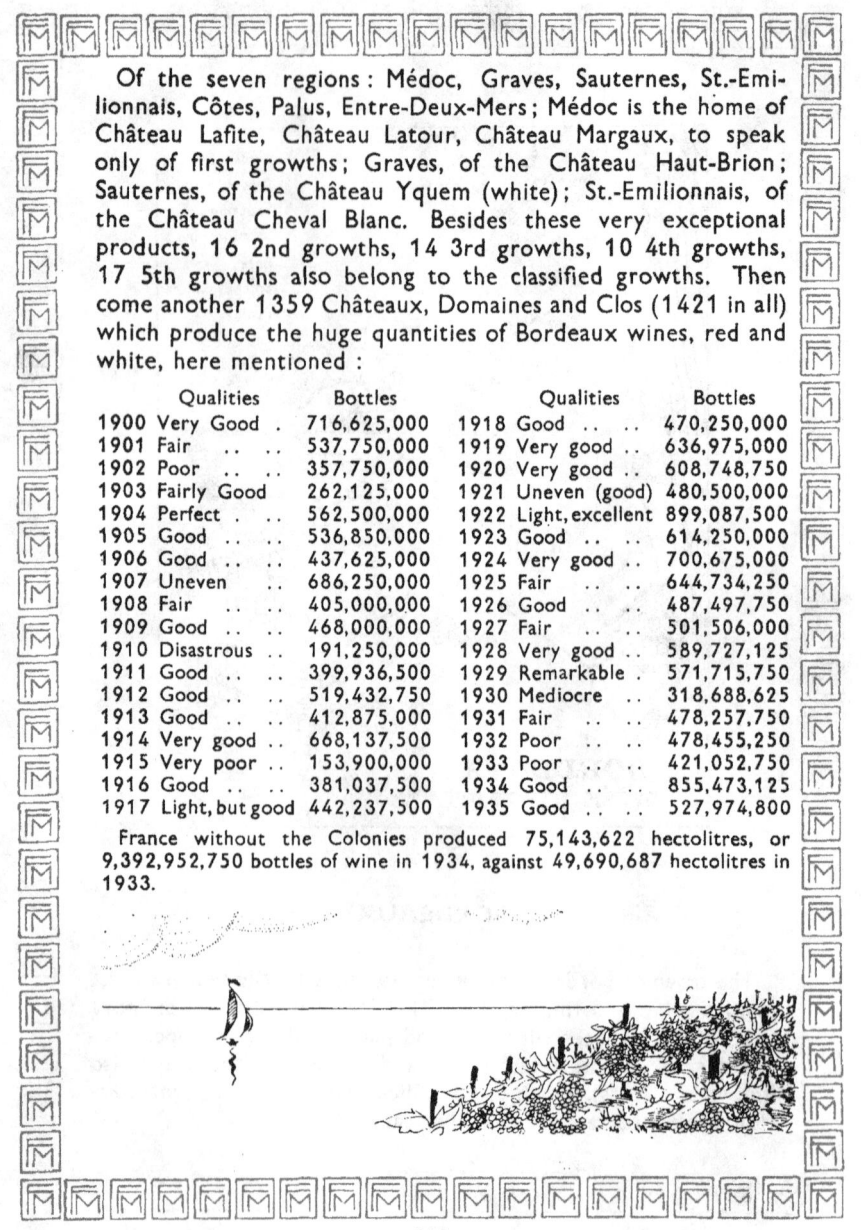

Of the seven regions: Médoc, Graves, Sauternes, St.-Emilionnais, Côtes, Palus, Entre-Deux-Mers; Médoc is the home of Château Lafite, Château Latour, Château Margaux, to speak only of first growths; Graves, of the Château Haut-Brion; Sauternes, of the Château Yquem (white); St.-Emilionnais, of the Château Cheval Blanc. Besides these very exceptional products, 16 2nd growths, 14 3rd growths, 10 4th growths, 17 5th growths also belong to the classified growths. Then come another 1359 Châteaux, Domaines and Clos (1421 in all) which produce the huge quantities of Bordeaux wines, red and white, here mentioned:

Qualities	Bottles	Qualities	Bottles
1900 Very Good	716,625,000	1918 Good	470,250,000
1901 Fair	537,750,000	1919 Very good	636,975,000
1902 Poor	357,750,000	1920 Very good	608,748,750
1903 Fairly Good	262,125,000	1921 Uneven (good)	480,500,000
1904 Perfect	562,500,000	1922 Light, excellent	899,087,500
1905 Good	536,850,000	1923 Good	614,250,000
1906 Good	437,625,000	1924 Very good	700,675,000
1907 Uneven	686,250,000	1925 Fair	644,734,250
1908 Fair	405,000,000	1926 Good	487,497,750
1909 Good	468,000,000	1927 Fair	501,506,000
1910 Disastrous	191,250,000	1928 Very good	589,727,125
1911 Good	399,936,500	1929 Remarkable	571,715,750
1912 Good	519,432,750	1930 Mediocre	318,688,625
1913 Good	412,875,000	1931 Fair	478,257,750
1914 Very good	668,137,500	1932 Poor	478,455,250
1915 Very poor	153,900,000	1933 Poor	421,052,750
1916 Good	381,037,500	1934 Good	855,473,125
1917 Light, but good	442,237,500	1935 Good	527,974,800

France without the Colonies produced 75,143,622 hectolitres, or 9,392,952,750 bottles of wine in 1934, against 49,690,687 hectolitres in 1933.

BURGUNDY

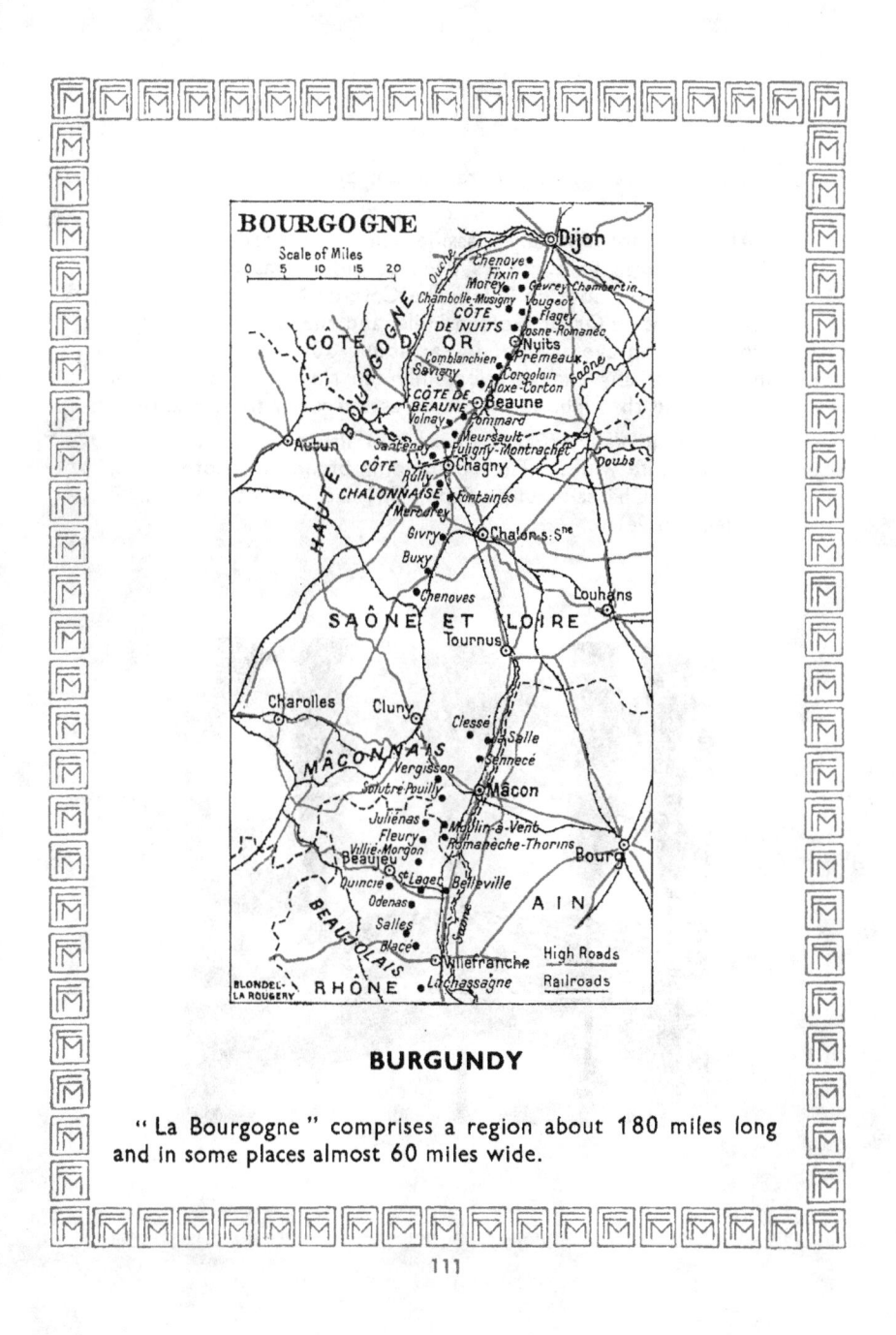

"La Bourgogne" comprises a region about 180 miles long and in some places almost 60 miles wide.

It produces the greatest, rarest and probably the most imitated of wine.

Although not officially classified like the Bordeaux wines, the Burgundies have always been considered as the kings of all wines. The Côte de Dijon, the Côte de Nuits and Côte de Beaune (Côte d'Or or Golden Hills) and the Côte Chalonnaise produce in an average good year about 300,000,000 bottles, and without any exaggeration fully ten times that amount of wine is sold throughout the world as Burgundy from France.

The Rhône Valley (Côtes du Rhône) also produces excellent red and white wines. The outstanding brands are Côte Rôtie, Hermitage, Châteauneuf-du-Pape, Château Grillet, and Tavel (couleur rosée).

CHAMPAGNE

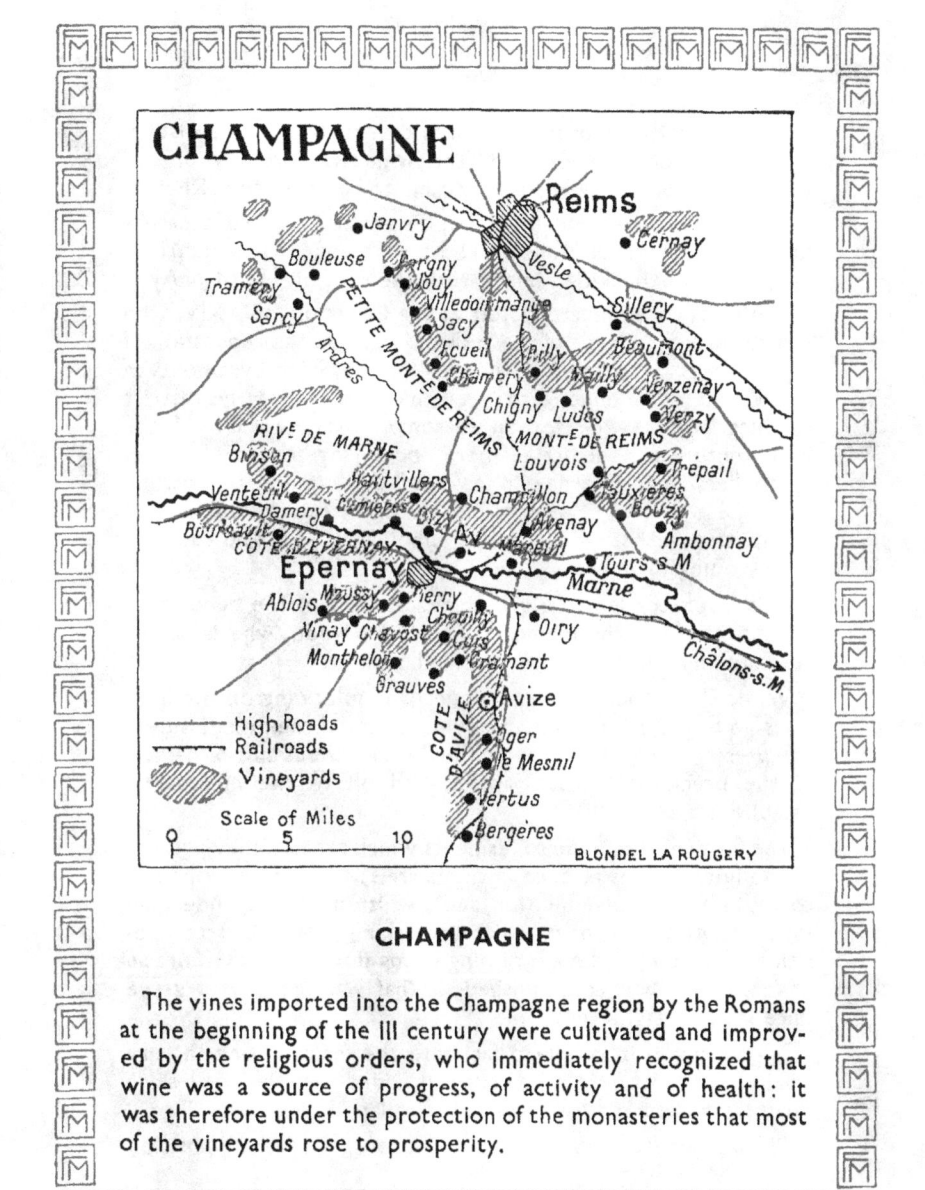

The vines imported into the Champagne region by the Romans at the beginning of the III century were cultivated and improved by the religious orders, who immediately recognized that wine was a source of progress, of activity and of health: it was therefore under the protection of the monasteries that most of the vineyards rose to prosperity.

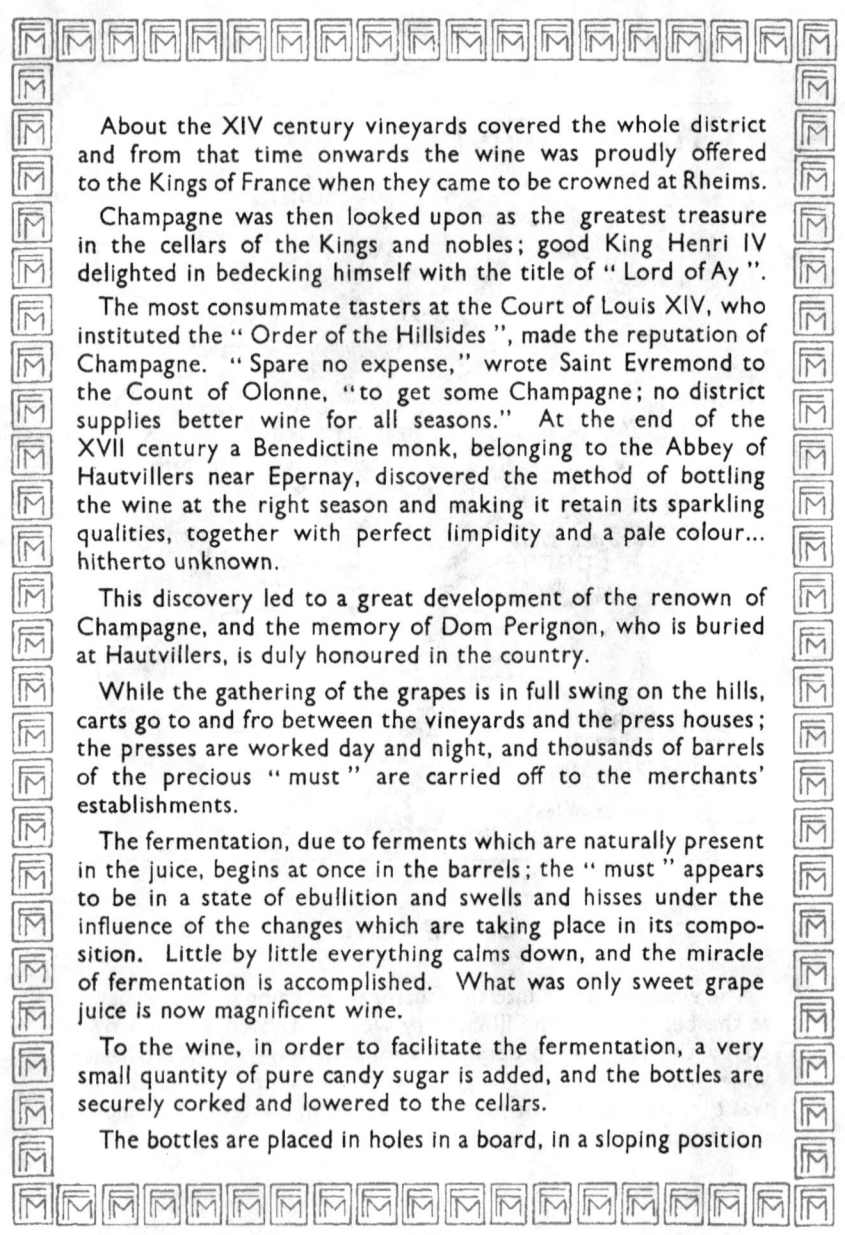

About the XIV century vineyards covered the whole district and from that time onwards the wine was proudly offered to the Kings of France when they came to be crowned at Rheims.

Champagne was then looked upon as the greatest treasure in the cellars of the Kings and nobles; good King Henri IV delighted in bedecking himself with the title of " Lord of Ay ".

The most consummate tasters at the Court of Louis XIV, who instituted the " Order of the Hillsides ", made the reputation of Champagne. " Spare no expense," wrote Saint Evremond to the Count of Olonne, "to get some Champagne; no district supplies better wine for all seasons." At the end of the XVII century a Benedictine monk, belonging to the Abbey of Hautvillers near Epernay, discovered the method of bottling the wine at the right season and making it retain its sparkling qualities, together with perfect limpidity and a pale colour... hitherto unknown.

This discovery led to a great development of the renown of Champagne, and the memory of Dom Perignon, who is buried at Hautvillers, is duly honoured in the country.

While the gathering of the grapes is in full swing on the hills, carts go to and fro between the vineyards and the press houses; the presses are worked day and night, and thousands of barrels of the precious " must " are carried off to the merchants' establishments.

The fermentation, due to ferments which are naturally present in the juice, begins at once in the barrels; the " must " appears to be in a state of ebullition and swells and hisses under the influence of the changes which are taking place in its composition. Little by little everything calms down, and the miracle of fermentation is accomplished. What was only sweet grape juice is now magnificent wine.

To the wine, in order to facilitate the fermentation, a very small quantity of pure candy sugar is added, and the bottles are securely corked and lowered to the cellars.

The bottles are placed in holes in a board, in a sloping position with the cork downwards; after several years of this treatment, the whole of the deposit collects close to the cork.

The cork is removed by the pressure from natural gas, it is actually driven out and the sediment with it. The wine is perfectly limpid now and before recorking the bottle the necessary sweetening is effected by adding still more pure candy sugar dissolved in Champagne of the best quality. The object of this is to meet the taste of the consumer, who, according to different countries, may prefer wines more or less sweetened.

Before shipping, the bottle is " dressed " with a capsule and label bearing the name of the firm and the word " Champagne " which is a legal guarantee of its origin.

The district which the French law has authorized to give the name of Champagne to its wine is small compared with other wine growing regions. The nature of the soil, the sorts of vine grown, and the special methods of cultivation in use result in the production of a high quality at the sacrifice of quantity; here, as elsewhere, quality is scarcely compatible with quantity.

The crop varies considerably from year to year and can only be estimated by taking an average over a long period. For 30 normal years the average production was 450,000 hectolitres or about 10,000,000 gallons a year, i.e. 60,000,000 bottles.

CONTENTS AND NAMES OF CHAMPAGNE BOTTLES

SPLIT (Quarter bottle)..	0.20 centil.	about	8 fl. ozs.
HALF..	0.40 ,,	,,	16 ,,
IMPERIAL PINT.	0.60 ,,	,,	24 ,,
BOTTLE (Quart)	0.80 ,,	,,	32 ,,
MAGNUM .	1.60 litres	,,	64 ,,
DOUBLE MAGNUM	3.20 ,,	,,	128 ,,
TRIPLE MAGNUM (Jeroboam)	4.80 ,,	,,	192 ,,
QUADRUPLE MAGNUM (Nebuchadnessar)	6.40 ,,	,,	256 ,,

Bottles holding twelve and sixteen quarts exist but are seldom used, except for publicity purposes.

SAUMUR

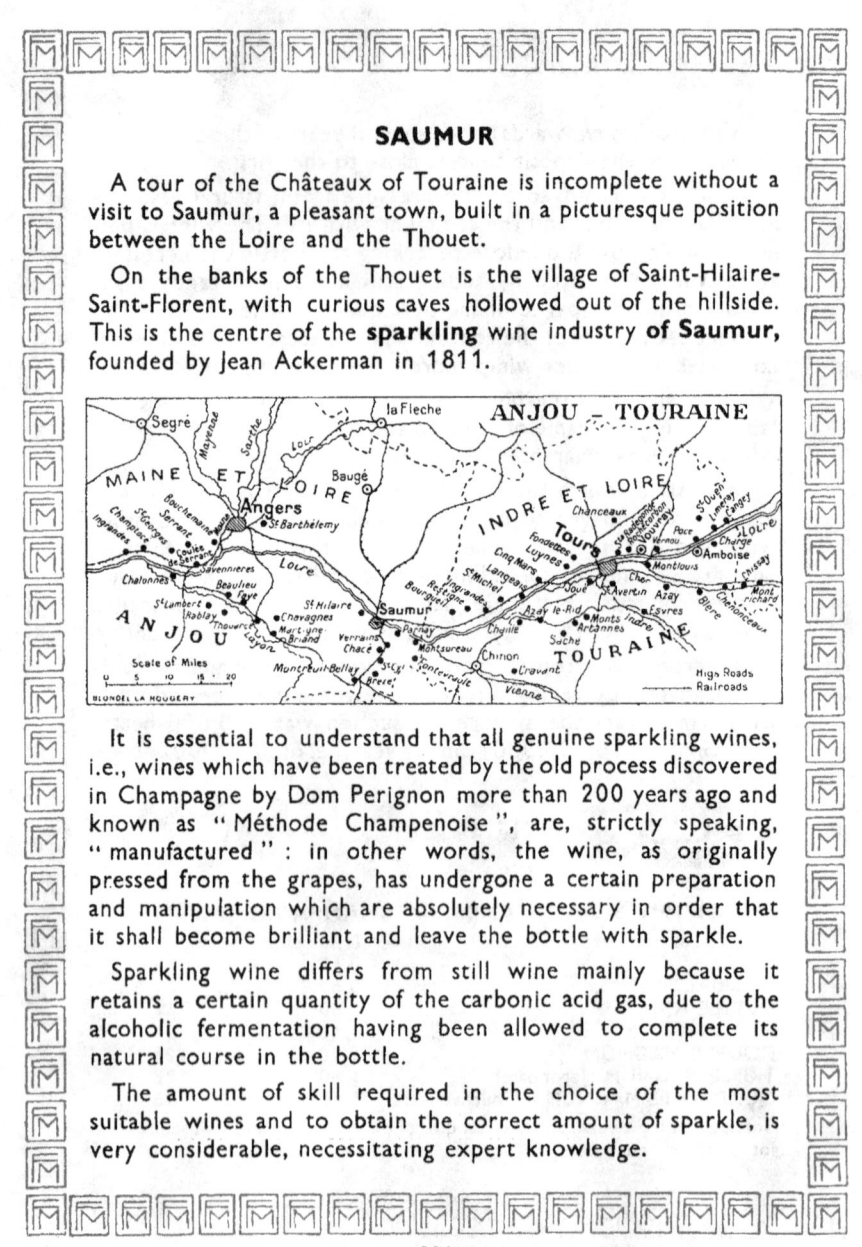

A tour of the Châteaux of Touraine is incomplete without a visit to Saumur, a pleasant town, built in a picturesque position between the Loire and the Thouet.

On the banks of the Thouet is the village of Saint-Hilaire-Saint-Florent, with curious caves hollowed out of the hillside. This is the centre of the **sparkling** wine industry **of Saumur**, founded by Jean Ackerman in 1811.

It is essential to understand that all genuine sparkling wines, i.e., wines which have been treated by the old process discovered in Champagne by Dom Perignon more than 200 years ago and known as "Méthode Champenoise", are, strictly speaking, "manufactured": in other words, the wine, as originally pressed from the grapes, has undergone a certain preparation and manipulation which are absolutely necessary in order that it shall become brilliant and leave the bottle with sparkle.

Sparkling wine differs from still wine mainly because it retains a certain quantity of the carbonic acid gas, due to the alcoholic fermentation having been allowed to complete its natural course in the bottle.

The amount of skill required in the choice of the most suitable wines and to obtain the correct amount of sparkle, is very considerable, necessitating expert knowledge.

The Douro District

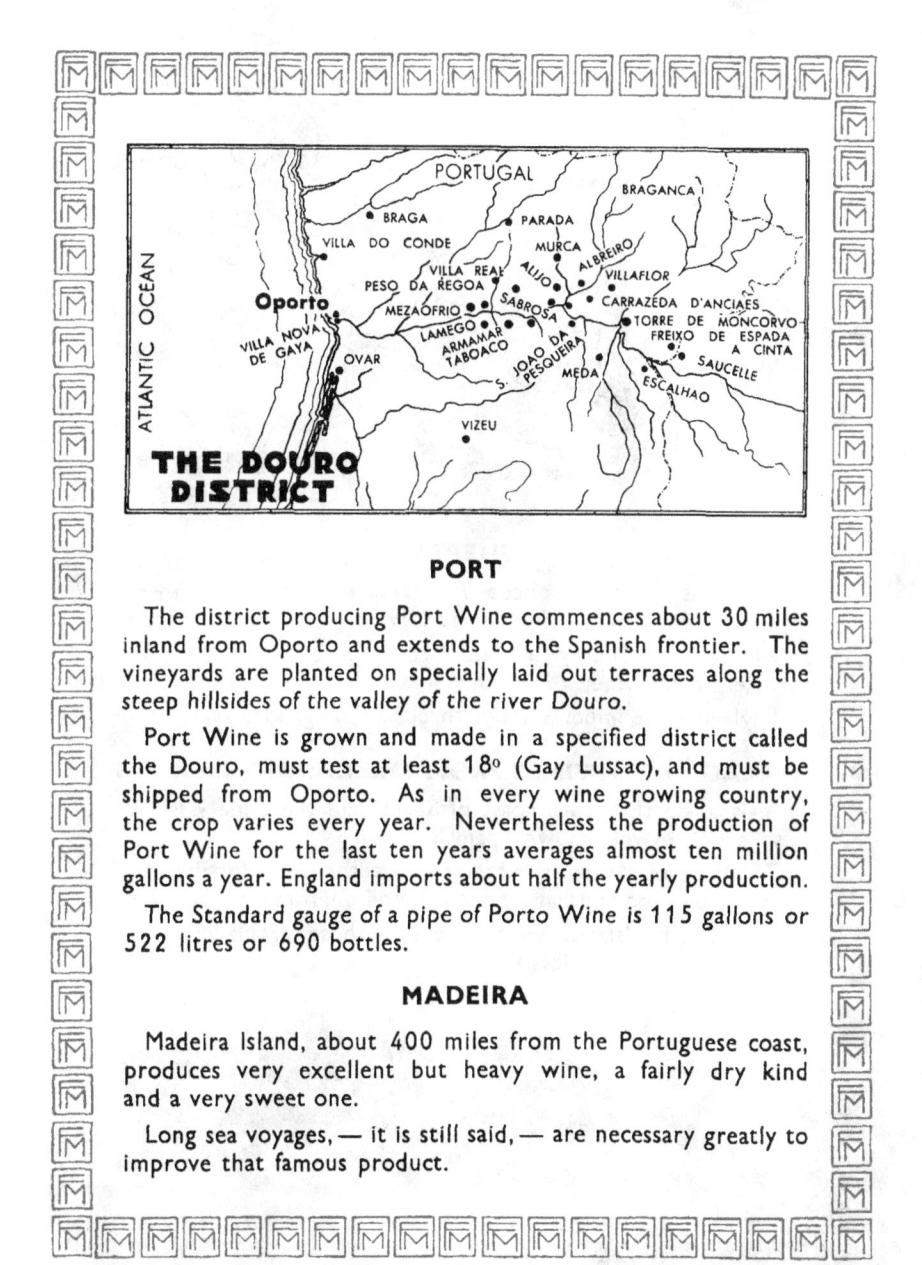

PORT

The district producing Port Wine commences about 30 miles inland from Oporto and extends to the Spanish frontier. The vineyards are planted on specially laid out terraces along the steep hillsides of the valley of the river Douro.

Port Wine is grown and made in a specified district called the Douro, must test at least 18º (Gay Lussac), and must be shipped from Oporto. As in every wine growing country, the crop varies every year. Nevertheless the production of Port Wine for the last ten years averages almost ten million gallons a year. England imports about half the yearly production.

The Standard gauge of a pipe of Porto Wine is 115 gallons or 522 litres or 690 bottles.

MADEIRA

Madeira Island, about 400 miles from the Portuguese coast, produces very excellent but heavy wine, a fairly dry kind and a very sweet one.

Long sea voyages, — it is still said, — are necessary greatly to improve that famous product.

THE SHERRY DISTRICT

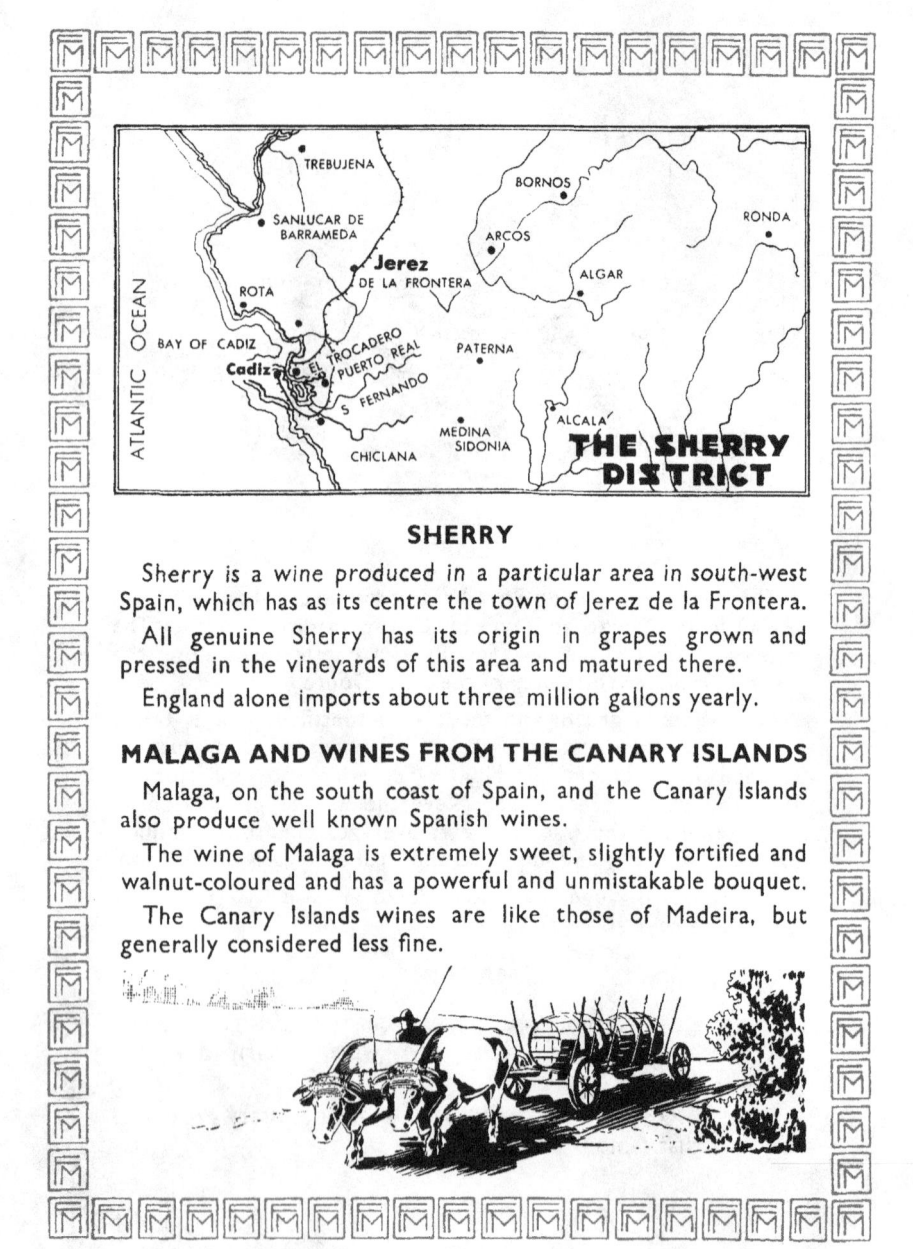

SHERRY

Sherry is a wine produced in a particular area in south-west Spain, which has as its centre the town of Jerez de la Frontera.

All genuine Sherry has its origin in grapes grown and pressed in the vineyards of this area and matured there.

England alone imports about three million gallons yearly.

MALAGA AND WINES FROM THE CANARY ISLANDS

Malaga, on the south coast of Spain, and the Canary Islands also produce well known Spanish wines.

The wine of Malaga is extremely sweet, slightly fortified and walnut-coloured and has a powerful and unmistakable bouquet.

The Canary Islands wines are like those of Madeira, but generally considered less fine.

COGNAC

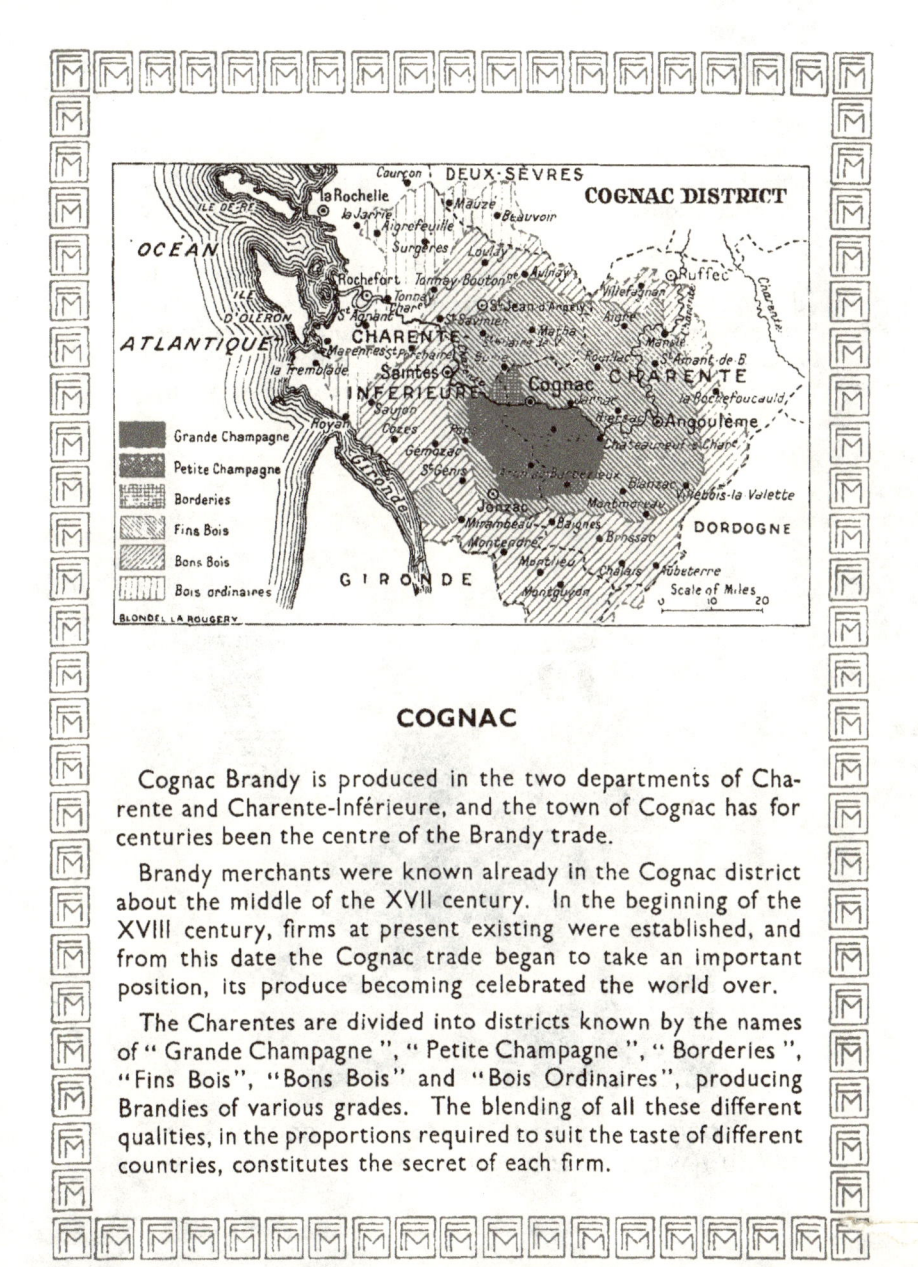

Cognac Brandy is produced in the two departments of Charente and Charente-Inférieure, and the town of Cognac has for centuries been the centre of the Brandy trade.

Brandy merchants were known already in the Cognac district about the middle of the XVII century. In the beginning of the XVIII century, firms at present existing were established, and from this date the Cognac trade began to take an important position, its produce becoming celebrated the world over.

The Charentes are divided into districts known by the names of " Grande Champagne ", " Petite Champagne ", " Borderies ", "Fins Bois", "Bons Bois" and "Bois Ordinaires", producing Brandies of various grades. The blending of all these different qualities, in the proportions required to suit the taste of different countries, constitutes the secret of each firm.

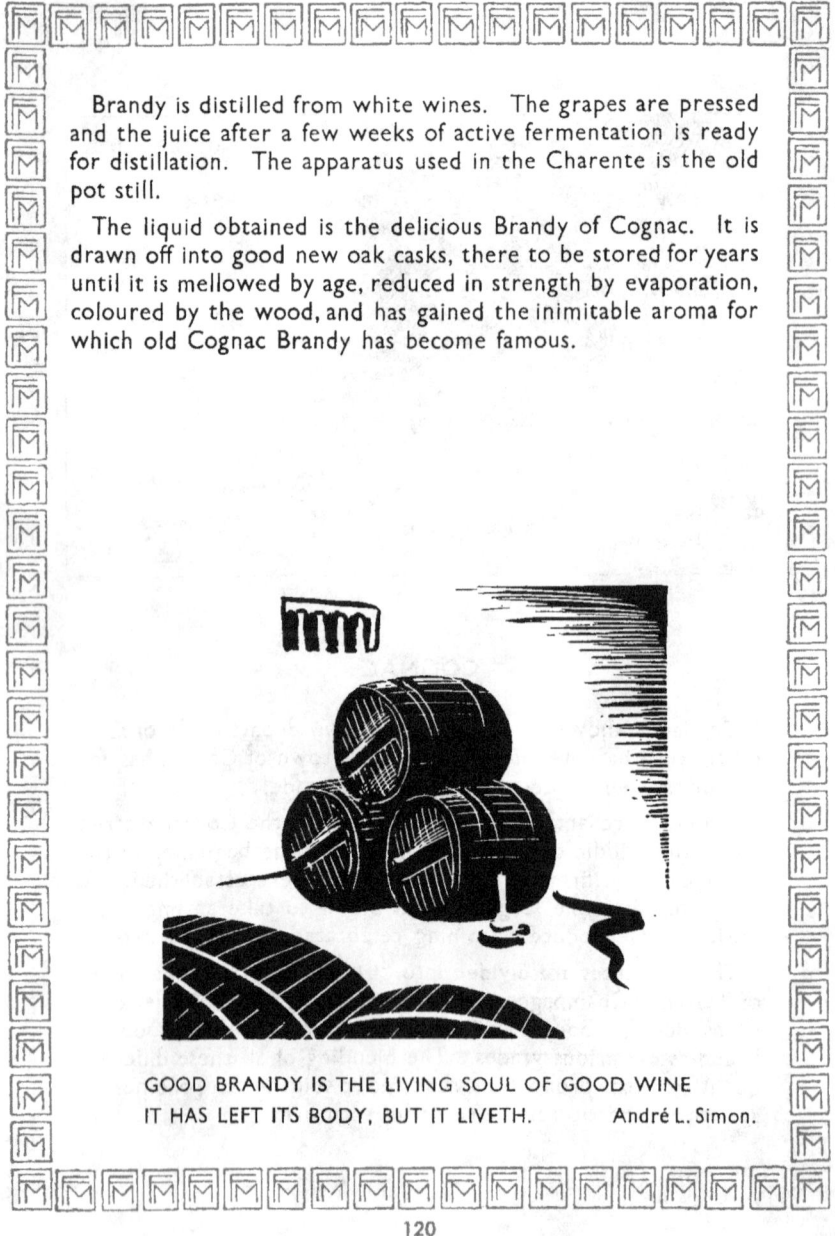

Brandy is distilled from white wines. The grapes are pressed and the juice after a few weeks of active fermentation is ready for distillation. The apparatus used in the Charente is the old pot still.

The liquid obtained is the delicious Brandy of Cognac. It is drawn off into good new oak casks, there to be stored for years until it is mellowed by age, reduced in strength by evaporation, coloured by the wood, and has gained the inimitable aroma for which old Cognac Brandy has become famous.

GOOD BRANDY IS THE LIVING SOUL OF GOOD WINE
IT HAS LEFT ITS BODY, BUT IT LIVETH.   André L. Simon.

ARMAGNAC

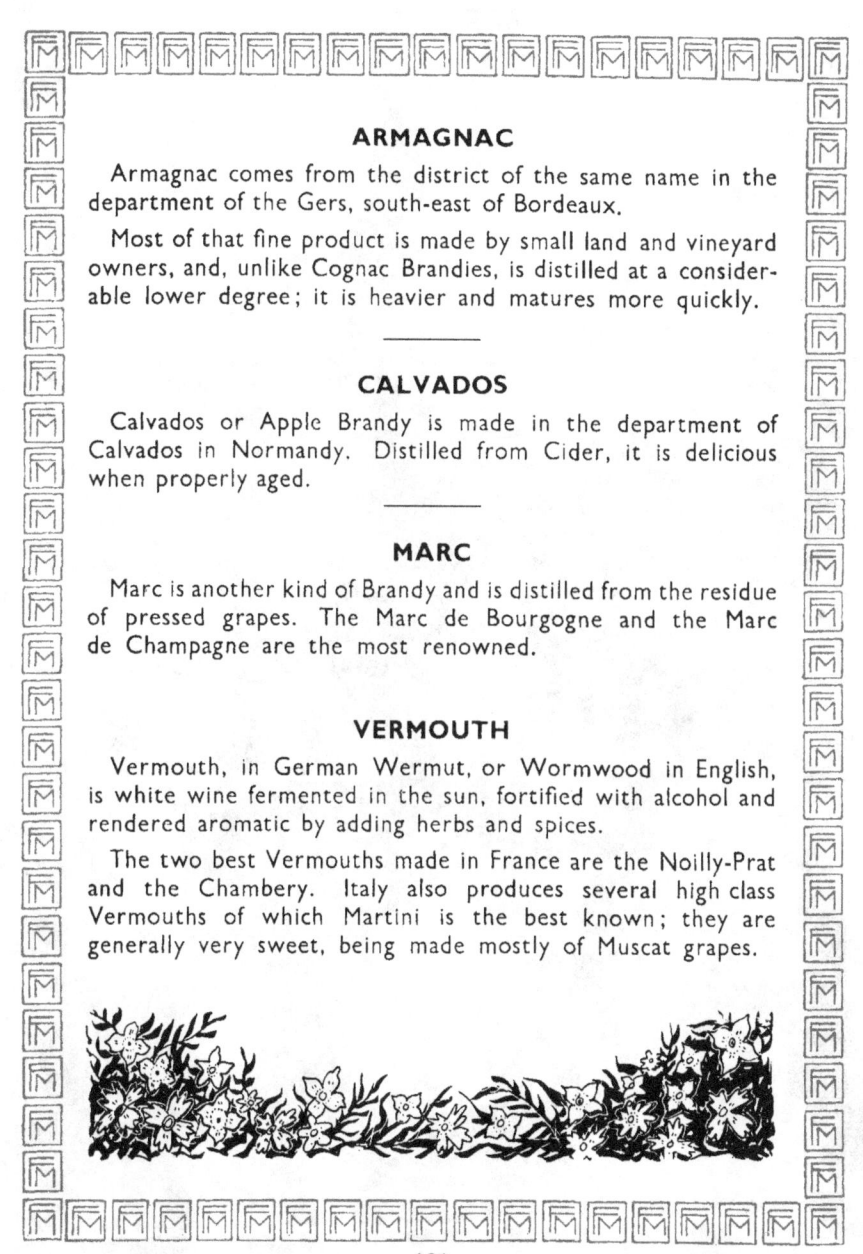

Armagnac comes from the district of the same name in the department of the Gers, south-east of Bordeaux.

Most of that fine product is made by small land and vineyard owners, and, unlike Cognac Brandies, is distilled at a considerable lower degree; it is heavier and matures more quickly.

CALVADOS

Calvados or Apple Brandy is made in the department of Calvados in Normandy. Distilled from Cider, it is delicious when properly aged.

MARC

Marc is another kind of Brandy and is distilled from the residue of pressed grapes. The Marc de Bourgogne and the Marc de Champagne are the most renowned.

VERMOUTH

Vermouth, in German Wermut, or Wormwood in English, is white wine fermented in the sun, fortified with alcohol and rendered aromatic by adding herbs and spices.

The two best Vermouths made in France are the Noilly-Prat and the Chambery. Italy also produces several high class Vermouths of which Martini is the best known; they are generally very sweet, being made mostly of Muscat grapes.

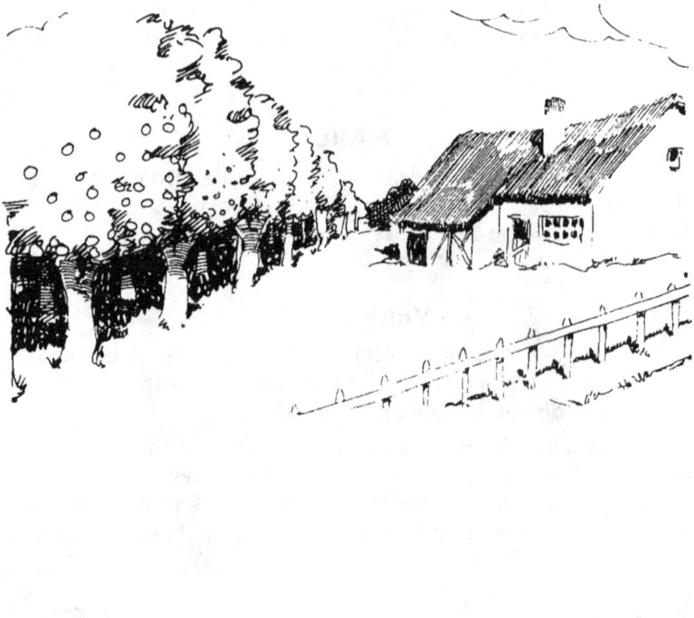

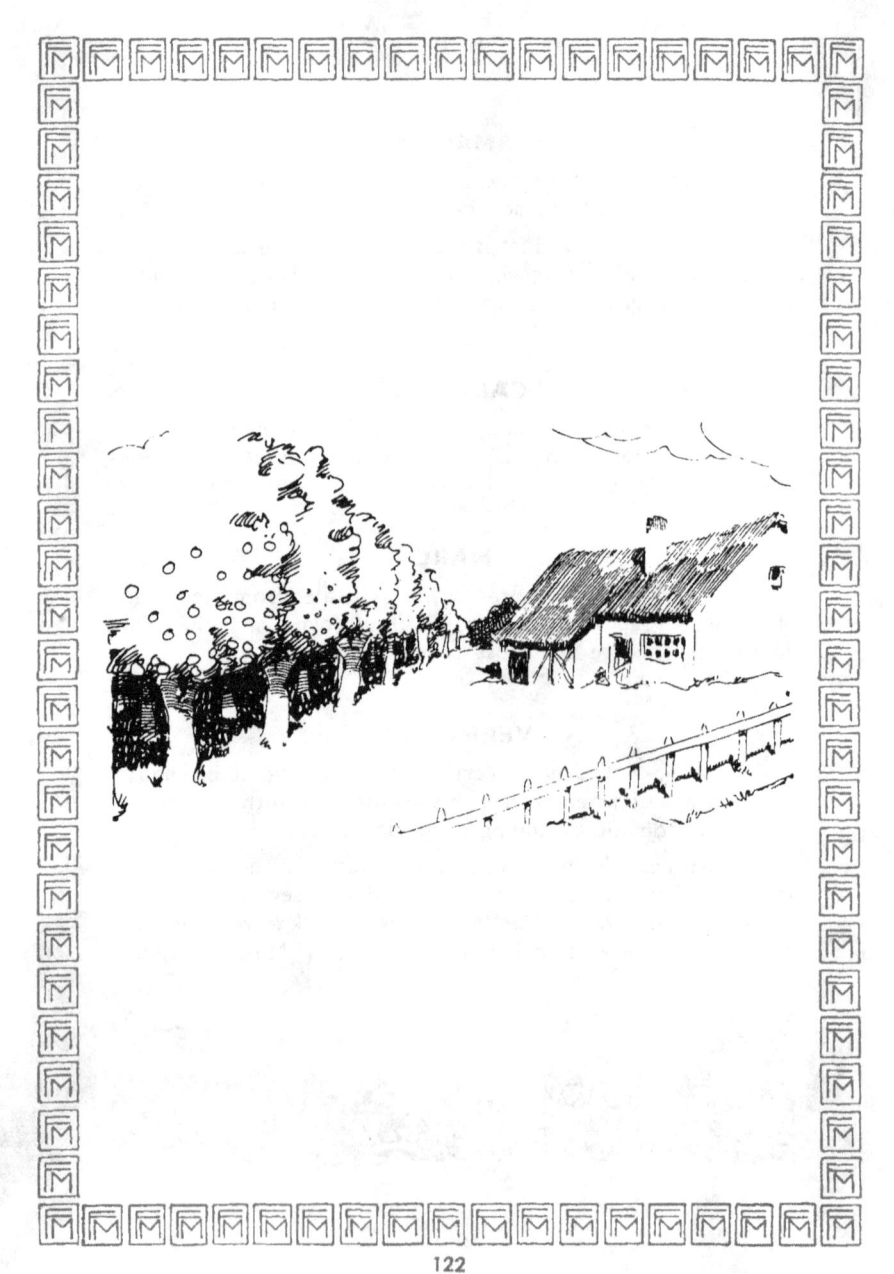

USEFUL FORMULAS

ALCOHOL
COMPARATIVE STRENGTHS

Gay Lussac	Sykes	American	Cartier
57·1	Proof	14·2	
57	0·2 u.p.	14	
56	2·0	12	21
55	3·7	10	
54	5·4	8	
53	7·1	6	20
52	8·8	4	
51	10·6	2	
50	12·3	Proof	
49	14·1	2 u.p.	19
48	15·9	4	
47	17·6	6	18
46	19·4	8	
45	21·2	10	
44	23·0	12	
43	24·8	14	
42	26·5	16	17
41	28·3	18	
40	30·0	20	
39	31·8	22	
38	33·6	24	16
37	35·4	26	
36	37·2	28	
35	38·9	30	
34	40·6	32	
33	42·3	34	
32	44·1	36	15
31	45·9	38	
30	47·6	40	
29	49·3	42	
28	51·0	44	

In Germany and Russia the Tralles system is in common use. It is the equivalent of the Gay Lussac system.

ANTIDOTES FOR POISONS

First — Send for a Physician. Second — Induce vomiting by tickling the throat with feather or finger; drink hot water, strong mustard and water; swallow sweet oil or whites of eggs.

Acids are antidotes for alkalis and vice versa.

POISONS AND THEIR ANTIDOTES

"Life's cares are a poison and Wine its best antidote"

Acids — Muriatic, Oxalic, Acetic, Sulphuric (Oil of Vitriol), Nitric (Aqua Fortis)	Soap-suds, magnesia, lime water.
Prussic acid	Ammonia in water. Dash water in face.
Carbolic Acid	Whiskey or dilute grain alcohol, flour and water, mucilaginous drinks.
Alkalis — Potash, Hartshorn, Lye, Ammonia.	Vinegar or Lemon juice in water.
Arsenic — Rat Poison, Paris Green	Milk, raw eggs, sweet oil, lime water, flour and water.
Bug Poison — Lead, Saltpetre, Corrosive Sublimate, Sugar of Lead, Blue Vitriol.. ..	Whites of eggs or milk in large doses.
Chloroform — Chloral, Ether	Dash cold water on head and chest. Artificial respiration.
Carbonate of Soda, Copperas, Cobalt	Soap-suds and mucilaginous drinks.
Iodine — Antimony, Tartar Emetic	Starch and water, astringent infusions, strong tea.
Mercury and its Salts	Whites of eggs, milk mucilages.
Opium — Morphine, Laudanum; Paregoric Soothing Powders or Syrup.	Strong black coffee, hot bath. Keep awake and moving at any cost.

DIFFERENCES OF TIME

NOON IN PARIS

Place	Time	Place	Time
Adelaide	9.30 p.m.	Mexico City	6. 0 a.m.
Amsterdam	12.20 —	Montreal	7. 0 —
Athens	2. 0 —	Moscow	2. 0 p.m.
Auckland, N.Z.	11.30 —	New Orleans	6. 0 a.m.
Berlin	1. 0 —	New York	7. 0 —
Bombay	5.30 —	Oslo	1. 0 p.m.
Brindisi	1. 0 —	Ottawa	7. 0 a.m.
Brisbane	10. 0 —	Panama	6.30 —
Brussels	12 noon	Peking	8. 0 p.m.
Bucharest	2. 0 p.m.	Perth (W.A.)	8. 0 —
Budapest	1. 0 —	Philippines	8. 0 —
Buenos Aires	8. 0 a.m.	Prague	1. 0 —
Cairo	2. 0 p.m.	Quebec	7. 0 a.m.
Calcutta	3.53 —	Rangoon	6.30 p.m.
Cape Town	2. 0 —	Rio de Janeiro	9. 0 a.m.
Ceylon	5.30 —	Rome	1. 0 p.m.
Chicago	6. 0 a.m.	San Francisco	4. 0 a.m.
Constantinople	2. 0 p.m.	Santiago, Chili	7. 0 —
Copenhagen	1. 0 —	Sardinia	1. 0 p.m.
Cuba	7. 0 a.m.	Singapore	7. 0 —
Gibraltar	12 noon	Sofia	2. 0 —
Hobart	10. 0 p.m.	St. Louis, U.S.A.	6. 0 a.m.
Hong Kong	8. 0 —	Stockholm	1. 0 p.m.
Jerusalem	2. 0 —	Suez	2. 0 —
Leningrad	2. 0 —	Sydney	10. 0 —
Lisbon	12 noon	Tokyo	9. 0 —
Madeira	11. 0 a.m.	Toronto	7. 0 a.m.
Madras	5.30 p.m.	Vancouver	4. 0 —
Madrid	12 noon	Vienna	1. 0 p.m.
Malta	1. 0 p.m.	Winnipeg	6. 0 a.m.
Mauritius	10. 0 —	Yokohama	9. 0 p.m.
Melbourne	9.30 —		

NAUTICAL MILES

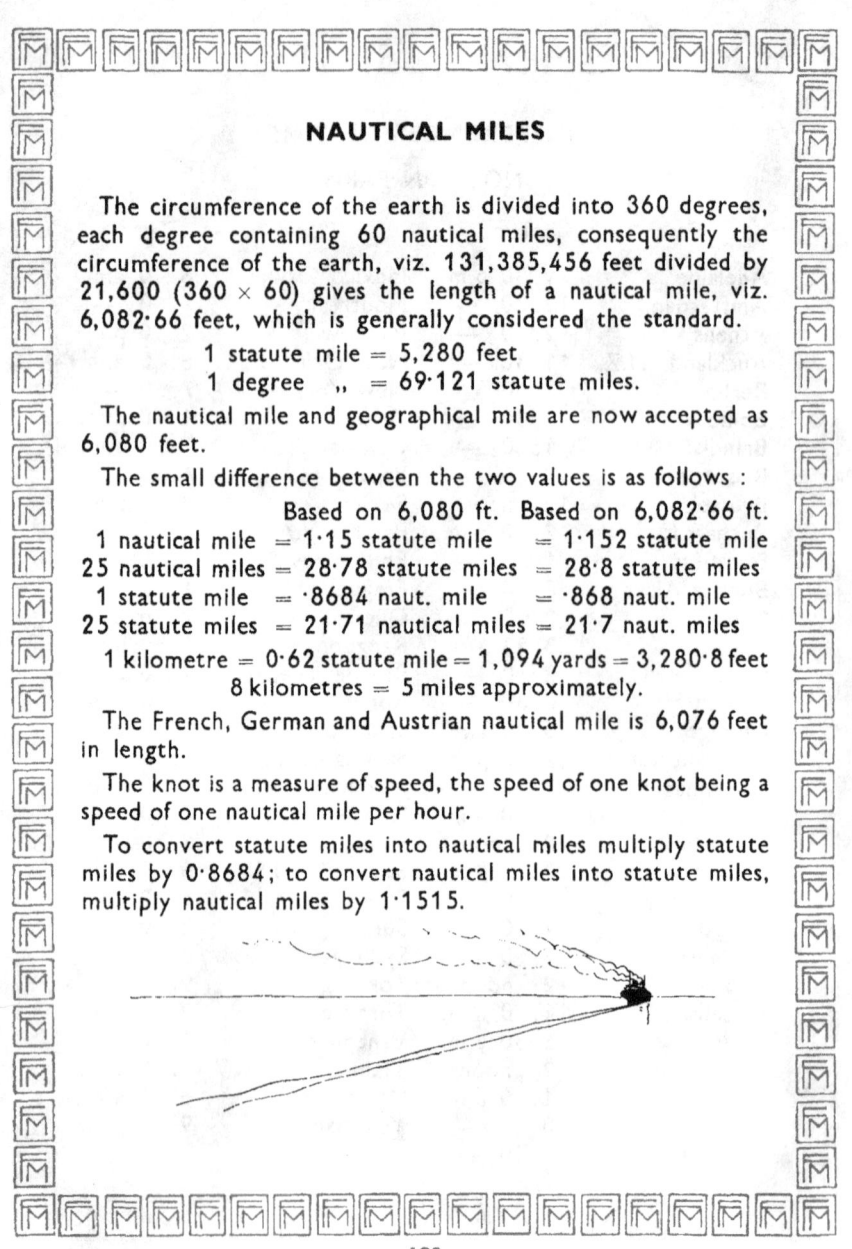

The circumference of the earth is divided into 360 degrees, each degree containing 60 nautical miles, consequently the circumference of the earth, viz. 131,385,456 feet divided by 21,600 (360 × 60) gives the length of a nautical mile, viz. 6,082·66 feet, which is generally considered the standard.

        1 statute mile = 5,280 feet
        1 degree ,,   = 69·121 statute miles.

The nautical mile and geographical mile are now accepted as 6,080 feet.

The small difference between the two values is as follows :

	Based on 6,080 ft.	Based on 6,082·66 ft.
1 nautical mile	= 1·15 statute mile	= 1·152 statute mile
25 nautical miles	= 28·78 statute miles	= 28·8 statute miles
1 statute mile	= ·8684 naut. mile	= ·868 naut. mile
25 statute miles	= 21·71 nautical miles	= 21·7 naut. miles

1 kilometre = 0·62 statute mile = 1,094 yards = 3,280·8 feet
        8 kilometres = 5 miles approximately.

The French, German and Austrian nautical mile is 6,076 feet in length.

The knot is a measure of speed, the speed of one knot being a speed of one nautical mile per hour.

To convert statute miles into nautical miles multiply statute miles by 0·8684; to convert nautical miles into statute miles, multiply nautical miles by 1·1515.

THE EARTH

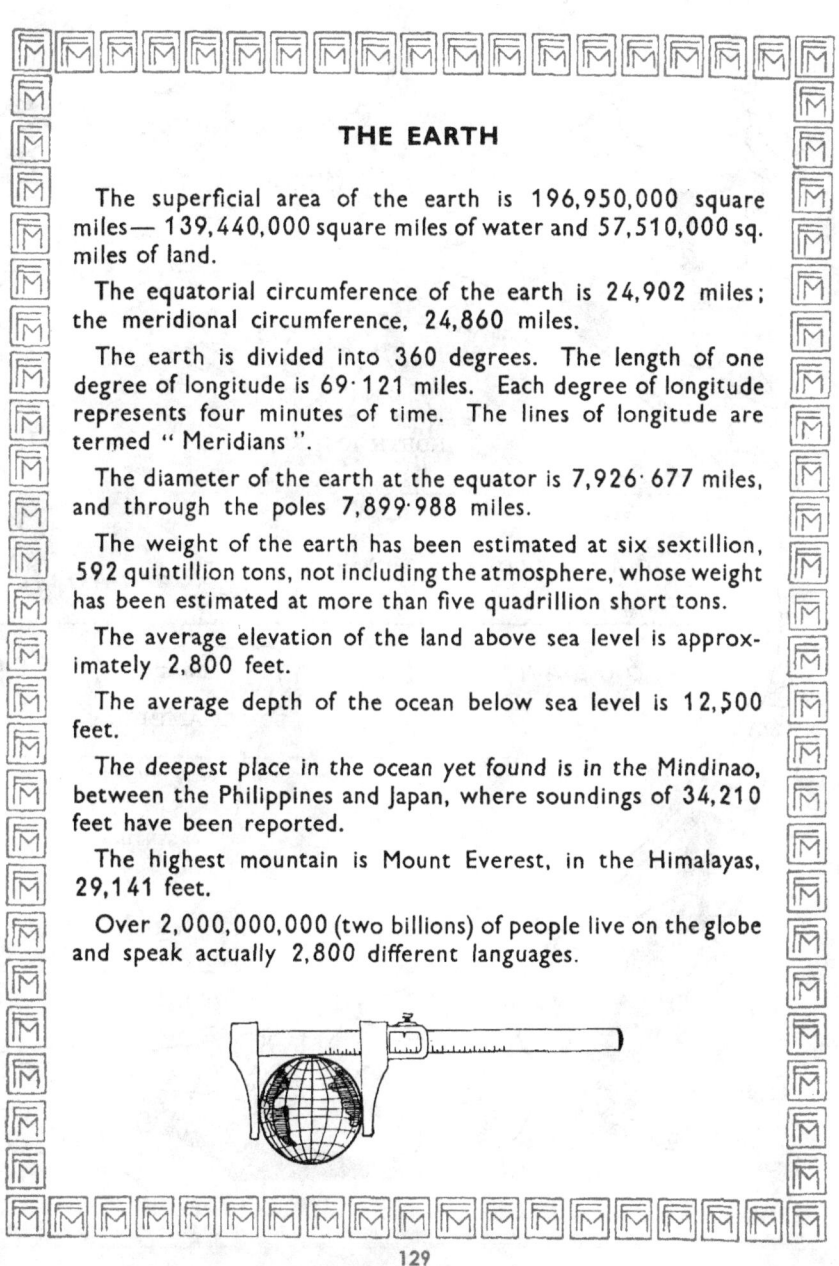

The superficial area of the earth is 196,950,000 square miles— 139,440,000 square miles of water and 57,510,000 sq. miles of land.

The equatorial circumference of the earth is 24,902 miles; the meridional circumference, 24,860 miles.

The earth is divided into 360 degrees. The length of one degree of longitude is 69·121 miles. Each degree of longitude represents four minutes of time. The lines of longitude are termed " Meridians ".

The diameter of the earth at the equator is 7,926·677 miles, and through the poles 7,899·988 miles.

The weight of the earth has been estimated at six sextillion, 592 quintillion tons, not including the atmosphere, whose weight has been estimated at more than five quadrillion short tons.

The average elevation of the land above sea level is approximately 2,800 feet.

The average depth of the ocean below sea level is 12,500 feet.

The deepest place in the ocean yet found is in the Mindinao, between the Philippines and Japan, where soundings of 34,210 feet have been reported.

The highest mountain is Mount Everest, in the Himalayas, 29,141 feet.

Over 2,000,000,000 (two billions) of people live on the globe and speak actually 2,800 different languages.

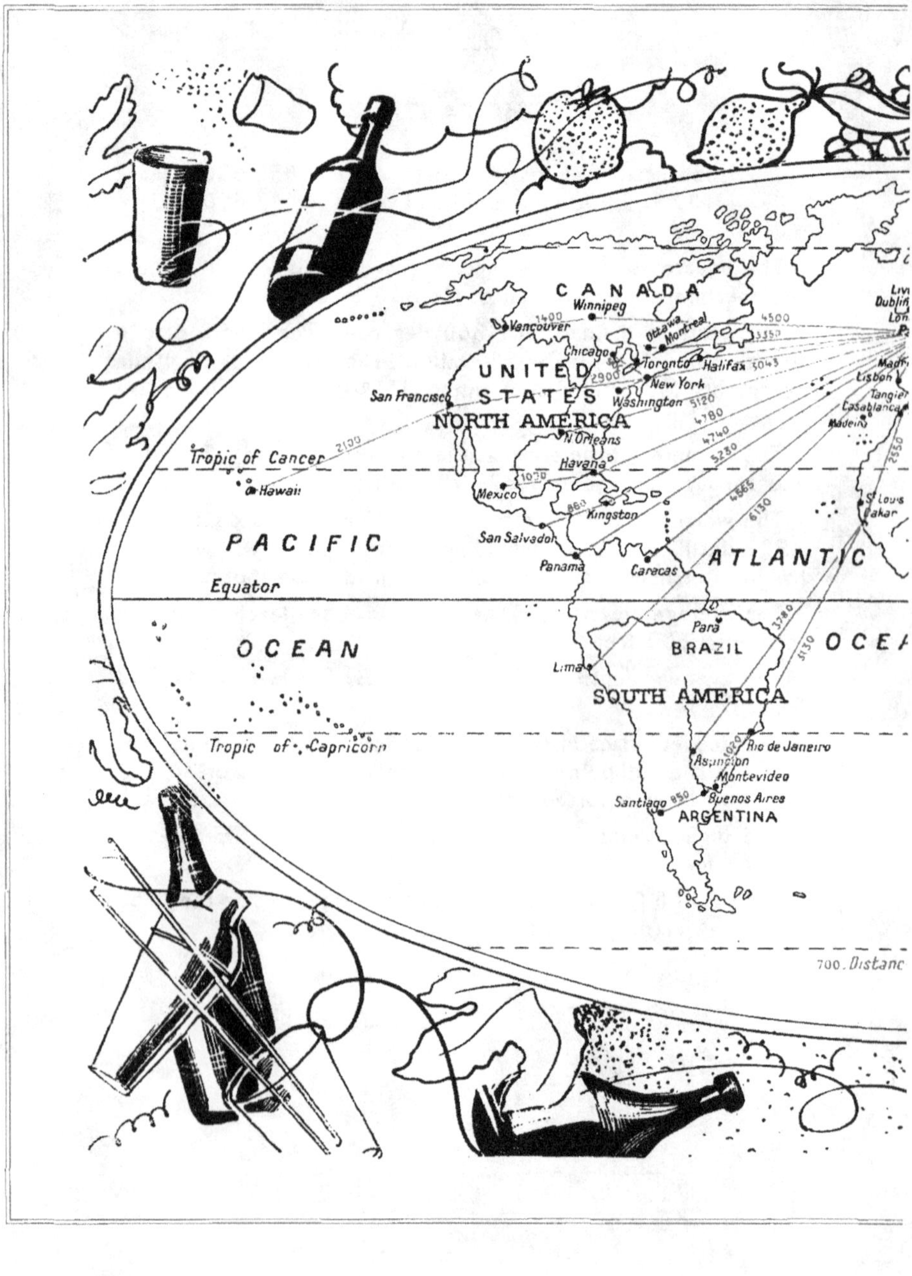

CANADA
Winnipeg
Vancouver
Ottawa
Montreal
Chicago
Toronto
Halifax
UNITED STATES
NORTH AMERICA
New York
Washington
San Francisco
N. Orleans
Havana
Mexico
Kingston
San Salvador
Panama
Caracas
Tropic of Cancer
Hawaii
PACIFIC
Equator
OCEAN
ATLANTIC
Lisbon
Casablanca
Madeira
St Louis
Dakar
Para
BRAZIL
Lima
SOUTH AMERICA
Tropic of Capricorn
Rio de Janeiro
Asuncion
Montevideo
Santiago
Buenos Aires
ARGENTINA
1400
4500
3350
5043
2900
5120
4780
4740
5230
4565
6130
2100
1030
860
2550
3780
3130
1020
850

SIBERIA
ASIA
CHINA
INDIA
JAPAN
PACIFIC
OCEAN
INDIAN
OCEAN
AUSTRALIA
NEW ZEALAND
Equator
Helsingfors
Leningrad
Riga
Moscow
Warsow
Vienna
Budapest
Bucarest
Belgrade
Rome
Sofia
Istambul
Ankara
Athens
Malta
Jerusalem
Tehran
Alex
Suez
Baghdad
Cairo
Mekka
Khartoum
Aden
Addis Ababa
Mukden
Vladivostok
Peking
Tokio
Yokohama
Shanghai
Canton
Calcutta
Hanoi
Hongkong
Bombay
Rangoon
Bangkok
Manila
Hyderabad
Madras
Saigon
Colombo
Johore Bahru
Singapore
Brazzaville
Nairobi
Zanzibar
Batavia
Tananarivo
Mauritius
Pretoria
Brisbane
Sydney
Auckland
Melbourne
Canberra
Red Sea
statute miles
DEL LA ROUGERY_PARIS

PRESSURE

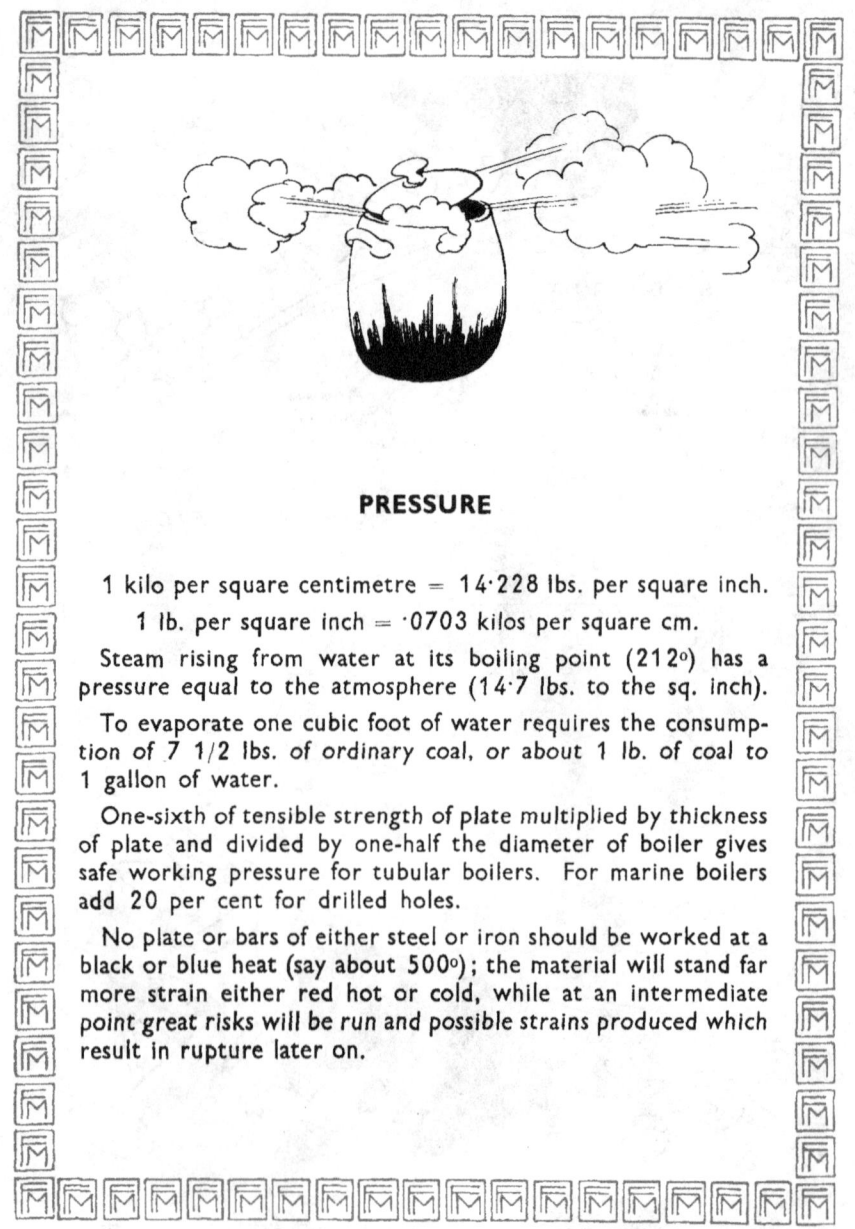

1 kilo per square centimetre = 14·228 lbs. per square inch.

1 lb. per square inch = ·0703 kilos per square cm.

Steam rising from water at its boiling point (212°) has a pressure equal to the atmosphere (14·7 lbs. to the sq. inch).

To evaporate one cubic foot of water requires the consumption of 7 1/2 lbs. of ordinary coal, or about 1 lb. of coal to 1 gallon of water.

One-sixth of tensible strength of plate multiplied by thickness of plate and divided by one-half the diameter of boiler gives safe working pressure for tubular boilers. For marine boilers add 20 per cent for drilled holes.

No plate or bars of either steel or iron should be worked at a black or blue heat (say about 500°); the material will stand far more strain either red hot or cold, while at an intermediate point great risks will be run and possible strains produced which result in rupture later on.

COMPARATIVE TEMPERATURES & MEASURES

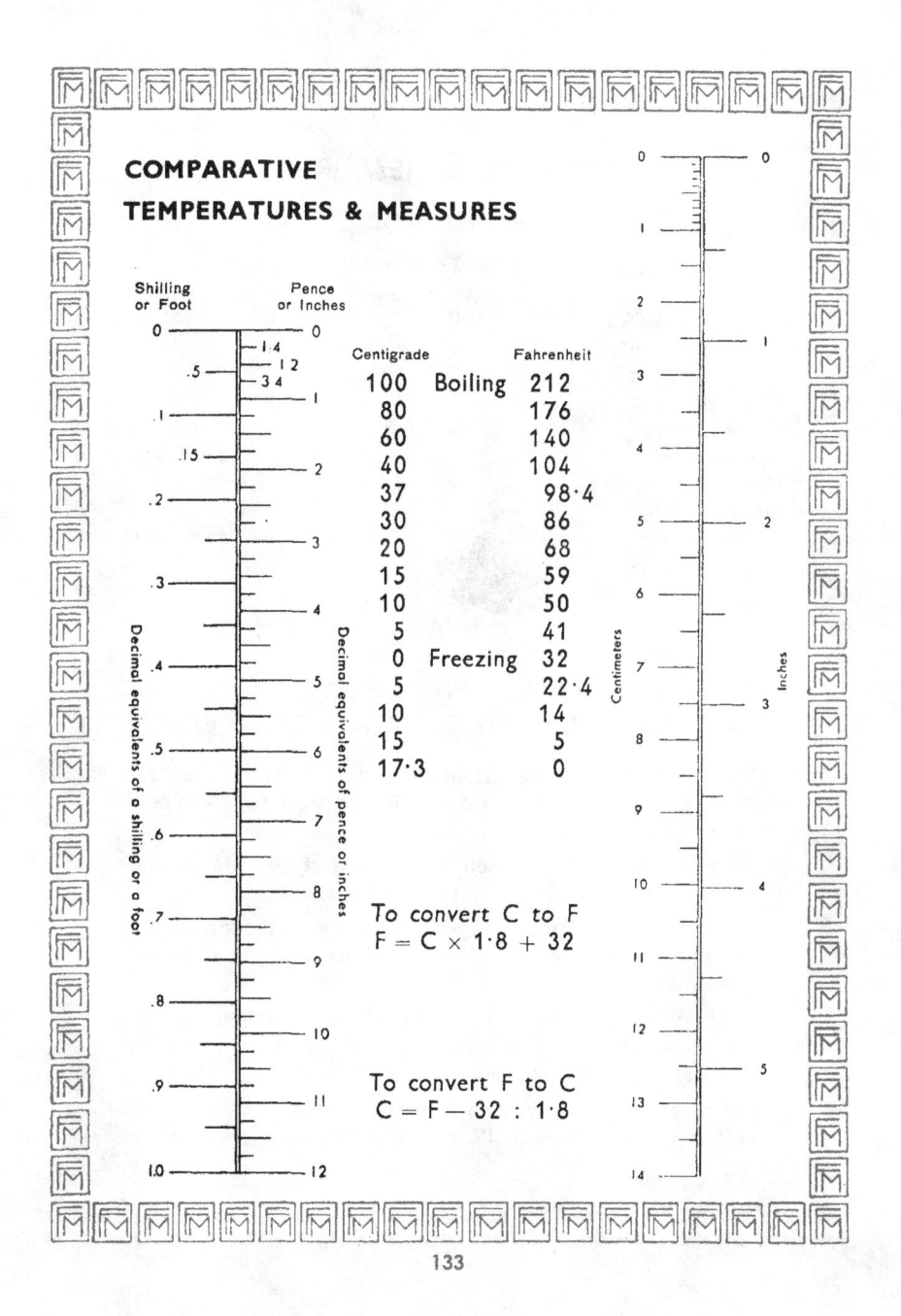

Centigrade		Fahrenheit
100	Boiling	212
80		176
60		140
40		104
37		98·4
30		86
20		68
15		59
10		50
5		41
0	Freezing	32
5		22·4
10		14
15		5
17·3		0

To convert C to F
F = C × 1·8 + 32

To convert F to C
C = F − 32 : 1·8

WEIGHTS & MEASURES

AVOIRDUPOIS

100 kilos = 267·93 lbs. Troy or 220·462 lbs. Avoir.

	Cwt.	Qrs.	St.	Lbs.	Oz.	Drs.	Grs.	Equivalents
Ton; tonneau	20	80	160	2240				1,016·0475 kilos
Hundredweight: quintal:		4	8	112				50·8024
Quarter;			2	28				12·7006 —
Stone; pierre :				14				6·3503 —
Pound; livre :					16	256	7000	453·5926 grs.
Ounce; once Avdp :						16	437½	28·3493 —
Dram; drachme							2711	1·7718 —
Grain Troy								6·4799 cgrs.

METRIC CARAT WEIGHTS
FOR PRECIOUS STONES, METALS AND PEARLS

The weight of precious stones is given in metric carats; a metric carat is divided into 100 cent-carats. A metric carat = 0·2 gramme.

For pearls the grain is used. The grain equals 1/4 carat or 0·05 gramme and is divided into 100 parts.

There are weights for the carat, multiples and submultiples. They are used for precious stones and pearls. Special weights in grains do not exist.

To obtain a weight in grains, multiply by 4 the weight in carats.
1 gramme = 5 carats = (5 × 4) 20 grains.
1 carat = 0·2 gramme; 1 grain = 0·05 gramme.

The carat is correctly used as expressing the degree of fineness, but not as a weight. Pure gold is described as 24 carats.

If a gold coin or any other gold article is of say 24, 22, 20, 18, 14, 9 carats, then it contains 24, 22, 20, 18, 14, 9 parts of pure gold, and the remaining parts are alloy.

Therefore we may consider that a golden jewel
at 22 carats has a standard of 0·915
— 20 — — 0·832
— 18 — — 0·750
— 14 — — 0·593
— 9 — — 0·375

but these standards are observed only when an official Law of Control is imposed, as it is in France.

0·950 is the standard for platinum used in jewels and works of art.

0·950 - 0·800 are the standards used for silverware.

CLOTH MEASURE

2 1/4 inches = 1 nail; 4 nails = 1 quarter; 4 quarters = 1 yard

CUBIC MEASURE

1,728 cubic inches = 1 cub. foot
27 cubic feet = 1 cub. yard
128 cubic feet = 1 cord (wood)
40 cubic feet = 1 ton (shipping)
231 cubic inches = 1 U.S. standard gallon
2150·42 cubic inches = 1 standard bushel
1 cubic foot = about four-fifths of a bushel

DRY MEASURE

2 pints = 1 quart   8 quarts = 1 peck
4 pecks = 1 bushel   36 bushels = 1 chaldron

APPROXIMATE LIQUID MEASURES AND EQUIVALENTS

1/4 gill	= 1 oz. 2 drams	= 03·5 centilitre	
1/2 ,,	= 2 ozs. 4 ,,	= 07·1 ,,	
1 ,,	= 5 ,,	= 14·2 centilitres	
4 gills	= 1 pint	= 0·568 litre	

2 pints = 1 quart   4 quarts = 1 imperial gallon or 160 ozs.
1 impl. gallon = 160 ozs. = 4·543 litres or 10 lbs. of pure water
1 litre = 35 1/2 ozs. = 1·76 pints.
31 1/2 gallons = 1 barrel   2 barrels = 1 hogshead

LONG MEASURE

12 inches	= 1 foot	40 rods	= 1 furlong
3 feet	= 1 yard	8 furlongs	= 1 statute mile
5 1/2 yards	= 1 rod	3 miles	= 1 league

METRIC EQUIVALENT MEASURES

1 millimetre	= 0·03937 inch
1 centimetre	= 0·3937 inch = 0·0328 foot
1 metre	= 39·37 in. = 1·0936 yards
1 decametre	= 1·9884 rods
1 kilometre	= 0·62137 mile
1 inch	= 2·54 centimetres
1 foot	= 3·048 decimetres
1 yard	= 0·9144 metre
1 rod	= 0·5929 decametre
1 mile	= 1·6093 kilometres

	Pole	Fath.	Yds.	Cubit	Ft.	In.	Equivalents	
Chain; Chaine	4	11	22	44	66	792	20·1164	metres
Pole, rod; perche:	2½	5½	11	16½	198		5·0291	—
Fathom; toise:		2	4	6	72		1·8288	—
Yard; verge :			2	3	36		91·4383	centim.
Cubit; coudée :				1½	18		45·7189	—
Foot; pied :					12		30·4792	—
Inch; pouce :							25·3994	millim.

1 sq. centimetre = 0·1550 square inch
1 sq. decimetre = 0·1076 square foot
1 sq. metre = 1·196 square yards
1 are = 3·954 square rods
1 hectare = 2·47 acres
1 sq. kilometre = 0·386 square mile
1 sq. inch = 6·452 sq. centimetres
1 sq. foot = 9·2903 sq. decimetres
1 sq. yard = 0·8361 sq. metre
1 sq. rod = 0·2529 are
1 acre = 0·4047 hectare
1 sq. mile = 2·59 sq. kilometres

1 acre = 0·4047 hectare = 40·47 ares = 4,840 sq. yards
= 160 sq. rods = 10 square chains.

1 sq. mile = 2·59 sq. kilometres = 259 hectares = 640 acres
or 3,097,600 sq. yds.

SQUARE MEASURE

144 sq. inches = 1 sq. foot.   40 sq. rods = 1 rood
9 sq. feet = 1 sq. yard   4 roods = 1 acre
30 1/4 sq. yds = 1 sq. rod   640 acres = 1 sq. mile

SURVEYOR'S MEASURE

7·92 inches = 1 link; 25 links = 1 rod; 4 rods = 1 chain
10 sq. chains or 160 sq. rods = 1 acre; 640 acres = 1 sq. mile
36 sq. miles (6 miles sq.) = 1 township

TIME

60 seconds = 1 minute   60 minutes = 1 hour
24 hours = 1 day   7 days = 1 week
28, 29, 30 or 31 days = 1 calendar month
30 days = 1 month in computing interest.
365 days = 1 year   366 days = 1 leap year

TROY

```
                  Ozs. Dwts.  Grs.    Mites
Pound; livre :     12  240   5760   115200   373·2419 grammes
Ounce; once :          20     480     9600    31·1035   —
Pennyweight; denier           24      480      1·5551   —
Grain Troy                             20      6·4799 centigr.
Mite; vingtième                                3·2399 milligr.
```

The Gold and Silver weight is the Troy pound of 12 ounces. The ounce is 20 dwt of 24 grains each. For Diamonds, the Troy ounce is divided into 151 ½ carats, making 6 carats equal to 19 grains nearly. For pearls, it is divided into 600 grains, making 5 pearl grains equal to 4 grains Troy.

```
1 Grain                ·06479 gramme
1 Oz. (Troy)          31·193  grammes
1 Lb. (Avoir.)         ·4536  kilogramme
1 Gramme              15·432  grains
1 Drachm               1·7718 grammes
```

USEFUL FORMULAS

To reduce inches to metres, multiply by ·0254
To reduce inches to centimetres, multiply by 2·54
To reduce centimetres to inches, multiply by ·3937
To reduce kilos to pounds, multiply by 2·2046
To reduce litres to gallons, multiply by ·22
To reduce gallons to litres, multiply by 4·548
To reduce grains to grammes, multiply by ·0648
To reduce ounces to grammes, multiply by 28·349

USEFUL INFORMATION

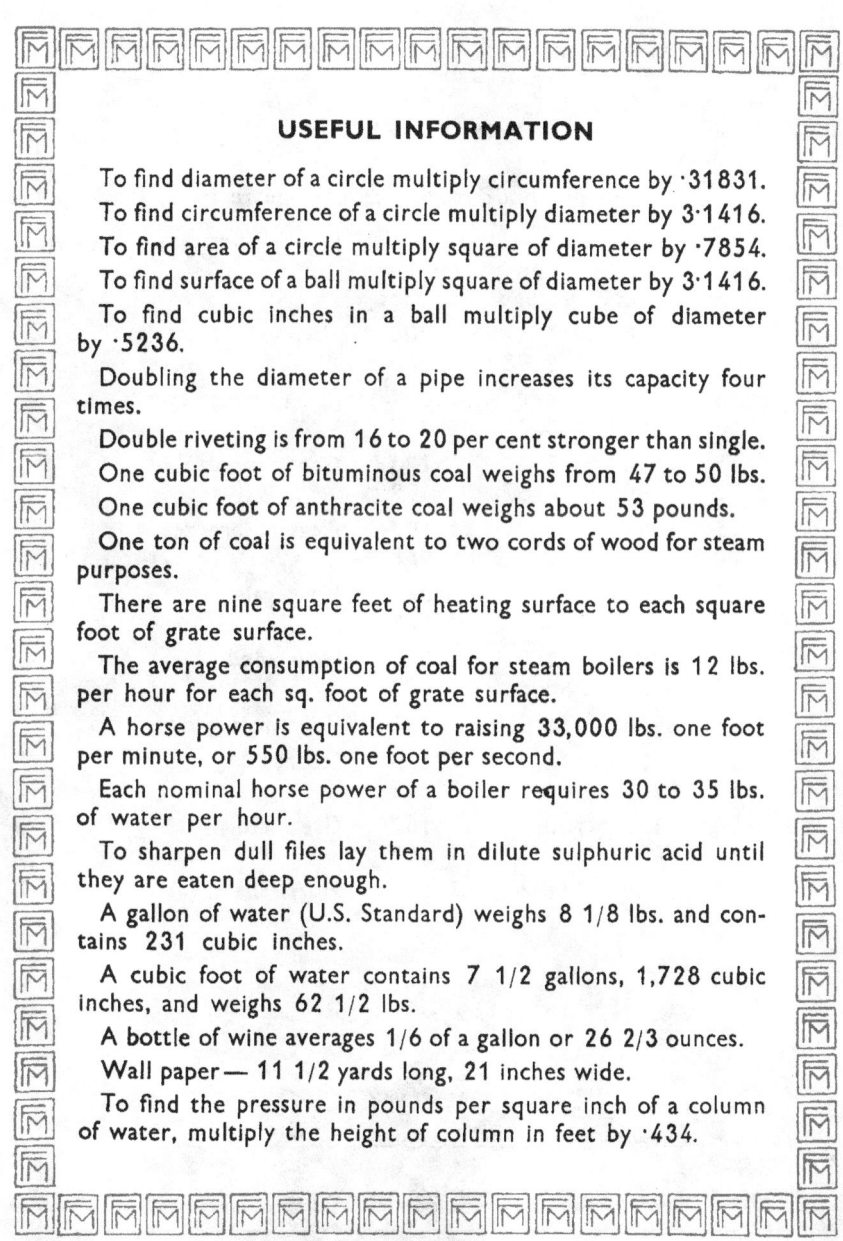

To find diameter of a circle multiply circumference by ·31831.
To find circumference of a circle multiply diameter by 3·1416.
To find area of a circle multiply square of diameter by ·7854.
To find surface of a ball multiply square of diameter by 3·1416.
To find cubic inches in a ball multiply cube of diameter by ·5236.

Doubling the diameter of a pipe increases its capacity four times.

Double riveting is from 16 to 20 per cent stronger than single.

One cubic foot of bituminous coal weighs from 47 to 50 lbs.

One cubic foot of anthracite coal weighs about 53 pounds.

One ton of coal is equivalent to two cords of wood for steam purposes.

There are nine square feet of heating surface to each square foot of grate surface.

The average consumption of coal for steam boilers is 12 lbs. per hour for each sq. foot of grate surface.

A horse power is equivalent to raising 33,000 lbs. one foot per minute, or 550 lbs. one foot per second.

Each nominal horse power of a boiler requires 30 to 35 lbs. of water per hour.

To sharpen dull files lay them in dilute sulphuric acid until they are eaten deep enough.

A gallon of water (U.S. Standard) weighs 8 1/8 lbs. and contains 231 cubic inches.

A cubic foot of water contains 7 1/2 gallons, 1,728 cubic inches, and weighs 62 1/2 lbs.

A bottle of wine averages 1/6 of a gallon or 26 2/3 ounces.

Wall paper— 11 1/2 yards long, 21 inches wide.

To find the pressure in pounds per square inch of a column of water, multiply the height of column in feet by ·434.

WIND PRESSURE

Miles per hour to pounds per square foot

Miles per hour	Feet per minute	Feet per second	Force in lbs. per sq. foot	Description
1	88	1·47	·005	Hardly perceptible
2	176	2·93	·020	
3	264	4·40	·044	Just perceptible
4	352	5·87	·079	
5	440	7·33	·123	Gentle breeze
10	880	14·67	·492	
15	1320	22	1·107	Pleasant breeze
20	1760	29·3	1·968	
25	2200	36·6	3·075	Brisk gale
30	2640	44	4·428	
35	3080	51·3	6·027	High wind
40	3520	58·6	7·872	
45	3960	66·0	9·963	Very high wind
50	4400	73·3	12:300	Storm
60	5280	88·0	17·712	
70	6160	102·7	24·107	Great storm
80	7040	117·3	31·488	
100	8800	146·6	49·200	Hurricane

FOR CLEANING VARIOUS SUBSTANCES

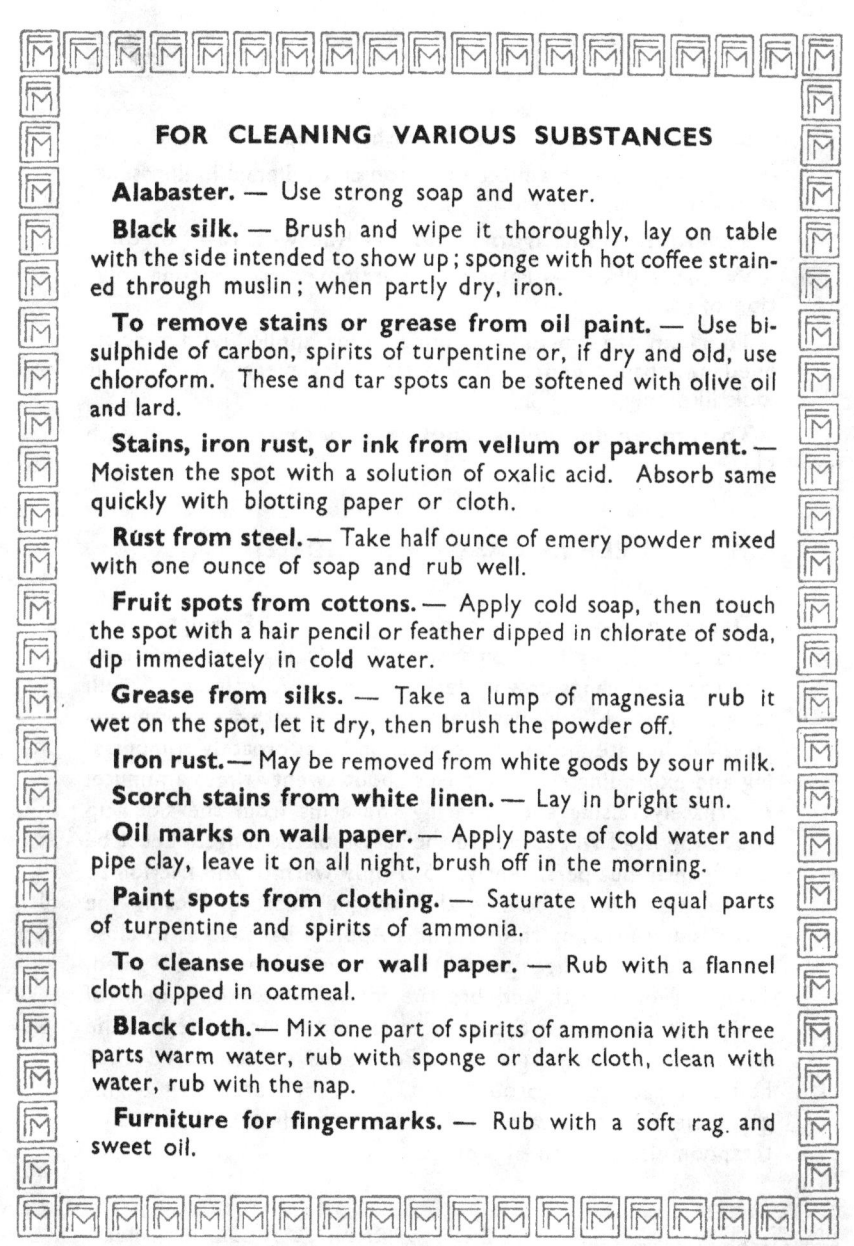

Alabaster. — Use strong soap and water.

Black silk. — Brush and wipe it thoroughly, lay on table with the side intended to show up; sponge with hot coffee strained through muslin; when partly dry, iron.

To remove stains or grease from oil paint. — Use bisulphide of carbon, spirits of turpentine or, if dry and old, use chloroform. These and tar spots can be softened with olive oil and lard.

Stains, iron rust, or ink from vellum or parchment. — Moisten the spot with a solution of oxalic acid. Absorb same quickly with blotting paper or cloth.

Rust from steel. — Take half ounce of emery powder mixed with one ounce of soap and rub well.

Fruit spots from cottons. — Apply cold soap, then touch the spot with a hair pencil or feather dipped in chlorate of soda, dip immediately in cold water.

Grease from silks. — Take a lump of magnesia rub it wet on the spot, let it dry, then brush the powder off.

Iron rust. — May be removed from white goods by sour milk.

Scorch stains from white linen. — Lay in bright sun.

Oil marks on wall paper. — Apply paste of cold water and pipe clay, leave it on all night, brush off in the morning.

Paint spots from clothing. — Saturate with equal parts of turpentine and spirits of ammonia.

To cleanse house or wall paper. — Rub with a flannel cloth dipped in oatmeal.

Black cloth. — Mix one part of spirits of ammonia with three parts warm water, rub with sponge or dark cloth, clean with water, rub with the nap.

Furniture for fingermarks. — Rub with a soft rag and sweet oil.

Chromos. — Go over lightly with a damp linen cloth.

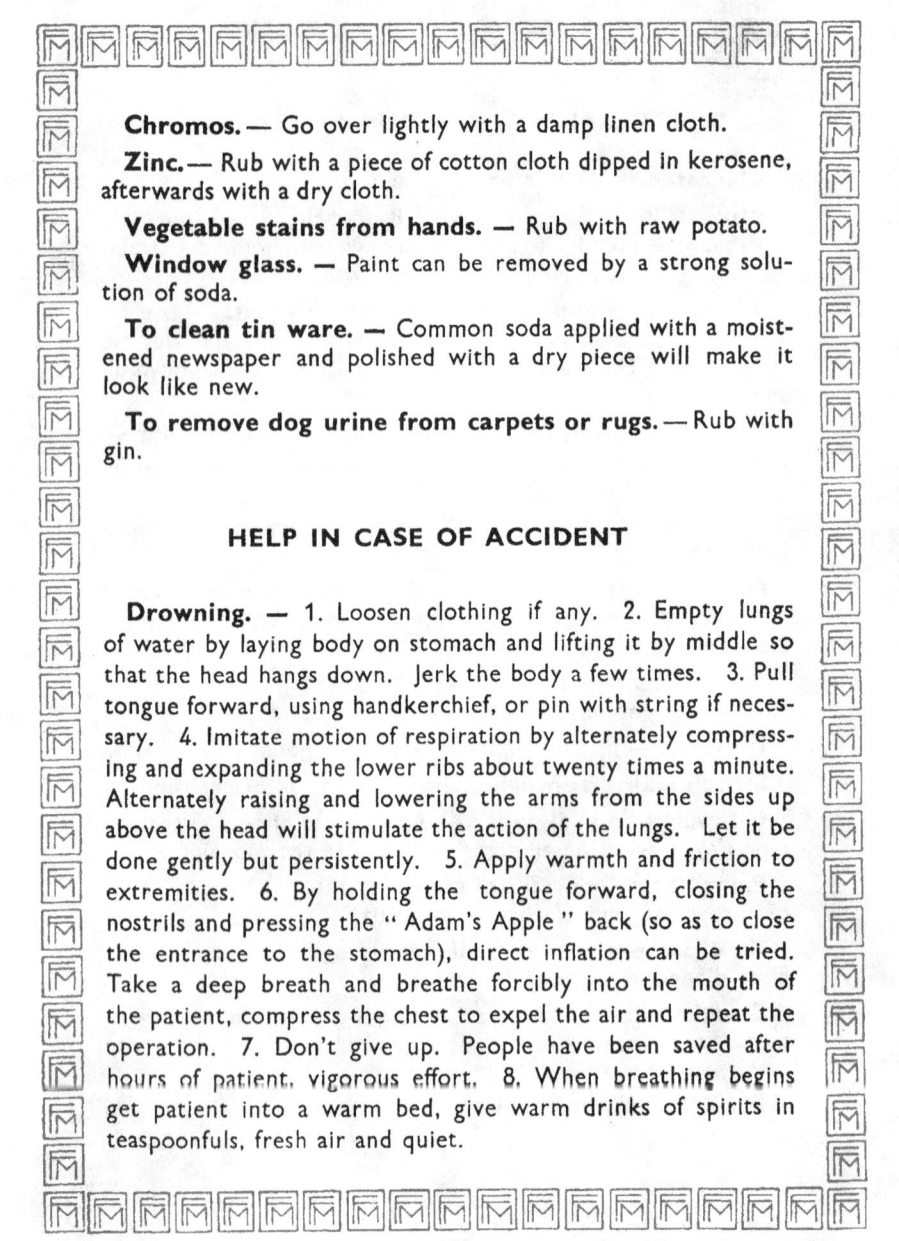

Zinc. — Rub with a piece of cotton cloth dipped in kerosene, afterwards with a dry cloth.

Vegetable stains from hands. — Rub with raw potato.

Window glass. — Paint can be removed by a strong solution of soda.

To clean tin ware. — Common soda applied with a moistened newspaper and polished with a dry piece will make it look like new.

To remove dog urine from carpets or rugs. — Rub with gin.

HELP IN CASE OF ACCIDENT

Drowning. — 1. Loosen clothing if any. 2. Empty lungs of water by laying body on stomach and lifting it by middle so that the head hangs down. Jerk the body a few times. 3. Pull tongue forward, using handkerchief, or pin with string if necessary. 4. Imitate motion of respiration by alternately compressing and expanding the lower ribs about twenty times a minute. Alternately raising and lowering the arms from the sides up above the head will stimulate the action of the lungs. Let it be done gently but persistently. 5. Apply warmth and friction to extremities. 6. By holding the tongue forward, closing the nostrils and pressing the " Adam's Apple " back (so as to close the entrance to the stomach), direct inflation can be tried. Take a deep breath and breathe forcibly into the mouth of the patient, compress the chest to expel the air and repeat the operation. 7. Don't give up. People have been saved after hours of patient, vigorous effort. 8. When breathing begins get patient into a warm bed, give warm drinks of spirits in teaspoonfuls, fresh air and quiet.

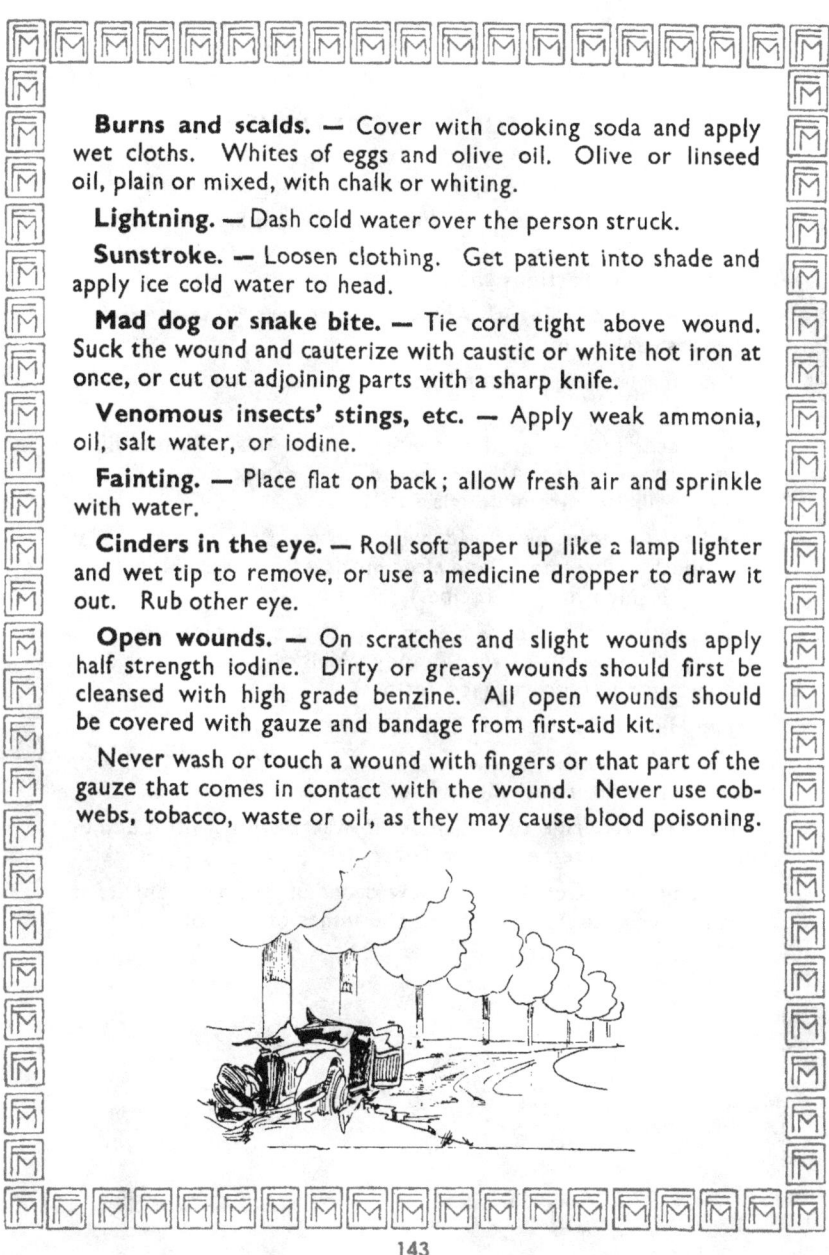

Burns and scalds. — Cover with cooking soda and apply wet cloths. Whites of eggs and olive oil. Olive or linseed oil, plain or mixed, with chalk or whiting.

Lightning. — Dash cold water over the person struck.

Sunstroke. — Loosen clothing. Get patient into shade and apply ice cold water to head.

Mad dog or snake bite. — Tie cord tight above wound. Suck the wound and cauterize with caustic or white hot iron at once, or cut out adjoining parts with a sharp knife.

Venomous insects' stings, etc. — Apply weak ammonia, oil, salt water, or iodine.

Fainting. — Place flat on back; allow fresh air and sprinkle with water.

Cinders in the eye. — Roll soft paper up like a lamp lighter and wet tip to remove, or use a medicine dropper to draw it out. Rub other eye.

Open wounds. — On scratches and slight wounds apply half strength iodine. Dirty or greasy wounds should first be cleansed with high grade benzine. All open wounds should be covered with gauze and bandage from first-aid kit.

Never wash or touch a wound with fingers or that part of the gauze that comes in contact with the wound. Never use cobwebs, tobacco, waste or oil, as they may cause blood poisoning.

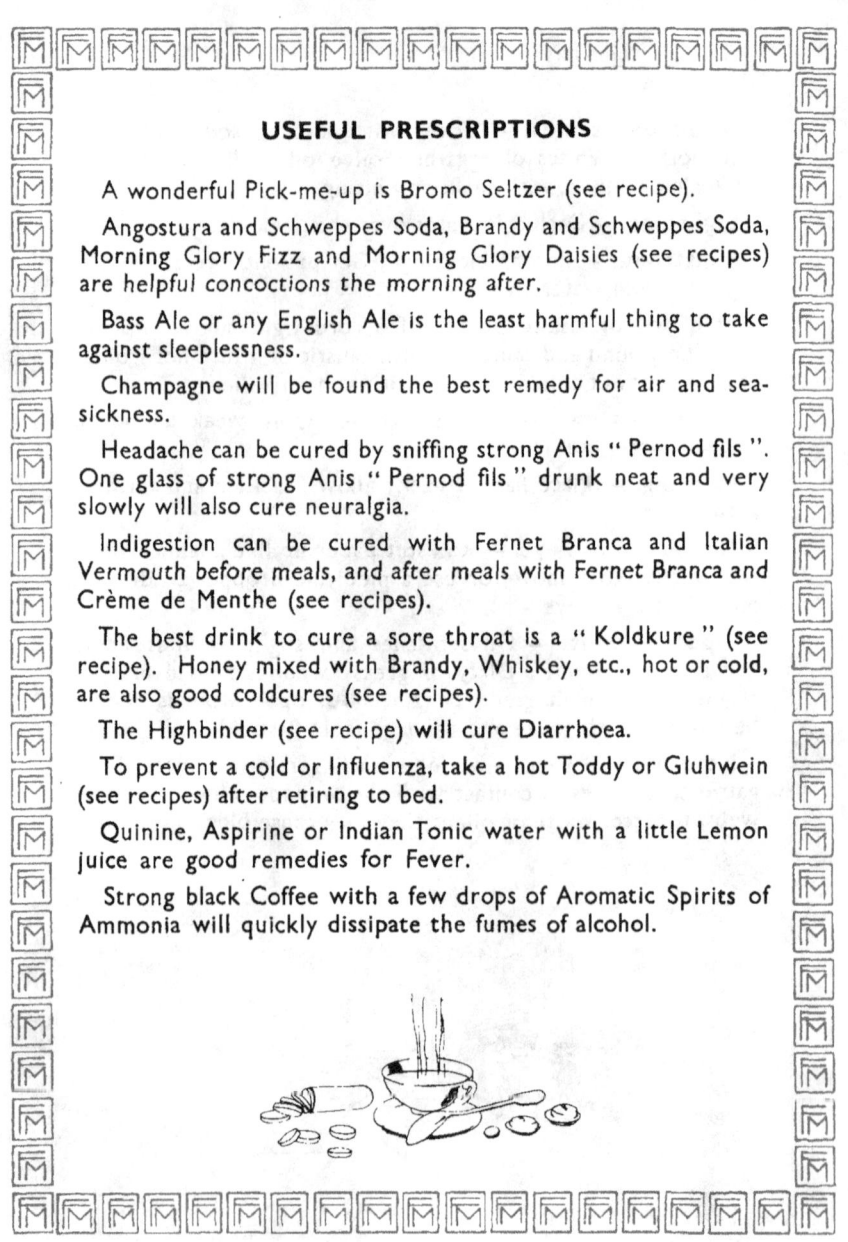

USEFUL PRESCRIPTIONS

A wonderful Pick-me-up is Bromo Seltzer (see recipe).

Angostura and Schweppes Soda, Brandy and Schweppes Soda, Morning Glory Fizz and Morning Glory Daisies (see recipes) are helpful concoctions the morning after.

Bass Ale or any English Ale is the least harmful thing to take against sleeplessness.

Champagne will be found the best remedy for air and seasickness.

Headache can be cured by sniffing strong Anis " Pernod fils ". One glass of strong Anis " Pernod fils " drunk neat and very slowly will also cure neuralgia.

Indigestion can be cured with Fernet Branca and Italian Vermouth before meals, and after meals with Fernet Branca and Crème de Menthe (see recipes).

The best drink to cure a sore throat is a " Koldkure " (see recipe). Honey mixed with Brandy, Whiskey, etc., hot or cold, are also good coldcures (see recipes).

The Highbinder (see recipe) will cure Diarrhoea.

To prevent a cold or Influenza, take a hot Toddy or Gluhwein (see recipes) after retiring to bed.

Quinine, Aspirine or Indian Tonic water with a little Lemon juice are good remedies for Fever.

Strong black Coffee with a few drops of Aromatic Spirits of Ammonia will quickly dissipate the fumes of alcohol.

HORSE RACING

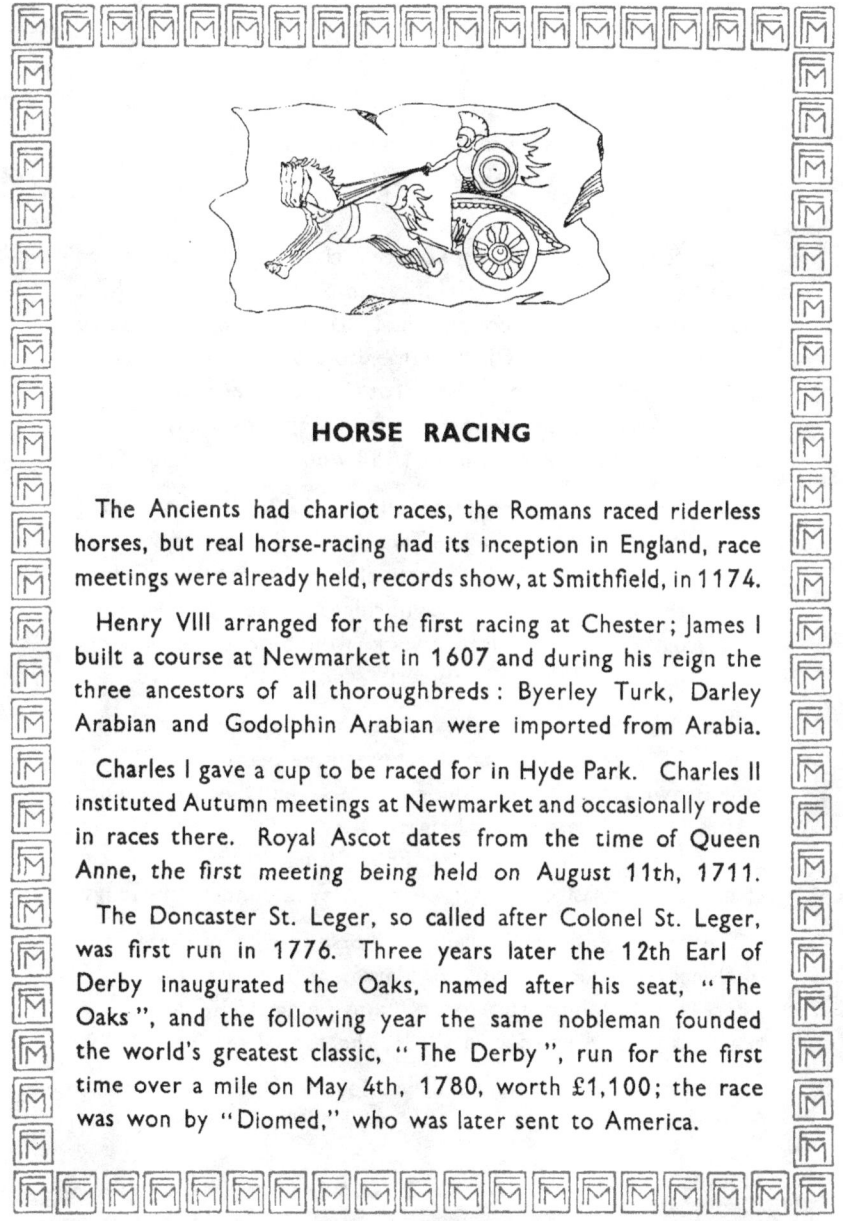

The Ancients had chariot races, the Romans raced riderless horses, but real horse-racing had its inception in England, race meetings were already held, records show, at Smithfield, in 1174.

Henry VIII arranged for the first racing at Chester; James I built a course at Newmarket in 1607 and during his reign the three ancestors of all thoroughbreds: Byerley Turk, Darley Arabian and Godolphin Arabian were imported from Arabia.

Charles I gave a cup to be raced for in Hyde Park. Charles II instituted Autumn meetings at Newmarket and occasionally rode in races there. Royal Ascot dates from the time of Queen Anne, the first meeting being held on August 11th, 1711.

The Doncaster St. Leger, so called after Colonel St. Leger, was first run in 1776. Three years later the 12th Earl of Derby inaugurated the Oaks, named after his seat, "The Oaks", and the following year the same nobleman founded the world's greatest classic, "The Derby", run for the first time over a mile on May 4th, 1780, worth £1,100; the race was won by "Diomed," who was later sent to America.

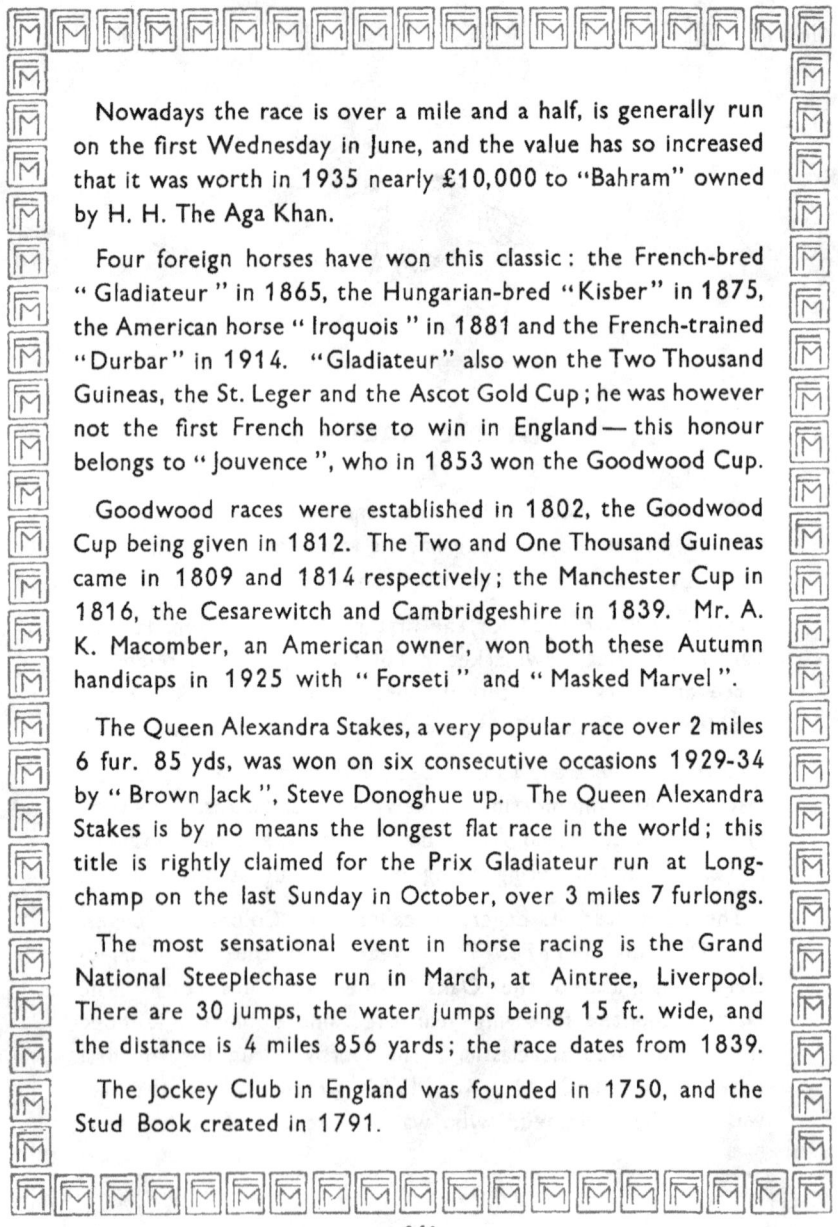

Nowadays the race is over a mile and a half, is generally run on the first Wednesday in June, and the value has so increased that it was worth in 1935 nearly £10,000 to "Bahram" owned by H. H. The Aga Khan.

Four foreign horses have won this classic: the French-bred " Gladiateur " in 1865, the Hungarian-bred "Kisber" in 1875, the American horse " Iroquois " in 1881 and the French-trained "Durbar" in 1914. "Gladiateur" also won the Two Thousand Guineas, the St. Leger and the Ascot Gold Cup; he was however not the first French horse to win in England — this honour belongs to " Jouvence ", who in 1853 won the Goodwood Cup.

Goodwood races were established in 1802, the Goodwood Cup being given in 1812. The Two and One Thousand Guineas came in 1809 and 1814 respectively; the Manchester Cup in 1816, the Cesarewitch and Cambridgeshire in 1839. Mr. A. K. Macomber, an American owner, won both these Autumn handicaps in 1925 with " Forseti " and " Masked Marvel ".

The Queen Alexandra Stakes, a very popular race over 2 miles 6 fur. 85 yds, was won on six consecutive occasions 1929-34 by " Brown Jack ", Steve Donoghue up. The Queen Alexandra Stakes is by no means the longest flat race in the world; this title is rightly claimed for the Prix Gladiateur run at Longchamp on the last Sunday in October, over 3 miles 7 furlongs.

The most sensational event in horse racing is the Grand National Steeplechase run in March, at Aintree, Liverpool. There are 30 jumps, the water jumps being 15 ft. wide, and the distance is 4 miles 856 yards; the race dates from 1839.

The Jockey Club in England was founded in 1750, and the Stud Book created in 1791.

The first racing recorded in France was in 1651, in gardens at the Muette in Paris. No organized meeting took place until 1776 when races were arranged on the Plaine des Sablons, the site of the present Longchamp, which in 1857, was rented by the Société d'Encouragement who built the famous course, and Napoleon III went from Paris by boat on the Seine to inaugurate it the same year. The French rules on racing were drawn up in 1780; these, during the Revolution, had been completely forgotten. Napoleon I revived racing in 1805, but had a wrong opinion of the thoroughbred, for he officially proclaimed that the half-bred was its superior; weight was allotted according to the horse's height and not for age or merit.

In 1806 a Grand Prix was instituted and called successively Prix Royal, Grand Prix Royal, Grand Prix National, Grand Prix Imperial, Grand Prix de l'Empereur and since 1869 Prix Gladiateur: therefore, the oldest race in France. The most famous French race is the Grand Prix de Paris; it was for several years the richest race in the world. In 1908 it was worth to Mr. W. K. Vanderbilt, owner of "Northeast", over 400,000 gold francs. Run at Longchamp on the last Sunday in June over 1 mile 7 furlongs, it was created in 1863 and won that year by " The Ranger ", an English horse, in front of the famous French filly " La Toucques ", the only filly to have won both French Oaks and Derby. 14 English horses have won the Grand Prix; "Galloper Light", "Comrade" and "Lemonora" are the winners since the resumption of that race after the world war.

Mr. Edmond Blanc, brother of Camille Blanc, of Monte Carlo fame, who raced very successfully for over forty years, won the Grand Prix on no fewer than seven occasions and in 1903 his colts " Quo Vadis ", " Caius " and " Vinicius " filled the first three places, a feat which will stand for many years. In 1899 he paid the colossal sum in those days of one million francs (about £40,000) for the English Derby winner " Flying Fox ".

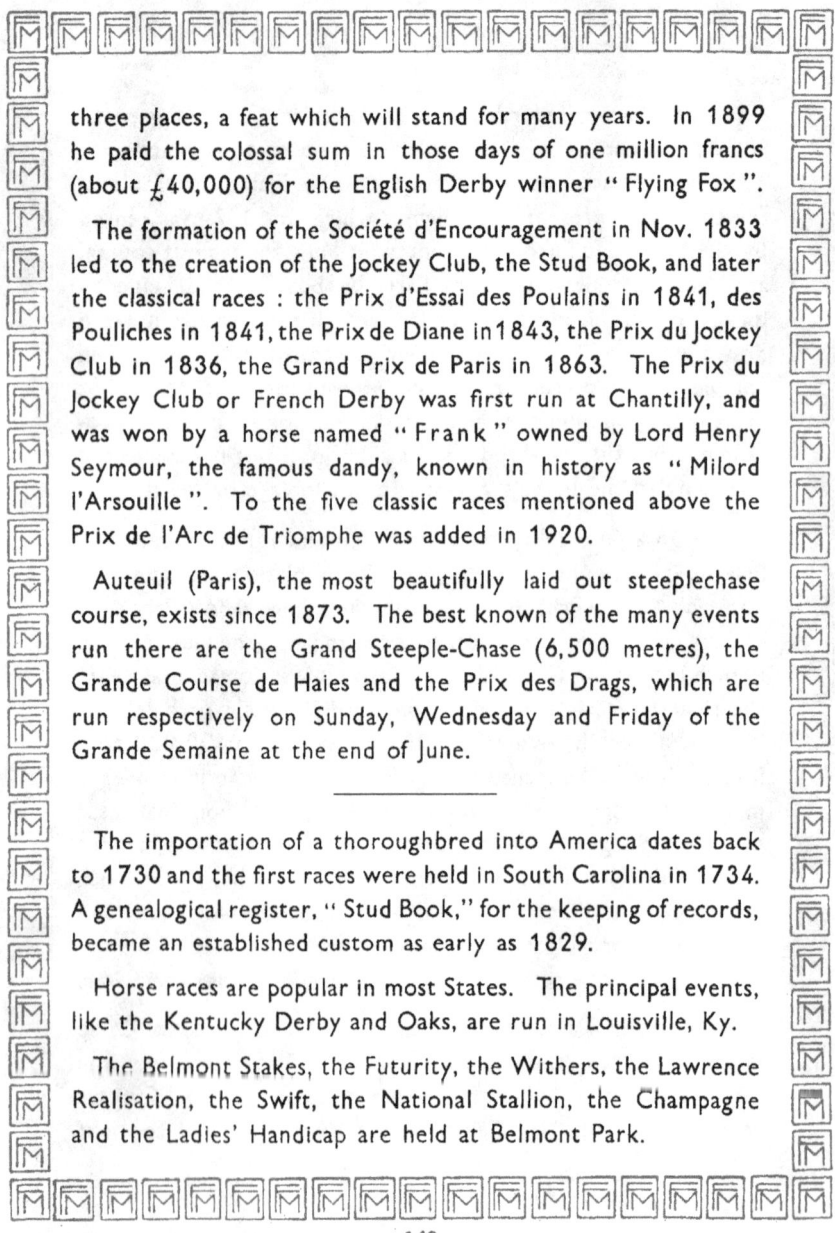

The formation of the Société d'Encouragement in Nov. 1833 led to the creation of the Jockey Club, the Stud Book, and later the classical races : the Prix d'Essai des Poulains in 1841, des Pouliches in 1841, the Prix de Diane in 1843, the Prix du Jockey Club in 1836, the Grand Prix de Paris in 1863. The Prix du Jockey Club or French Derby was first run at Chantilly, and was won by a horse named " Frank " owned by Lord Henry Seymour, the famous dandy, known in history as " Milord l'Arsouille ". To the five classic races mentioned above the Prix de l'Arc de Triomphe was added in 1920.

Auteuil (Paris), the most beautifully laid out steeplechase course, exists since 1873. The best known of the many events run there are the Grand Steeple-Chase (6,500 metres), the Grande Course de Haies and the Prix des Drags, which are run respectively on Sunday, Wednesday and Friday of the Grande Semaine at the end of June.

The importation of a thoroughbred into America dates back to 1730 and the first races were held in South Carolina in 1734. A genealogical register, " Stud Book," for the keeping of records, became an established custom as early as 1829.

Horse races are popular in most States. The principal events, like the Kentucky Derby and Oaks, are run in Louisville, Ky.

The Belmont Stakes, the Futurity, the Withers, the Lawrence Realisation, the Swift, the National Stallion, the Champagne and the Ladies' Handicap are held at Belmont Park.

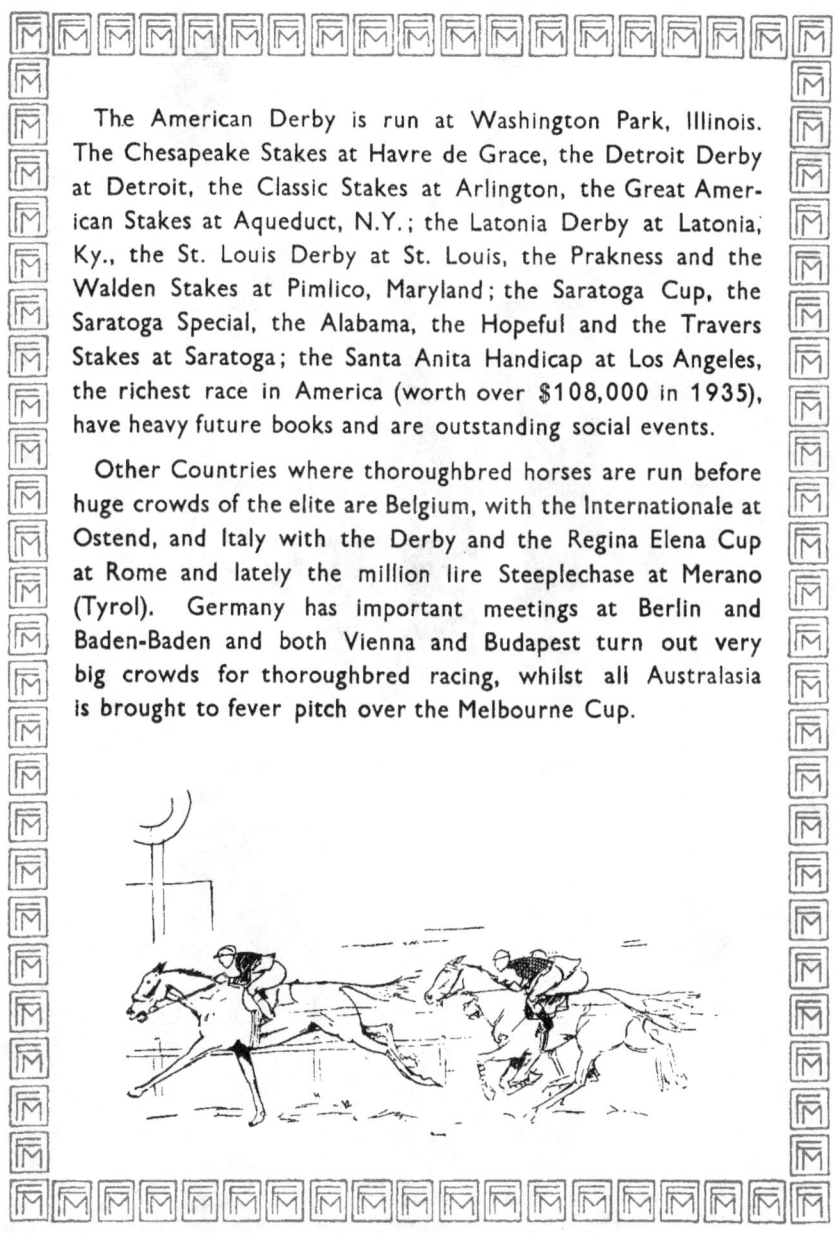

The American Derby is run at Washington Park, Illinois. The Chesapeake Stakes at Havre de Grace, the Detroit Derby at Detroit, the Classic Stakes at Arlington, the Great American Stakes at Aqueduct, N.Y.; the Latonia Derby at Latonia, Ky., the St. Louis Derby at St. Louis, the Prakness and the Walden Stakes at Pimlico, Maryland; the Saratoga Cup, the Saratoga Special, the Alabama, the Hopeful and the Travers Stakes at Saratoga; the Santa Anita Handicap at Los Angeles, the richest race in America (worth over $108,000 in 1935), have heavy future books and are outstanding social events.

Other Countries where thoroughbred horses are run before huge crowds of the elite are Belgium, with the Internationale at Ostend, and Italy with the Derby and the Regina Elena Cup at Rome and lately the million lire Steeplechase at Merano (Tyrol). Germany has important meetings at Berlin and Baden-Baden and both Vienna and Budapest turn out very big crowds for thoroughbred racing, whilst all Australasia is brought to fever pitch over the Melbourne Cup.

in sparkling wine

WHOLESALE AGENTS

PARIS
A. Rouland, 14, Rue Vignon

LONDON
Anderson, Dobson & C. Ltd.

NEW-YORK
Francis Draz & Cº Inc.

BOSTON
S. S. Pierce & Company

ACKERMAN-LAURANCE
Established 1811
St-Hilaire - St-Florent (Maine, Loire), FRANCE
THE FAVORITE FOR COCKTAILS AT THE RITZ BAR - PARIS

AIR FRANCE

WORLDS LEADING AIR SERVICES

PARIS TO LONDON IN LESS THAN 60 MINUTES

SERVICES TO 87 CITIES 29 COUNTRIES
(4 CONTINENTS)
Télep. OPERA 4100   PARIS OFFICES 9 rue AUBER

THE PERFECT CRISTAL COCKTAIL GLASS SHOULD BEAR THE BACCARAT TRADE MARK

CRISTALLERIES DE BACCARAT
30 bis RUE DE PARADIS. PARIS

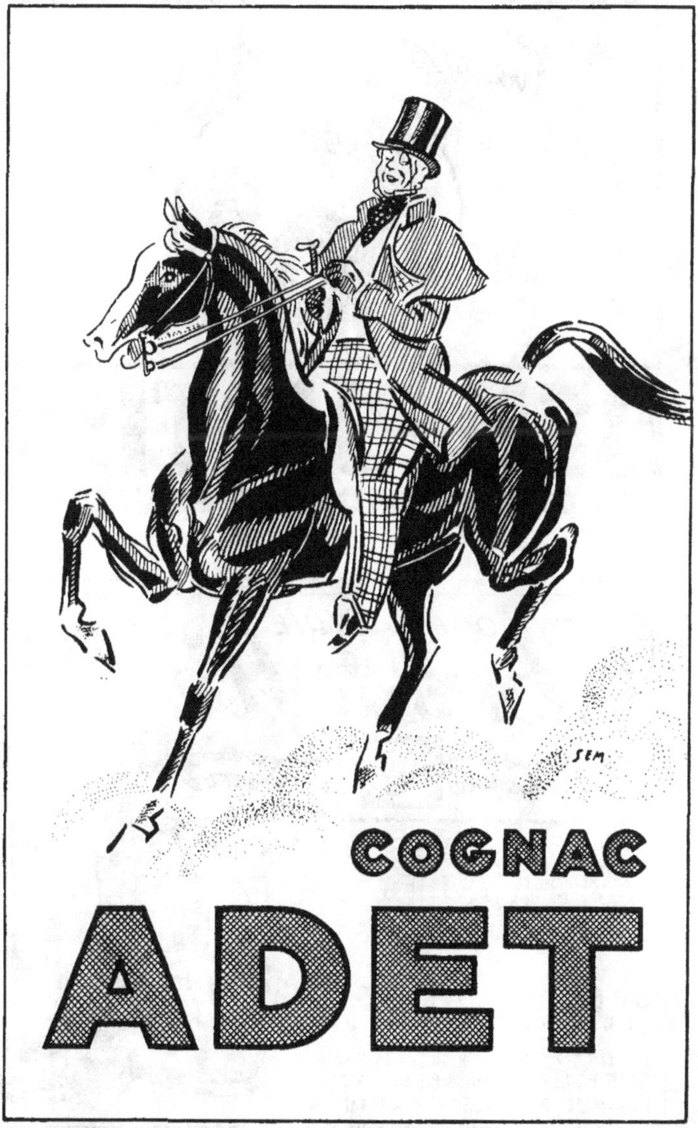
SEM
COGNAC
ADET

the world's best cordial

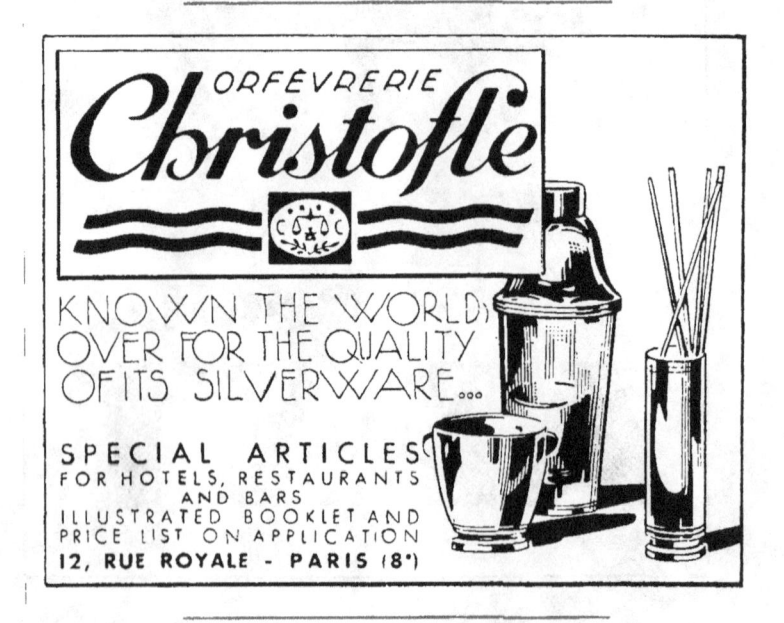

BÉNÉDICTINE
"LA GRANDE LIQUEUR FRANÇAISE"

ORFÉVRERIE Christofle

KNOWN THE WORLD OVER FOR THE QUALITY OF ITS SILVERWARE...

SPECIAL ARTICLES
FOR HOTELS, RESTAURANTS AND BARS
ILLUSTRATED BOOKLET AND PRICE LIST ON APPLICATION
12, RUE ROYALE - PARIS (8°)

DA SILVA'S PORT

ESTABLISHED IN 1813

LARGE PROPERTIES :
SITUATED IN THE ALTO CORGO (HIGH DOURO)

IMPORTANT STOCK :
OF OVER 6000 PIPES ABOUT 700 000 GALLONS OF RARE OLD WINES

OUSTANDING REPUTATION

THE BEST SHERRIES GROWN IN THE PAGO DE MACHARNUDO DISTRICT

AGUSTIN BLAZQUEZ

ESTABLISHED IN 1825
JEREZ (SPAIN)

LEOPOLD DE LYS LTD
1, RUE DES ITALIENS, 1
PARIS (IX)

CANNES

SPEND YOUR WINTER AT CANNES
OPEN FROM DECEMBER TO MAY

LA VILLE DES FLEURS ET DES SPORTS ÉLÉGANTS

THE MOST FASHIONABLE WINTER RESORT
HOTELS AND PALACES .. LUXURY VERY REASONABLE PRICES

CASINO MUNICIPAL
BACCARA — TRENTE ET QUARANTE — ROULETTE
RESTAURANT DES AMBASSADEURS

FLAT and HURDLE RACES · GOLF · TENNIS · POLO · REGATTAS
FROM LONDON 6 HOURS BY AIR FRANCE, 4 HOURS FROM PARIS · BY LUXE TRAIN 12 HOURS FROM PARIS

---

from easter ... to october

LEADING HOTELS
NORMANDY - ROYAL - HOTEL du GOLF

baccarat, roulette **CASINO** *trente et quarante*
RESTAURANT DES AMBASSADEURS

GOLF POLO TENNIS REGATTAS
FLAT and HURDLE RACES 3.000.000 frs of Prices)

From PARIS, 2 hours by Train, 186 km. by Road
From LONDON, 90 minutes by Plane (Banco Air Service)

DEAUVILLE
LA PLAGE FLEURIE

MARQUÉS DEL MÉRITO

JEREZ

PRODUCE OF SPAIN

LE SHERRY DE QUALITÉ

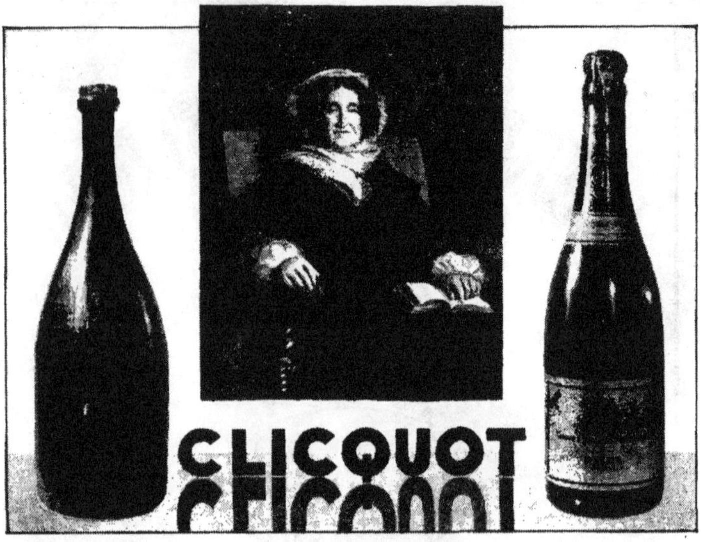
CLICQUOT

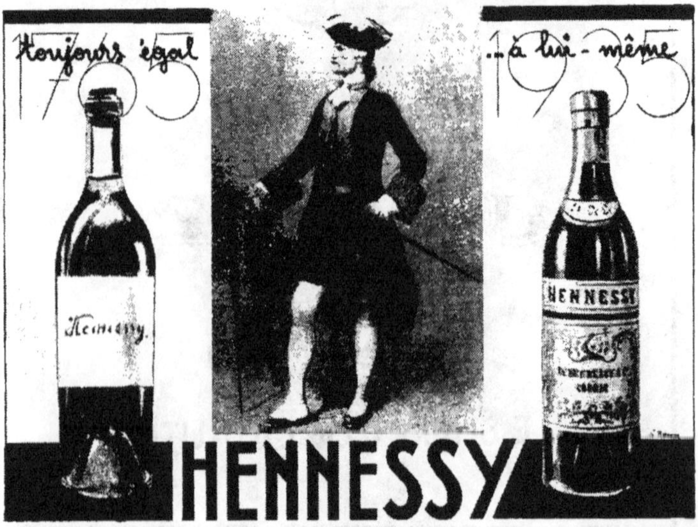
Toujours égal
... à lui-même
Hennessy
HENNESSY

GILBEY'S SPEY ROYAL

Has the mellowness that only age can impart

CRYSTAL CLEAR

W & A Gilbey
LTD.

Pantheon, Oxford Street, London, W.1

CUSENIER

Liqueurs de luxe

Made specially to prevent sore throats

CRAVEN "A" Cigarettes are made from the finest imported matured Virginia Tobacco guaranteed pure and absolutely free from adulteration of any kind

CRAVEN 'A' CORK TIPPED

CARRERAS LIMITED
(ESTD 1788)
ARCADIA WORKS, LONDON, ENGLAND

GORDON'S
DRY GIN
THE HEART OF A
GOOD COCKTAIL
SOLE AGENTS IN FRANCE
SIMON FRERES LTD
16, Rue d'Aguesseau
PARIS 8e - ANJOU 16-25
In quoting "that Supreme Gin which is the heart of a good cocktail," I mean Gordon's

DENIS - MOUNIE & C°
COGNAC

By Appointment

Purveyors to His Majesty King GEORGE V
also Purveyors to
His Late Majesty King EDWARD VII

Sole Agents :

MACKESSON ROBBINS & C°, Inc.
111 Eighth Avenue
New York City, N. Y.

CUNNINGHAM RIVIERE & NEWMAN
7 The Crescent
Minories
London, E. C. 3

Your Lighter gets thirsty too!

The best pick-me-up for any lighter is

DUNHILL'S "BENZIQUE"

On sale everywhere, in patent unbreakable containers.

ALFRED DUNHILL
15, Rue de la Paix, Paris

LONDON   NEW YORK   TORONTO

LUCKY STRIKE
"IT'S TOASTED"
CIGARETTES
LUCKY STRIKE
The Cream of the Crop
The clean center leaves are the mildest leaves
They Taste Better!

Supreme—
"King George IV"
GOLD LABEL

OLD SCOTCH WHISKY

THE PRODUCTS OF THE MOST FAMOUS SCOTS DISTILLERIES
ARE USED TO OBTAIN ITS OUTSTANDING QUALITY

CHAMPAGNE

EXTRA **KRUG** SEC

REIMS

Established 1843

PRIVATE CUVÉE

CHAMPAGNE

MOËT & CHANDON

ESTABLISHED IN 1743

★

BRUT IMPÉRIAL

The Cigarette
that makes a cocktail perfect
ED. LAURENS
"LE KHÉDIVE"
HIGH CLASS EGYPTIAN
CIGARETTES
ALEXANDRIA
CAIRO
ON SALE EVERYWHERE

MARTINI
ROSSI
MARTINI & ROSSI
APÉRITIF ROSSI
A LA GENTIANE
DRY
MARTINI
MARTINI
SEC
FOR ALL YOUR COCKTAILS

IN EVERY BOTTLE OF

Cheerfulness

champagne

POMMERY & GRENO

REIMS

148. Bᵈ HAUSSMANN
PARIS

James Pile
tailor

LONDON
ESTABLISHED 1784

PARIS
27, Rue Cambon
Tel.: Caumartin 33-56

BIARRITZ
13, Rue Mazagran

MONTE CARLO

Bunting

R. R. BUNTING

BOOT AND SHOEMAKER
to the Principal Courts of Europe

117 Wigmore Street, W. 1
LONDON
Phone: Welbeck 8970

233 Rue Saint-Honoré
PARIS
Phone: Opéra 8334

Noted for Quality, Fashion & Workmanship

A. ROULAND

14, RUE VIGNON - PARIS

AGENCE GENERALE ET DEPOT

Vins de Champagne	REIMS	Whisky Irlandais.	DUBLIN...
Vins de Bordeaux.	Own Growth	London Dry Gin.	LONDRES..
Vins de Bourgogne.	BEAUNE	Rye Whisky.	MONTREAL.
Vins Mousseux.	SAUMUR	Canadian Whisky.	MONTREAL.
Vins de Porto	OPORTO	Bourbon Whisky.	MONTREAL.
Vins de Xérès.	JEREZ	Angostura Bitters.	TRINIDAD..
Vins de Madère.	MADÈRE	Vins du Rhin	
Vins de Malaga.	MALAGA	et de la Moselle.	COBLENCE.
Whisky Ecossais.	MARKINCH	Plymouth Gin.	PLYMOUTH.

VOUVRAY NATURE ET CHAMPAGNE NATURE

Entrepôts à Neuilly-sur-Seine
134 à 140, Rue Perronet

Téléphone : OPERA 43-80   Télégrammes : Roulanvins, Paris

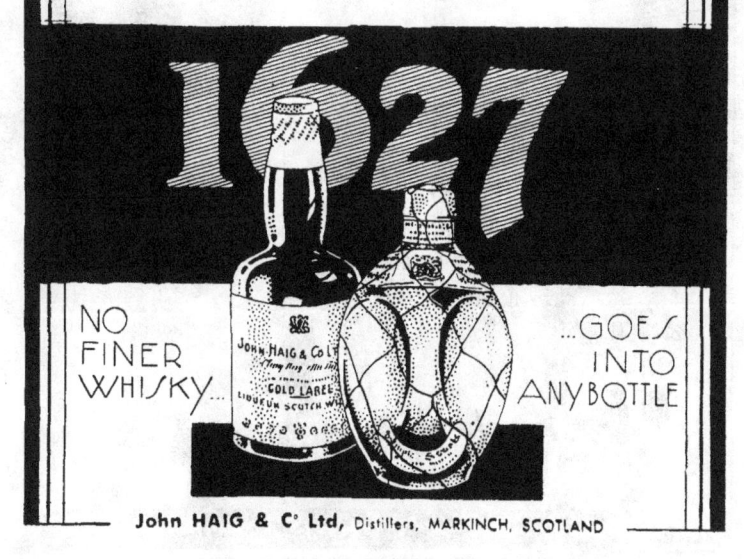

1627

NO FINER WHISKY... ...GOES INTO ANY BOTTLE

John HAIG & C° Ltd, Distillers, MARKINCH, SCOTLAND

After your cocktail,
After a good lunch
or a good dinner
smoke
PUNCH
cigars
Havana's finest

Georges Rosell
1 Rue d'ALGER
PARIS
PHONE :
OPE. 40.93
CAU. 28.71
cocktail parties and light suppers at your own home

Seagram's

DISTILLERS SINCE 1857

Rye *Bourbon*

The World's favourites

PIC SALTED CASHEW NUTS

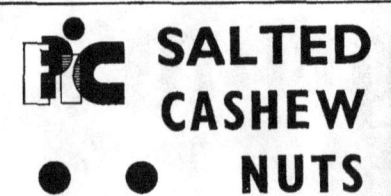

NO BAR IS UP TO DATE WITHOUT THEM

Some of the Premier Bars using them are :—

Ritz Hotel	Paris
Hotel Crillon	Paris
Hotel George V	Paris
Ritz Hotel	London
Savoy Hotel	London
Carlton Hotel	London
Dorchester Hotel	London
Berkeley Hotel	London

WRITE FOR FULL DETAILS TO
EPIC NUT & FOOD PRODUCTS, LTD.
19, BERKELEY ST., LONDON, W.1.
Telephones : Mayfair 1292, 1033
Telegrams : Epicnut, Piccy, London.

Daily Mail

WHEN TRAVELLING ON THE CONTINENT, READ THE "CONTINENTAL DAILY MAIL" ON SALE EVERYWHERE

FRANK'S special

UNITED STATES LINES
MANHATTAN
and WASHINGTON
cocktails

**ASK FOR THEM EN ROUTE TO NEW YORK
ON AMERICA'S NEW LUXURY LINERS**

UNITED STATES LINES
PARIS : 10 RUE AUBER   LONDON : 7 HAYMARKET S.W. 1
HAMBURG : ALSTERTHOR AND FERDINANDSTRASSE   AND ALL TRAVEL AGENTS

BY APPOINTMENT TO HIS MAJESTY THE KING

White Horse Scotch **Whisky**

QUALITY NEVER VARIES

the old blend whiskey of the white horse cellar from the original recipe 1746

ALSATIAN WINE	Riquewihr, Alsace
BRANDY	Cognac
CHAMPAGNE	Epernay
GIN	London
PORT	Porto, Portugal
SHERRY	Jerez, Spain
VERMOUTH	Torino
WHISKY	Glasgow

GÉNÉRAL AGENT
M. L. DREYFUS
76 et 78, Avenue des Champs-Élysées
PARIS — Tél. : Élysées 68-04 — 68-05

INTERNATIONAL GENEVA ASSOCIATION

25.000 MEMBERS — 360 SECTIONS

INTERNATIONAL ASSOCIATION
OF BAR HOTEL AND RESTAURANT EMPLOYEES
National Administrations in Every Country
Central Office in Zurich - Switzerland

OFFICES IN FRANCE: 5, RUE MARIOTTE. - PARIS (17e)

BISHOP & SONS

NORD 58-15

FRANK'S SPECIAL PRINTERS

61 & 63, RUE BICHAT, PARIS

ADDITIONS

INDEX

	Page
Foreword and Introduction	7—12
How to enjoy Cocktails at Home	13—16
Various Specialities and their Origin	17—19

PART I

COCKTAILS in alphabetical order	21—43

PART II

MIXED DRINKS

After-Dinner	47	Lemonades	69
Cobblers	48	Miscellaneous	
Collins	49	(see next page)	70—77
Coolers	50	Non Alcoholic	78—79
Crustas	51	Puffs	80
Cups	52—54	Punches	81—84
Daisies	55	Rickeys	85
Egg Nogs	56	Sangarees	86
Fixes	57	Scaffas	87
Fizzes	58—62	Seapea	61
Flips	63	Shrubs	88
Highballs	64	Slings	89
Hot Drinks	65—67	Smashes	90
Iced Liqueurs	47	Sours	91
Juleps	68	Toddies	92
Kalte Ente	53	Zooms	93

ADDITIONS

PART III

MISCELLANEOUS DRINKS (70—77)

Page

American Beauty
Americano
American Rose
Ammonia & Water
Angostura & Ginger Ale
Angostura & Soda

Barbotage au Champagne
Barman's Delight
Bishop
Bismarck or Black Velvet
Black Rose
Black Stripe
Bordeaux Champagne
Bosom Caresser
Brandy & Honey
Byrrh Cassis

Café & Kirsch (cold)
Cassisco
Chambery Fraise
Columbia Skin
Corpse Reviver No. 2

Dog's Nose
Dubonnet Citron

Eskimo
Eye Opener

Fog Horn
Frank's Refresher

Gin Buck
Gin Spider
Gin & Tonic
Green Hat
Grenadine & Kirsch

Horse's Neck

Irish Rose

Kalte Ente 53
King's Peg or
    Brandy & Champagne
Koldkure

Macka
Magnolia
Mamy Taylor
Mimosa or Champagne Orange
Morning Bracer
Morning Smile

Pick-me-up
Picon Grenadine
Prince of Wales

Queen's Peg or
    Gin & Champagne

Rainbow
Rhine Wine or
    Moselle & Seltzer
Rock & Rye

Seapea 61
Shandy Gaff
Sherry & Egg
Soyer au Champagne
Stone Fence
Stone Wall

Toison d'Or
Tomate

Vermouth Cassis

White Plush

ADDITIONS

PART IV
Page
SANDWICHES.. 95—102

PART V
WINES... 107—121

PART VI
USEFUL FORMULAS

Alcohol comparative strengths	125	Long Measure	136
Antidotes for Poisons	126	Metric equivalent Measures	136
Poisons and their Antidotes	126	Square Measure	137
Differences of Time	127	Surveyor's Measure	137
Nautical Miles	128	Time	137
The Earth	129	Troy	138
Pressure	132	Useful Formulas	138
Comparative Temperatures and Measures	133	Useful Information	139
Metric Carat Weights	134	Wind Pressure	140
Cloth Measure	135	For cleaning various substances	141
Cubic Measure	135	Help in case of Accident	142
Dry Measure	135	Useful Prescriptions	144
Approximate Liquid Measures and Equivalents	136	Horse Racing	145

LIST OF ADVERTISERS

Ackerman-Laurance	151	Dreyfus	174
Adet	153	Dunhill	162
Air France	152	Geneva Association	175
Baccarat	152	Gilbey	159
Benedictine	154	Gordon	161
Bishop & Sons	175	Hennessy	158
Bunting	168	"King George IV"	164
Cannes	156	Krug	164
Cashew Nuts "Epic"	172	Laurens	166
Christofle	154	Lucky Strike	163
Clicquot	158	Martini-Rossi	166
Craven A	160	Moet & Chandon	165
Cusenier	160	Pile	168
Da Silva	155	Pommery-Greno	167
Daily Mail	172	Punch Cigars	170
Deauville	156	Rosell (Georges)	170
Del Mérito (Jerez)	157	Rouland	169
Denis-Mounie	162	Seagram	171

U. S. Lines 173

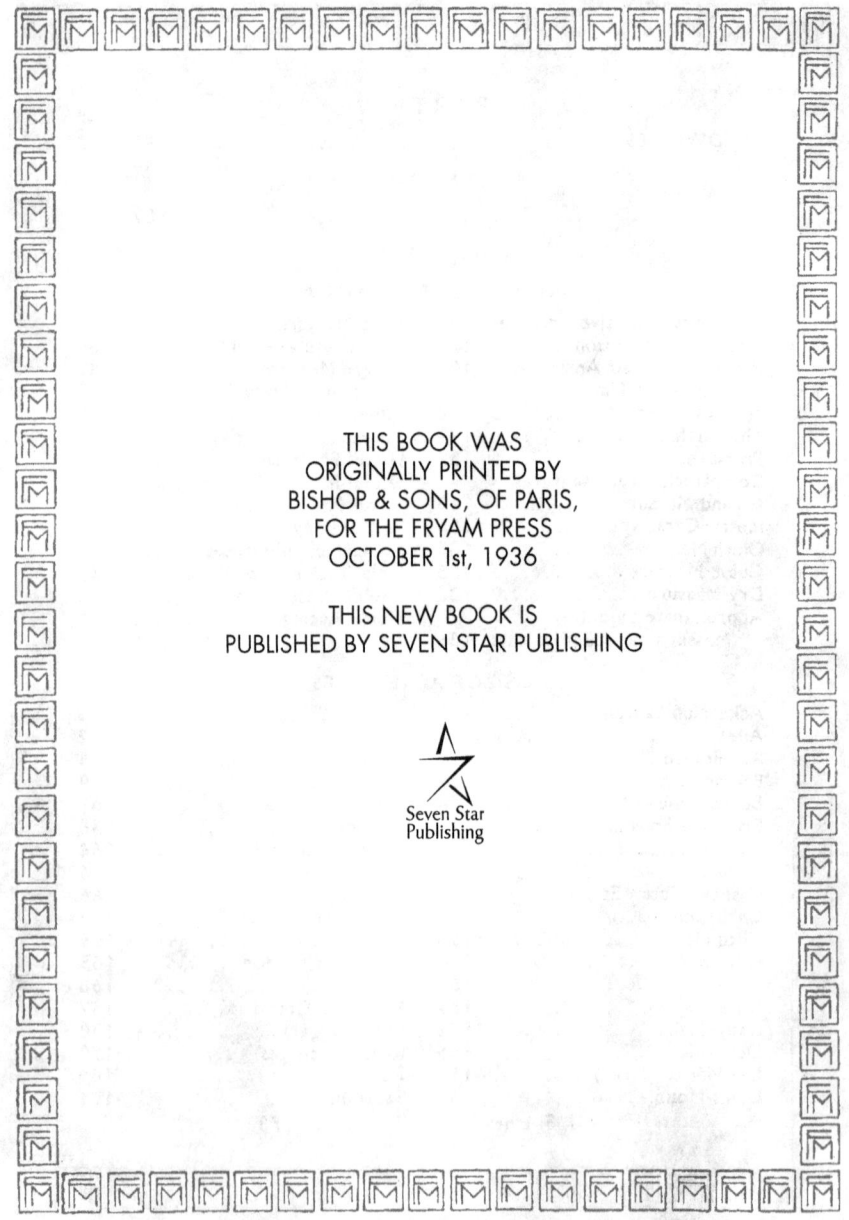

THIS BOOK WAS
ORIGINALLY PRINTED BY
BISHOP & SONS, OF PARIS,
FOR THE FRYAM PRESS
OCTOBER 1st, 1936

THIS NEW BOOK IS
PUBLISHED BY SEVEN STAR PUBLISHING

Seven Star
Publishing